MW01611525

Introduction to

LITERATURE

pearson custom library

College of DuPage
HUMNT 1110:
The Arts and Cultural Diversity
Professor John P. Frazier
The Arts and Cultural Diversity Textbook

PEARSON
Custom
Publishing

Director of Database Publishing: Michael Payne
Sponsoring Editor: Natalie Danner
Development Editor: Katherine R. Gehan
Editorial Assistant: Laura Krier
Marketing Manager: Kerry Chapman
Operations Manager: Eric M. Kenney
Production Managers: Kathleen Adams and Jennifer Berry
Database Project Specialist: Jennifer Carfagna
Rights Editor: Francesca Marcantonio
Cover Designer: Renée Sartell

Cover Art: Photography by Chris Beaudoin.

Copyright © 2006 by Pearson Custom Publishing.

All rights reserved.

This copyright covers material written expressly for this volume by the editor/s
as well as the compilation itself. It does not cover the individual selections herein that
first appeared elsewhere. Permission to reprint these has been obtained by Pearson
Custom Publishing for this edition only. Further reproduction by any means, elec-
tronic or mechanical, including photocopying and recording, or by any information
storage or retrieval system, must be arranged with the individual copyright holders
noted.

Printed in the United States of America

Please visit our website at *www.pearsoncustom.com*
Attention Bookstores: For permission to return any unsold stock, contact
Pearson Custom Publishing at 1-800-777-6872.

ISBN: **0536192928**

PEARSON CUSTOM PUBLISHING
75 Arlington Street, Suite 300, Boston, MA 02116
A Pearson Education Company

Introduction to
LITERATURE
pearson custom library

Editorial Board

Kathleen Shine Cain, Merrimack College

Kathleen Fitzpatrick, Pomona College

Janice Neuleib, Illinois State University

Stanley Orr, University of Hawai'i

Paige Reynolds, College of the Holy Cross

Stephen Ruffus, Salt Lake City Community College

Acknowledgements

A project as broad, far-reaching, challenging, and path-breaking as *The Pearson Custom Library: Introduction to Literature* could not be undertaken or accomplished without the support and participation of many colleagues. For their contributions, research, ideas, and suggestions, the editors particularly wish to thank David L.G. Arnold, University of Wisconsin, Stevens Point; Lydia M. Barovero, Providence College; Lisa Bickmore, Salt Lake City Community College; Claire Connolly, University of Wales-Cardiff; Allison Fernley, Salt Lake City Community College; Lisa Fluet, Boston College; Clint Gardner, Salt Lake City Community College; Curtis Gruenler, Hope College; Hilary Justice, Illinois State University; Martin Kevorkian, University of Texas, Austin; Lynn Kilpatrick, University of Utah; Susanne Liaw; Mark Lovely, Merrimack College; James J. Lu, California Baptist University; Sarah McKibben, Cristanne Miller, Pomona College; University of Notre Dame; Jim Miracky, College of the Holy Cross; Bill Miskinis, College of the Holy Cross; Bill Morgan, Illinois State University; Mark Morrison, Pennsylvania State University; John Mulrooney, College of the Holy Cross; Jamil Mustafa, Lewis University; Lisa Perdigao, Florida Institute of Technology; Jason Pickavance, Salt Lake City Community College; Robin Schulze, Pennsylvania State University; Mary Trotter, University of Wisconsin-Madison; Steve Vineberg, College of the Holy Cross; Helen Whall, College of the Holy Cross; Mario Pereira, Brown University; and Janice Wiggins.

Your *Introduction to Literature* purchase includes access to online resources designed to complement your readings. This Companion Website is located at the following URL:

http://www.pearsoncustom.com/dbintrolit/introlit/student

When prompted, enter the User Name: **ilstudent** and Password: **illearn**

(*Note:* The User Name and Password are case-sensitive, so be sure to use upper and lower case characters exactly as shown above.)

Once logged in, you will have access to the following resources:

Link Library. A collection of vetted web links organized by key terms and literary figures which offer you background and context for many of the selections you'll be reading.

The Writing Process. Advice that can aid you during the writing process. Included are guidelines and suggestions for each phase of writing, from start to finish.

Plagiarism. Suggestions to help you maintain academic honesty, with illustrative examples.

Grammar Guide. Spells out some of the rules and conventions of standard written English.

MLA Style. A brief guide to help you follow MLA style in citing your sources. The Modern Language Association style is widely used for papers in English composition, literature, and foreign languages.

We invite you to explore!

Contents

IX

Martin Luther King Jr.

GWENDOLYN BROOKS

A man went forth with gifts.
He was a prose poem.
He was a tragic grace.
He was a warm music.

He tried to heal the vivid volcanoes.   *5*
His ashes are
reading the world.

His Dream still wishes to anoint
the barricades of faith and of control.

His word still burns the center of the sun,   *10*
above the thousands and the
hundred thousands.

The word was Justice. It was spoken.

So it shall be spoken.
So it shall be done.   *15*

[1970]

Reprinted by permission from *Riot.* Copyright © 1970 by Gwendolyn Brooks.

"I Have A Dream"

Speech by Martin Luther King

Reading Questions: What is the message of Dr. King's speech? Would Dr. King be proud of the racial progress that the United States has made since the 1960's? Why or why not?

Delivered on the steps at the Lincoln Memorial in Washington D.C. on August 28, 1963.

Five score years ago, a great American, in whose symbolic shadow we stand signed the Emancipation Proclamation. This momentous decree came as a great beacon light of hope to millions of Negro slaves who had been seared in the flames of withering injustice. It came as a joyous daybreak to end the long night of captivity. But one hundred years later, we must face the tragic fact that the Negro is still not free. One hundred years later, the life of the Negro is still sadly crippled by the manacles of segregation and the chains of discrimination. One hundred years later, the Negro lives on a lonely island of poverty in the midst of a vast ocean of material prosperity. One hundred years later, the Negro is still languishing in the corners of American society and finds himself an exile in his own land.

So we have come here today to dramatize an appalling condition. In a sense we have come to our nation's capital to cash a check. When the architects of our republic wrote the magnificent words of the Constitution and the Declaration of Independence, they were signing a promissory note to which every American was to fall heir.

This note was a promise that all men would be guaranteed the inalienable rights of life, liberty, and the pursuit of happiness. It is obvious today that America has defaulted on this promissory note insofar as her citizens of color are concerned. Instead of honoring this sacred obligation, America has given the Negro people a bad check which has come back marked "insufficient funds." But we refuse to believe that the bank of justice is bankrupt. We refuse to believe that there are insufficient funds in the great vaults of opportunity of this nation.

So we have come to cash this check -- a check that will give us upon demand the riches of freedom and the security of justice. We have also come to this hallowed spot to remind America of the fierce urgency of now. This is no time to engage in the luxury of cooling off or to take the tranquilizing drug of gradualism. Now is the time to rise from the dark and desolate valley of segregation to the sunlit path of racial justice. Now is the time to open the doors of opportunity to all of God's children. Now is the time to lift our nation from the quicksands of racial injustice to the solid rock of brotherhood. It would be fatal for the nation to overlook the urgency of the moment and to underestimate the determination of the Negro. This sweltering summer of the Negro's legitimate discontent will not pass until there is an invigorating autumn of freedom and equality. Nineteen sixty-three is not an end, but a beginning. Those who hope that the

Negro needed to blow off steam and will now be content will have a rude awakening if the nation returns to business as usual. There will be neither rest nor tranquility in America until the Negro is granted his citizenship rights.

The whirlwinds of revolt will continue to shake the foundations of our nation until the bright day of justice emerges. But there is something that I must say to my people who stand on the warm threshold which leads into the palace of justice. In the process of gaining our rightful place we must not be guilty of wrongful deeds. Let us not seek to satisfy our thirst for freedom by drinking from the cup of bitterness and hatred. We must forever conduct our struggle on the high plane of dignity and discipline. we must not allow our creative protest to degenerate into physical violence. Again and again we must rise to the majestic heights of meeting physical force with soul force. The marvelous new militancy which has engulfed the Negro community must not lead us to distrust of all white people, for many of our white brothers, as evidenced by their presence here today, have come to realize that their destiny is tied up with our destiny and their freedom is inextricably bound to our freedom.

We cannot walk alone. And as we walk, we must make the pledge that we shall march ahead. We cannot turn back. There are those who are asking the devotees of civil rights, "When will you be satisfied?" we can never be satisfied as long as our bodies, heavy with the fatigue of travel, cannot gain lodging in the motels of the highways and the hotels of the cities. We cannot be satisfied as long as the Negro's basic mobility is from a smaller ghetto to a larger one. We can never be satisfied as long as a Negro in Mississippi cannot vote and a Negro in New York believes he has nothing for which to vote. No, no, we are not satisfied, and we will not be satisfied until justice rolls down like waters and righteousness like a mighty stream.

I am not unmindful that some of you have come here out of great trials and tribulations. Some of you have come fresh from narrow cells. Some of you have come from areas where your quest for freedom left you battered by the storms of persecution and staggered by the winds of police brutality. You have been the veterans of creative suffering. Continue to work with the faith that unearned suffering is redemptive. Go back to Mississippi, go back to Alabama, go back to Georgia, go back to Louisiana, go back to the slums and ghettos of our northern cities, knowing that somehow this situation can and will be changed. Let us not wallow in the valley of despair. I say to you today, my friends, that in spite of the difficulties and frustrations of the moment, I still have a dream. It is a dream deeply rooted in the American dream.

I have a dream that one day this nation will rise up and live out the true meaning of its creed: "We hold these truths to be self-evident: that all men are created equal." I have a dream that one day on the red hills of Georgia the sons of former slaves and the sons of former slaveowners will be able to sit down together at a table of brotherhood. I have a dream that one day even the state of Mississippi, a desert state, sweltering with the heat of injustice and oppression, will be transformed into an oasis of freedom and justice. I have a dream that my four children will one day live in a nation where they will not be judged by the color of their skin but by the content of their character. I have a dream today.

I have a dream that one day the state of Alabama, whose governor's lips are presently dripping with the words of interposition and nullification, will be transformed into a situation where little black boys and black girls will be able to join hands with little white boys and white girls and walk together as sisters and brothers. I have a dream today. I have a dream that one day every valley shall be exalted, every hill and mountain shall be made low, the rough places will be made plain, and the crooked places will be made straight, and the glory of the Lord shall be revealed, and all flesh shall see it together. This is our hope. This is the faith with which I return to the South. With this faith we will be able to hew out of the mountain of despair a stone of hope. With this faith we will be able to transform the jangling discords of our nation into a beautiful symphony of brotherhood. With this faith we will be able to work together, to pray together, to struggle together, to go to jail together, to stand up for freedom together, knowing that we will be free one day.

This will be the day when all of God's children will be able to sing with a new meaning, "My country, 'tis of thee, sweet land of liberty, of thee I sing. Land where my fathers died, land of the pilgrim's pride, from every mountainside, let freedom ring." And if America is to be a great nation, this must become true. So let freedom ring from the prodigious hilltops of New Hampshire. Let freedom ring from the mighty mountains of New York. Let freedom ring from the heightening Alleghenies of Pennsylvania! Let freedom ring from the snowcapped Rockies of Colorado! Let freedom ring from the curvaceous peaks of California! But not only that; let freedom ring from Stone Mountain of Georgia! Let freedom ring from Lookout Mountain of Tennessee! Let freedom ring from every hill and every molehill of Mississippi. From every mountainside, let freedom ring.

When we let freedom ring, when we let it ring from every village and every hamlet, from every state and every city, we will be able to speed up that day when all of God's children, black men and white men, Jews and Gentiles, Protestants and Catholics, will be able to join hands and sing in the words of the old Negro spiritual, "Free at last! free at last! thank God Almighty, we are free at last!"

The Analects

K'UNG FU-TSU (CONFUCIUS)

Book 1

1-1. The Master said, "Is it not pleasant to learn with a constant perseverance and application?

"Is it not delightful to have friends coming from distant quarters?

"Is he not a man of complete virtue, who feels no discomposure though men may take no note of him?"

1-2. The philosopher Yu said, "They are few who, being filial and fraternal, are fond of offending against their superiors. There have been none, who, not liking to offend against their superiors, have been fond of stirring up confusion.

"The superior man bends his attention to what is radical. That being established, all practical courses naturally grow up. Filial piety and fraternal submission,—are they not the root of all benevolent actions?"

1-3. The Master said, "Fine words and an insinuating appearance are seldom associated with true virtue."

1-4. The philosopher Tsang said, "I daily examine myself on three points:— whether, in transacting business for others, I may have been not faithful;— whether, in intercourse with friends, I may have been not sincere;—whether I may have not mastered and practiced the instructions of my teacher."

1-5. The Master said, "To rule a country of a thousand chariots, there must be reverent attention to business, and sincerity; economy in expenditure, and love for men; and the employment of the people at the proper seasons."

1-6. The Master said, "A youth, when at home, should be filial, and, abroad, respectful to his elders. He should be earnest and truthful. He should overflow

Reprinted from *The Analects of Confucius,* translated by Arthur Waley (1938), Simon & Schuster, Inc.

in love to all, and cultivate the friendship of the good. When he has time and opportunity, after the performance of these things, he should employ them in polite studies."

1-7. Tsze-hsia said, "If a man withdraws his mind from the love of beauty, and applies it as sincerely to the love of the virtuous; if, in serving his parents, he can exert his utmost strength; if, in serving his prince, he can devote his life; if, in his intercourse with his friends, his words are sincere:—although men say that he has not learned, I will certainly say that he has.

1-8. The Master said, "If the scholar be not grave, he will not call forth any veneration, and his learning will not be solid.

"Hold faithfulness and sincerity as first principles.

"Have no friends not equal to yourself.

"When you have faults, do not fear to abandon them."

1-9. The philosopher Tsang said, "Let there be a careful attention to perform the funeral rites to parents, and let them be followed when long gone with the ceremonies of sacrifice;—then the virtue of the people will resume its proper excellence."

1-10. Tsze-ch'in asked Tsze-kung saying, "When our master comes to any country, he does not fail to learn all about its government. Does he ask his information? or is it given to him?"

Tsze-kung said, "Our master is benign, upright, courteous, temperate, and complaisant and thus he gets his information. The master's mode of asking information,—is it not different from that of other men?"

1-11. The Master said, "While a man's father is alive, look at the bent of his will; when his father is dead, look at his conduct. If for three years he does not alter from the way of his father, he may be called filial."

1-12. The philosopher Yu said, "In practicing the rules of propriety, a natural ease is to be prized. In the ways prescribed by the ancient kings, this is the excellent quality, and in things small and great we follow them.

"Yet it is not to be observed in all cases. If one, knowing how such ease should be prized, manifests it, without regulating it by the rules of propriety, this likewise is not to be done."

1-13. The philosopher Yu said, "When agreements are made according to what is right, what is spoken can be made good. When respect is shown according to what is proper, one keeps far from shame and disgrace. When the parties upon whom a man leans are proper persons to be intimate with, he can make them his guides and masters."

1-14. The Master said, "He who aims to be a man of complete virtue in his food does not seek to gratify his appetite, nor in his dwelling place does he seek the appliances of ease; he is earnest in what he is doing, and careful in his speech; he frequents the company of men of principle that he may be rectified:—such a person may be said indeed to love to learn."

1-15. Tsze-kung said, "What do you pronounce concerning the poor man who yet does not flatter, and the rich man who is not proud?" The Master replied, "They will do; but they are not equal to him, who, though poor, is yet cheerful, and to him, who, though rich, loves the rules of propriety."

Tsze-kung replied, "It is said in the Book of Poetry, 'As you cut and then file, as you carve and then polish.'—The meaning is the same, I apprehend, as that which you have just expressed."

The Master said, "With one like Ts'ze, I can begin to talk about the odes. I told him one point, and he knew its proper sequence."

The Master said, "I will not be afflicted at men's not knowing me; I will be afflicted that I do not know men."

Book 2

2-1. The Master said, "He who exercises government by means of his virtue may be compared to the north polar star, which keeps its place and all the stars turn towards it."

2-2. The Master said, "In the Book of Poetry are three hundred pieces, but the design of them all may be embraced in one sentence 'Having no depraved thoughts.'"

2-3. The Master said, "If the people be led by laws, and uniformity sought to be given them by punishments, they will try to avoid the punishment, but have no sense of shame.

"If they be led by virtue, and uniformity sought to be given them by the rules of propriety, they will have the sense of shame, and moreover will become good."

2-4. The Master said, "At fifteen, I had my mind bent on learning.
"At thirty, I stood firm.
"At forty, I had no doubts.

"At fifty, I knew the decrees of Heaven.

"At sixty, my ear was an obedient organ for the reception of truth.

"At seventy, I could follow what my heart desired, without transgressing what was right."

2-5. Mang I asked what filial piety was. The Master said, "It is not being disobedient."

Soon after, as Fan Ch'ih was driving him, the Master told him, saying, "Mang-sun asked me what filial piety was, and I answered him,—'not being disobedient.'"

Fan Ch'ih said, "What did you mean?" The Master replied, "That parents, when alive, be served according to propriety; that, when dead, they should be buried according to propriety; and that they should be sacrificed to according to propriety."

2-6. Mang Wu asked what filial piety was. The Master said, "Parents are anxious lest their children should be sick."

2-7. Tsze-yu asked what filial piety was. The Master said, "The filial piety nowadays means the support of one's parents. But dogs and horses likewise are able to do something in the way of support;—without reverence, what is there to distinguish the one support given from the other?"

2-8. Tsze-hsia asked what filial piety was. The Master said, "The difficulty is with the countenance. If, when their elders have any troublesome affairs, the young take the toil of them, and if, when the young have wine and food, they set them before their elders, is THIS to be considered filial piety?"

2-9. The Master said, "I have talked with Hui for a whole day, and he has not made any objection to anything I said;—as if he were stupid. He has retired, and I have examined his conduct when away from me, and found him able to illustrate my teachings. Hui!—He is not stupid."

2-10. The Master said, "See what a man does.

"Mark his motives.

"Examine in what things he rests.

"How can a man conceal his character? How can a man conceal his character?"

2-11. The Master said, "If a man keeps cherishing his old knowledge, so as continually to be acquiring new, he may be a teacher of others."

2-12. The Master said, "The accomplished scholar is not a utensil."

2-13. Tsze-kung asked what constituted the superior man. The Master said, "He acts before he speaks, and afterwards speaks according to his actions."

2-14. The Master said, "The superior man is catholic and not partisan. The mean man is partisan and not catholic."

2-15. The Master said, "Learning without thought is labor lost; thought without learning is perilous."

2-16. The Master said, "To attack a task from the wrong end can do nothing but harm."

2-17. The Master said, "Yu, shall I teach you what knowledge is? When you know a thing, to hold that you know it; and when you do not know a thing, to allow that you do not know it;—this is knowledge."

2-18. Tsze-chang was learning with a view to official emolument.

The Master said, "Hear much and put aside the points of which you stand in doubt, while you speak cautiously at the same time of the others:—then you will afford few occasions for blame. See much and put aside the things which seem perilous, while you are cautious at the same time in carrying the others into practice: then you will have few occasions for repentance. When one gives few occasions for blame in his words, and few occasions for repentance in his conduct, he is in the way to get emolument."

2-19. Duke Ai asked, saying, "What should be done in order to secure the submission of the people?"

Confucius replied, "Advance the upright and set aside the crooked, then the people will submit. Advance the crooked and set aside the upright, then the people will not submit."

2-20. Chi K'ang asked how to cause the people to reverence their ruler, to be faithful to him, and to go on to nerve themselves to virtue.

The Master said, "Let him preside over them with gravity;—then they will reverence him. Let him be final and kind to all;—then they will be faithful to him. Let him advance the good and teach the incompetent;—then they will eagerly seek to be virtuous."

2-21. Some one addressed Confucius, saying, "Sir, why are you not engaged in the government?"

The Master said, "What does the *Book of History* say of filial piety?—'You are final, you discharge your brotherly duties. These qualities are displayed in government.' This then also constitutes the exercise of government. Why must there be THAT—making one be in the government?"

2-22. The Master said, "I do not know how a man without truthfulness is to get on. How can a large carriage be made to go without the crossbar for yoking the oxen to, or a small carriage without the arrangement for yoking the horses?"

2-23. Tsze-chang asked whether the affairs of ten ages from now could be known.

Confucius said, "The Yin dynasty followed the regulations of the Hsia: wherein it took from or added to them may be known. The Chau dynasty has followed the regulations of Yin: wherein it took from or added to them may be known. Some other may follow the Chau, but though it should be at the distance of a hundred ages, its affairs may be known."

2-24. The Master said, "For a man to sacrifice to a spirit which does not belong to him is flattery.

"To see what is right and not to do it is want of courage."

Edward Said

[1935–2003]

EDWARD SAID *has been described as one of the United States's few genuine "public intellectuals," a writer whose ideas and opinions resonate inside the academy, and in the world beyond. His writing draws connections between literary representations and cultural politics, between language and power. Said was born in Palestine and educated in Western schools in Jerusalem, Cairo, and the United States; he was throughout his life a highly active and public proponent of Palestinian rights and a respected commentator on Middle Eastern affairs. In his critical work, Said was interested in the tension between individual self-expression in writing and the larger cultural forces that attempt to regulate what the individual is able to say. In his most influential text,* Orientalism *(1978), he argues that two centuries of Western scholarship on and literary representations of the Orient—or the system of discourse that he refers to collectively as Orientalism—determined what can and cannot be known about the region by creating indelible and stereotypical preconceptions that have influenced all further writing. For Said, Orientalism is grounded in a cluster of principles: that the Orient is less rational, less developed, and less civilized than the West. Such discourse inevitably has imperial effects, but Orientalism, for Said, has been given birth and legitimacy not by politicians or military officials but by scholars, whose ostensible "objectivity" allowed such assumptions to become "fact." In* Orientalism, *Said calls attention to the inevitable conjunction of knowledge and power; he continues this project in subsequent books, including* The Question of Palestine *(1979),* Covering Islam *(1981), and* Culture and Imperialism *(1994).*

from *Orientalism*

EDWARD SAID

Knowing the Oriental

ON JUNE 13, 1910, Arthur James Balfour lectured the House of Commons on "the problems with which we have to deal in Egypt." These, he said, "belong to a wholly different category" than those "affecting the Isle of Wight or the West Riding of Yorkshire." He spoke with the authority of a long-time member of Parliament, former private secretary to Lord Salisbury, former chief secretary for Ireland, former secretary for Scotland, former prime minister, veteran of numerous overseas crises, achievements, and changes. During his involvement in imperial affairs Balfour served a monarch who in 1876 had been declared Empress of India; he had been especially well placed in positions of uncommon influence to follow the Afghan and Zulu wars, the British occupation of Egypt in 1882, the death of General Gordon in the Sudan, the Fashoda Incident, the battle of Omdurman, the Boer War, the Russo-Japanese War. In addition his remarkable social eminence, the breadth of his learning and wit—he could write on such varied subjects as Bergson, Handel, theism, and golf—his education at Eton and Trinity College, Cambridge, and his apparent command over imperial affairs all gave considerable authority to what he told the Commons in June 1910. But there was still more to Balfour's speech, or at least to his need for giving it so didactically and moralistically. Some members were questioning the necessity for "England in Egypt," the subject of Alfred Milner's enthusiastic book of 1892, but here designating a once-profitable occupation that had become a source of trouble now that Egyptian nationalism was on the rise and the continuing British presence in Egypt no longer so easy to defend. Balfour, then, to inform and explain.

Recalling the challenge of J. M. Robertson, the member of Tyneside, Balfour himself put Robertson's question again: "What right have you to take up these airs of superiority with regard to people whom you choose to call Oriental?" The choice of "Oriental" was canonical; it had been employed by Chaucer and Mandeville, by Shakespeare, Dryden, Pope, and Byron. It designated Asia or the East, geographically, morally, culturally. One could speak in Europe of an Oriental personality, an Oriental atmosphere, an Oriental tale,

Reprinted from *Orientalism* by permission of Pantheon Books, a division of Random House, Inc. Copyright © 1978 by Edward W. Said.

Oriental despotism, or an Oriental mode of production, and be understood. Marx had used the word, and now Balfour was using it; his choice was understandable and called for no comment whatever.

> I take up no attitude of superiority. But I ask [Robertson and anyone else] . . . who has even the most superficial knowledge of history, if they will look in the face the facts with which a British statesman has to deal when he is put in a position of supremacy over great races like the inhabitants of Egypt and countries in the East. We know the civilization of Egypt better than we know the civilization of any other country. We know it further back; we know it more intimately; we know more about it. It goes far beyond the petty span of the history of our race, which is lost in the prehistoric period at a time when the Egyptian civilisation had already passed its prime. Look at all the Oriental countries. Do not talk about superiority or inferiority.

Two great themes dominate his remarks here and in what will follow: knowledge and power, the Baconian themes.[1] As Balfour justifies the necessity for British occupation of Egypt, supremacy in his mind is associated with "our" knowledge of Egypt and not principally with military or economic power. Knowledge to Balfour means surveying a civilization from its origins to its prime to its decline—and of course, it means *being able to do that*. Knowledge means rising above immediacy, beyond self, into the foreign and distant. The object of such knowledge is inherently vulnerable to scrutiny; this object is a "fact" which, if it develops, changes, or otherwise transforms itself in the way that civilizations frequently do, nevertheless is fundamentally, even ontologically stable. To have such knowledge of such a thing is to dominate it, to have authority over it. And authority here means for "us" to deny autonomy to "it"—the Oriental country—since we know it and it exists, in a sense, *as* we know it. British knowledge of Egypt *is* Egypt for Balfour, and the burdens of knowledge make such questions as inferiority and superiority seem petty ones. Balfour nowhere denies British superiority and Egyptian inferiority; he takes them for granted as he describes the consequences of knowledge.

> First of all, look at the facts of the case. Western nations as soon as they emerge into history show the beginnings of those capacities for self-government . . . having merits of their own. . . . You may look through the whole history of the Orientals in what is called, broadly speaking, the East, and you never find traces of self-government. All their great centuries—and they have been very great—have been passed under despotisms, under absolute government. All their great contributions to civilisation—and they have been great—have been made under that form of government. Conqueror has succeeded conqueror; one domination has followed another;

---

[1]The reference is to Sir Francis Bacon (1561–1626), English philosopher and scientist, and originator of the expression "Knowledge is power." [Ed. note.]

but never in all the revolutions of fate and fortune have you seen one of those nations of its own motion establish what we, from a Western point of view, call self-government. That is the fact. It is not a question of superiority and inferiority. I suppose a true Eastern sage would say that the working government which we have taken upon ourselves in Egypt and elsewhere is not a work worthy of a philosopher—that it is the dirty work, the inferior work, of carrying on the necessary labour.

Since these facts are facts, Balfour must then go on to the next part of his argument.

> Is it a good thing for these great nations—I admit their greatness—that this absolute government should be exercised by us? I think it is a good thing. I think that experience shows that they have got under it far better government than in the whole history of the world they ever had before, and which not only is a benefit to them, but is undoubtedly a benefit to the whole of the civilised West. . . . We are in Egypt not merely for the sake of the Egyptians, though we are there for their sake; we are there also for the sake of Europe at large.

Balfour produces no evidence that Egyptians and "the races with whom we deal" appreciate or even understand the good that is being done them by colonial occupation. It does not occur to Balfour, however, to let the Egyptian speak for himself, since presumably any Egyptian who would speak out is more likely to be "the agitator [who] wishes to raise difficulties" than the good native who overlooks the "difficulties" of foreign domination. And so, having settled the ethical problems, Balfour turns at last to the practical ones. "If it is our business to govern, with or without gratitude, with or without the real and genuine memory of all the loss of which we have relieved the population [Balfour by no means implies, as part of that loss, the loss or at least the indefinite post-ponement of Egyptian independence] and no vivid imagination of all the benefits which we have given to them; if that is our duty, how is it to be performed?" England exports "our very best to these countries." These selfless administrators do their work "amidst tens of thousands of persons belonging to a different creed, a different race, a different discipline, different conditions of life." What makes their work of governing possible is their sense of being supported at home by a government that endorses what they do. Yet

> directly the native populations have that instinctive feeling that those with whom they have got to deal have not behind them the might, the authority, the sympathy, the full and ungrudging support of the country which sent them there, those populations lose all that sense of order which is the very basis of their civilisation, just as our officers lose all that sense of power and authority, which is the very basis of everything they can do for the benefit of those among whom they have been sent.

Balfour's logic here is interesting, not least for being completely consistent with the premises of his entire speech. England knows Egypt; Egypt is what England knows; England knows that Egypt cannot have self-government; England confirms that by occupying Egypt; for the Egyptians, Egypt is what England has occupied and now governs; foreign occupation therefore becomes "the very basis" of contemporary Egyptian civilization; Egypt requires, indeed insists upon, British occupation. But if the special intimacy between governor and governed in Egypt is disturbed by Parliament's doubts at home, then "the authority of what . . . is the dominant race—and as I think ought to remain the dominant race—has been undermined." Not only does English prestige suffer; "it is vain for a handful of British officials—endow them how you like, give them all the qualities of character and genius you can imagine—it is impossible for them to carry out the great task which in Egypt, not we only, but the civilised world have imposed upon them."[2]

As a rhetorical performance Balfour's speech is significant for the way in which he plays the part of, and represents, a variety of characters. There are of course "the English," for whom the pronoun "we" is used with the full weight of a distinguished, powerful man who feels himself to be representative of all that is best in his nation's history. Balfour can also speak for the civilized world, the West, and the relatively small corps of colonial officials in Egypt. If he does not speak directly for the Orientals, it is because they after all speak another language; yet he knows how they feel since he knows their history, their reliance upon such as he, and their expectations. Still, he does speak for them in the sense that what they might have to say, were they to be asked and might they be able to answer, would somewhat uselessly confirm what is already evident: that they are a subject race, dominated by a race that knows them and what is good for them better than they could possibly know themselves. Their great moments were in the past; they are useful in the modern world only because the powerful and up-to-date empires have effectively brought them out of the wretchedness of their decline and turned them into rehabilitated residents of productive colonies.

Egypt in particular was an excellent case in point, and Balfour was perfectly aware of how much right he had to speak as a member of his country's parliament on behalf of England, the West, Western civilization, about modern Egypt. For Egypt was not just another colony: it was the vindication of

---

[2]This and the preceding quotations from Arthur James Balfour's speech to the House of Commons are from Great Britain, *Parliamentary Debates* (Commons), 5th ser., 17 (1910): 1140–46. See also A. P. Thornton, *The Imperial Idea and Its Enemies: A Study in British Power* (London: MacMillan & Co., 1959), pp. 357–60. Balfour's speech was a defense of Eldon Gorst's policy in Egypt; for a discussion of that see Peter John Dreyfus Mellini, "Sir Eldon Gorst and British Imperial Policy in Egypt," unpublished Ph.D. dissertation, Stanford University, 1971.

Western imperialism; it was, until its annexation by England, an almost academic example of Oriental backwardness; it was to become the triumph of English knowledge and power. Between 1882, the year in which England occupied Egypt and put an end to the nationalist rebellion of Colonel Arabi, and 1907, England's representative in Egypt, Egypt's master, was Evelyn Baring (also known as "Over-baring"), Lord Cromer. On July 30, 1907, it was Balfour in the Commons who had supported the project to give Cromer a retirement prize of fifty thousand pounds as a reward for what he had done in Egypt. Cromer *made* Egypt, said Balfour:

> Everything he has touched he has succeeded in. . . . Lord Cromer's services during the past quarter of a century have raised Egypt from the lowest pitch of social and economic degradation until it now stands among Oriental nations, I believe, absolutely alone in its prosperity, financial and moral.[3]

How Egypt's moral prosperity was measured, Balfour did not venture to say. British exports to Egypt equaled those to the whole of Africa; that certainly indicated a sort of financial prosperity, for Egypt and England (somewhat unevenly) together. But what really mattered was the unbroken, all-embracing Western tutelage of an Oriental country, from the scholars, missionaries, businessmen, soldiers, and teachers who prepared and then implemented the occupation to the high functionaries like Cromer and Balfour who saw themselves as providing for, directing, and sometimes even forcing Egypt's rise from Oriental neglect to its present lonely eminence.

If British success in Egypt was as exceptional as Balfour said, it was by no means an inexplicable or irrational success. Egyptian affairs had been controlled according to a general theory expressed both by Balfour in his notions about Oriental civilization and by Cromer in his management of everyday business in Egypt. The most important thing about the theory during the first decade of the twentieth century was that it worked, and worked staggeringly well. The argument, when reduced to its simplest form, was clear, it was precise, it was easy to grasp. There are Westerners, and there are Orientals. The former dominate; the latter must be dominated, which usually means having their land occupied, their internal affairs rigidly controlled, their blood and treasure put at the disposal of one or another Western power. That Balfour and Cromer, as we shall soon see, could strip humanity down to such ruthless cultural and racial essences was not at all an indication of their particular

---

[3]Denis Judd, *Balfour and the British Empire: A Study in Imperial Evolution*, 1874–1932 (London: MacMillan & Co., 1968), p. 286. See also p. 292: as late as 1926 Balfour spoke—without irony—of Egypt as an "independent nation."

viciousness. Rather it was an indication of how streamlined a general doctrine had become by the time they put it to use—how streamlined and effective.

Unlike Balfour, whose theses on Orientals pretended to objective universality, Cromer spoke about Orientals specifically as what he had ruled or had to deal with, first in India, then for the twenty-five years in Egypt during which he emerged as the paramount consul-general in England's empire. Balfour's "Orientals" are Cromer's "subject races," which he made the topic of a long essay published in the *Edinburgh Review* in January 1908. Once again, knowledge of subject races or Orientals is what makes their management easy and profitable; knowledge gives power, more power requires more knowledge, and so on in an increasingly profitable dialectic of information and control. Cromer's notion is that England's empire will not dissolve if such things as militarism and commercial egotism at home and "free institutions" in the colony (as opposed to British government "according to the Code of Christian morality") are kept in check. For if, according to Cromer, logic is something "the existence of which the Oriental is disposed altogether to ignore," the proper method of ruling is not to impose ultrascientific measures upon him or to force him bodily to accept logic. It is rather to understand his limitations and "endeavor to find, in the contentment of the subject race, a more worthy and, it may be hoped, a stronger bond of union between the rulers and the ruled." Lurking everywhere behind the pacification of the subject race is imperial might, more effective for its refined understanding and infrequent use than for its soldiers, brutal tax gatherers, and incontinent force. In a word, the Empire must be wise; it must temper its cupidity with selflessness, and its impatience with flexible discipline.

> To be more explicit, what is meant when it is said that the commercial spirit should be under some control is this—that in dealing with Indians or Egyptians, or Shilluks, or Zulus, the first question is to consider what these people, who are all, nationally speaking, more or less *in statu pupillari*, themselves think is best in their own interests, although this is a point which deserves serious consideration. But it is essential that each special issue should be decided mainly with reference to what, by the light of Western knowledge and experience tempered by local considerations, we conscientiously think is best for the subject race, without reference to any real or supposed advantage which may accrue to England as a nation, or—as is more frequently the case—to the special interests represented by some one or more influential classes of Englishmen. If the British nation as a whole persistently bears this principle in mind, and insists sternly on its application, though we can never create a patriotism akin to that based on affinity of race or community of language, we may perhaps foster some sort of cosmopolitan allegiance grounded on the respect always accorded to superior talents and unselfish conduct, and on the gratitude derived both from favours conferred and from those to come. There may then at all events

be some hope that the Egyptian will hesitate before he throws in his lot with any future Arabi. . . . Even the Central African savage may eventually learn to chant a hymn in honour of Astraea Redux, as represented by the British official who denies him gin but gives him justice. More than this, commerce will gain.[4]

How much "serious consideration" the ruler ought to give proposals from the subject race was illustrated in Cromer's total opposition to Egyptian nationalism. Free native institutions, the absence of foreign occupation, a self-sustaining national sovereignty: these unsurprising demands were consistently rejected by Cromer, who asserted unambiguously that "the real future of Egypt . . . lies not in the direction of a narrow nationalism, which will only embrace native Egyptians . . . but rather in that of an enlarged cosmopolitanism."[5] Subject races did not have it in them to know what was good for them. Most of them were Orientals, of whose characteristics Cromer was very knowledgeable since he had had experience with them both in India and Egypt. One of the convenient things about Orientals for Cromer was that managing them, although circumstances might differ slightly here and there, was almost everywhere nearly the same.[6] This was, of course, because Orientals were almost everywhere nearly the same.

Now at last we approach the long-developing core of essential knowledge, knowledge both academic and practical, which Cromer and Balfour inherited from a century of modern Western Orientalism: knowledge about and knowledge of Orientals, their race, character, culture, history, traditions, society, and possibilities. This knowledge was effective: Cromer believed he had put it to use in governing Egypt. Moreover, it was tested and unchanging knowledge, since "Orientals" for all practical purposes were a Platonic essence, which any Orientalist (or ruler of Orientals) might examine, understand, and expose. Thus in the thirty-fourth chapter of his two-volume work *Modern Egypt*, the magisterial record of his experience and achievement, Cromer puts down a sort of personal canon of Orientalist wisdom:

> Sir Alfred Lyall once said to me: "Accuracy is abhorrent to the Oriental mind. Every Anglo-Indian should always remember that maxim." Want of accuracy, which easily degenerates into untruthfulness, is in fact the main characteristic of the Oriental mind.

---

[4]Evelyn Baring, Lord Cromer, *Political and Literary Essays*, 1908–1913 (1913; reprint ed., Freeport, N. Y.: Books for Libraries Press, 1969), pp. 40, 53, 12–14.

[5]Ibid., p. 171.

[6]Roger Owen, "The Influence of Lord Cromer's Indian Experience on British Policy in Egypt 1883–1907," in *Middle Eastern Affairs, Number Four: St. Antony's Papers Number 17*, ed. Albert Hourani (London: Oxford University Press, 1965), pp. 109–39.

The European is a close reasoner; his statements of fact are devoid of any ambiguity; he is a natural logician, albeit he may not have studied logic; he is by nature sceptical and requires proof before he can accept the truth of any proposition; his trained intelligence works like a piece of mechanism. The mind of the Oriental, on the other hand, like his picturesque streets, is eminently wanting in symmetry. His reasoning is of the most slipshod description. Although the ancient Arabs acquired in a somewhat higher degree the science of dialectics, their descendants are singularly deficient in the logical faculty. They are often incapable of drawing the most obvious conclusions from any simple premises of which they may admit the truth. Endeavor to elicit a plain statement of facts from any ordinary Egyptian. His explanation will generally be lengthy, and wanting in lucidity. He will probably contradict himself half-a-dozen times before he has finished his story. He will often break down under the mildest process of cross-examination.

Orientals or Arabs are thereafter shown to be gullible, "devoid of energy and initiative," much given to "fulsome flattery," intrigue, cunning, and unkindness to animals; Orientals cannot walk on either a road or a pavement (their disordered minds fail to understand what the clever European grasps immediately, that roads and pavements are made for walking); Orientals are inveterate liars, they are "lethargic and suspicious," and in everything oppose the clarity, directness, and nobility of the Anglo-Saxon race.[7]

Cromer makes no effort to conceal that Orientals for him were always and only the human material he governed in British colonies. "As I am only a diplomatist and an administrator, whose proper study is also man, but from the point of view of governing him," Cromer says, ". . . I content myself with noting the fact that somehow or other the Oriental generally acts, speaks, and thinks in a manner exactly opposite to the European."[8] Cromer's descriptions are of course based partly on direct observation, yet here and there he refers to orthodox Orientalist authorities (in particular Ernest Renan and Constantin de Volney[9]) to support his views. To these authorities he also defers when it comes to explaining why Orientals are the way they are. He has no doubt that *any* knowledge of the Oriental will confirm his views, which, to judge from his description of the Egyptian breaking under cross-examination,

---

[7] Evelyn Baring, Lord Cromer, *Modern Egypt* (New York: Macmillan Co., 1908), 2: 146–67. For a British view of British policy in Egypt that runs totally counter to Cromer's, see Wilfrid Scawen Blunt, *Secret History of the English Occupation of Egypt: Being a Personal Narrative of Events* (New York: Alfred A. Knopf, 1922). There is a valuable discussion of Egyptian opposition to British rule in Mounah A. Khouri, *Poetry and the Making of Modern Egypt, 1882–1922* (Leiden: E. J. Brill, 1971).

[8] Cromer, *Modern Egypt*, 2: 164.

[9] Ernest Renan (1823–1892), French philosopher and scholar of the Hebrew language and culture; Constantin de Volney (1757–1820), French scholar and author of *Voyage en Syrie at en Egypte* (1787). [Ed. note.]

find the Oriental to be guilty. The crime was that the Oriental was an Oriental, and it is an accurate sign of how commonly acceptable such a tautology was that it could be written without even an appeal to European logic or symmetry of mind. Thus any deviation from what were considered the norms of Oriental behavior was believed to be unnatural; Cromer's last annual report from Egypt consequently proclaimed Egyptian nationalism to be an "entirely novel idea" and "a plant of exotic rather than of indigenous growth."[10]

We would be wrong, I think, to underestimate the reservoir of accredited knowledge, the codes of Orientalist orthodoxy, to which Cromer and Balfour refer everywhere in their writing and in their public policy. To say simply that Orientalism was a rationalization of colonial rule is to ignore the extent to which colonial rule was justified in advance by Orientalism, rather than after the fact. Men have always divided the world up into regions having either real or imagined distinction from each other. The absolute demarcation between East and West, which Balfour and Cromer accept with such complacency, had been years, even centuries, in the making. There were of course innumerable voyages of discovery; there were contacts through trade and war. But more than this, since the middle of the eighteenth century there had been two principal elements in the relation between East and West. One was a growing systematic knowledge in Europe about the Orient, knowledge reinforced by the colonial encounter as well as by the widespread interest in the alien and unusual, exploited by the developing sciences of ethnology, comparative anatomy, philology, and history; furthermore, to this systematic knowledge was added a sizable body of literature produced by novelists, poets, translators, and gifted travelers. The other feature of Oriental-European relations was that Europe was always in a position of strength, not to say domination. There is no way of putting this euphemistically. True, the relationship of strong to weak could be disguised or mitigated, as when Balfour acknowledged the "greatness" of Oriental civilizations. But the essential relationship, on political, cultural, and even religious grounds, was seen—in the West, which is what concerns us here—to be one between a strong and a weak partner.

Many terms were used to express the relation: Balfour and Cromer, typically, used several. The Oriental is irrational, depraved (fallen), childlike, "different"; thus the European is rational, virtuous, mature, "normal." But the way of enlivening the relationship was everywhere to stress the fact that the Oriental lived in a different but thoroughly organized world of his own, a world with its own national, cultural, and epistemological boundaries and principles of internal coherence. Yet what gave the Oriental's world its intelligibility and identity was not the result of his own efforts but rather the whole

---

[10]Cited in John Marlowe, *Cromer in Egypt* (London: Elek Books, 1970), p. 271.

complex series of knowledgeable manipulations by which the Orient was identified by the West. Thus the two features of cultural relationship I have been discussing come together. Knowledge of the Orient, because generated out of strength, in a sense *creates* the Orient, the Oriental, and his world. In Cromer's and Balfour's language the Oriental is depicted as something one judges (as in a court of law), something one studies and depicts (as in a curriculum), something one disciplines (as in a school or prison), something one illustrates (as in a zoological manual). The point is that in each of these cases the Oriental is *contained* and *represented* by dominating frameworks. Where do these come from?

Cultural strength is not something we can discuss very easily—and one of the purposes of the present work is to illustrate, analyze, and reflect upon Orientalism as an exercise of cultural strength. In other words, it is better not to risk generalizations about so vague and yet so important a notion as cultural strength until a good deal of material has been analyzed first. But at the outset one can say that so far as the West was concerned during the nineteenth and twentieth centuries, an assumption had been made that the Orient and everything in it was, if not patently inferior to, then in need of corrective study by the West. The Orient was viewed as if framed by the classroom, the criminal court, the prison, the illustrated manual. Orientalism, then, is knowledge of the Orient that places things Oriental in class, court, prison, or manual for scrutiny, study, judgment, discipline, or governing.

During the early years of the twentieth century, men like Balfour and Cromer could say what they said, in the way they did, because a still earlier tradition of Orientalism than the nineteenth-century one provided them with a vocabulary, imagery, rhetoric, and figures with which to say it. Yet Orientalism reinforced, and was reinforced by, the certain knowledge that Europe or the West literally commanded the vastly greater part of the earth's surface. The period of immense advance in the institutions and content of Orientalism coincides exactly with the period of unparalleled European expansion; from 1815 to 1914 European direct colonial dominion expanded from about 35 percent of the earth's surface to about 85 percent of it.[11] Every continent was affected, none more so than Africa and Asia. The two greatest empires were the British and the French; allies and partners in some things, in others they were hostile rivals. In the Orient, from the eastern shores of the Mediterranean to Indochina and Malaya, their colonial possessions and imperial spheres of influence were adjacent, frequently overlapped, often were fought over. But it was in

---

[11]Harry Magdoff, "Colonialism (1763–c. 1970)," *Encyclopaedia Britannica*, 15th ed. (1974), pp. 893–4. See also D. K. Fieldhouse, *The Colonial Empires: A Comparative Survey from the Eighteenth Century* (New York: Delacorte Press, 1967), p. 178.

the Near Orient, the lands of the Arab Near East, where Islam was supposed to define cultural and racial characteristics, that the British and the French encountered each other and "the Orient" with the greatest intensity, familiarity, and complexity. For much of the nineteenth century, as Lord Salisbury put it in 1881, their common view of the Orient was intricately problematic: "When you have got a . . . faithful ally who is bent on meddling in a country in which you are deeply interested—you have three courses open to you. You may renounce—or monopolize—or share. Renouncing would have been to place the French across our road to India. Monopolizing would have been very near the risk of war. So we resolved to share."[12]

And share they did, in ways that we shall investigate presently. What they shared, however, was not only land or profit or rule; it was the kind of intellectual power I have been calling Orientalism. In a sense Orientalism was a library or archive of information commonly and, in some of its aspects, unanimously held. What bound the archive together was a family of ideas[13] and a unifying set of values proven in various ways to be effective. These ideas explained the behavior of Orientals; they supplied Orientals with a mentality, a genealogy, an atmosphere; most important, they allowed Europeans to deal with and even to see Orientals as a phenomenon possessing regular characteristics. But like any set of durable ideas, Orientalist notions influenced the people who were called Orientals as well as those called Occidental, European, or Western; in short, Orientalism is better grasped as a set of constraints upon and limitations of thought than it is simply as a positive doctrine. If the essence of Orientalism is the ineradicable distinction between Western superiority and Oriental inferiority, then we must be prepared to note how in its development and subsequent history Orientalism deepened and even hardened the distinction. When it became common practice during the nineteenth century for Britain to retire its administrators from India and elsewhere once they had reached the age of fifty-five, then a further refinement in Orientalism had been achieved; no Oriental was ever allowed to see a Westerner as he aged and degenerated, just as no Westerner needed ever to see himself, mirrored in the eyes of the subject race, as anything but a vigorous, rational, ever-alert young Raj.[14]

---

[12]Quoted in Afaf Lutfi al-Sayyid, *Egypt and Cromer: A Study in Anglo-Egyptian Relations* (New York: Frederick A. Praeger, 1969), p. 3.

[13]The phrase is to be found in Ian Hacking, *The Emergence of Probability: A Philosophical Study of Early Ideas About Probability, Induction and Statistical Inference* (London: Cambridge University Press, 1975), p. 17.

[14]V. G. Kiernan, *The Lords of Human Kind: Black Man, Yellow Man, and White Man in an Age of Empire* (Boston: Little, Brown & Co., 1969), p. 55.

Orientalist ideas took a number of different forms during the nineteenth and twentieth centuries. First of all, in Europe there was a vast literature about the Orient inherited from the European past. What is distinctive about the late eighteenth and early nineteenth centuries, which is where this study assumes modern Orientalism to have begun, is that an Oriental renaissance took place, as Edgar Quinet phrased it.[15] Suddenly it seemed to a wide variety of thinkers, politicians, and artists that a new awareness of the Orient, which extended from China to the Mediterranean, had arisen. This awareness was partly the result of newly discovered and translated Oriental texts in languages like Sanskrit, Zend, and Arabic; it was also the result of a newly perceived relationship between the Orient and the West. For my purposes here, the keynote of the relationship was set for the Near East and Europe by the Napoleonic invasion of Egypt in 1798, an invasion which was in many ways the very model of a truly scientific appropriation of one culture by another, apparently stronger one. For with Napoleon's occupation of Egypt processes were set in motion between East and West that still dominate our contemporary cultural and political perspectives. And the Napoleonic expedition, with its great collective monument of erudition, the *Description de l'Egypte*, provided a scene or setting for Orientalism, since Egypt and subsequently the other Islamic lands were viewed as the live province, the laboratory, the theater of effective Western knowledge about the Orient. I shall return to the Napoleonic adventure a little later.

With such experiences as Napoleon's the Orient as a body of knowledge in the West was modernized, and this is a second form in which nineteenth- and twentieth-century Orientalism existed. From the outset of the period I shall be examining there was everywhere amongst Orientalists the ambition to formulate their discoveries, experiences, and insights suitably in modern terms, to put ideas about the Orient in very close touch with modern realities. Renan's linguistic investigations of Semitic in 1848, for example, were couched in a style that drew heavily for its authority upon contemporary comparative grammar, comparative anatomy, and racial theory; these lent his Orientalism prestige and—the other side of the coin—made Orientalism vulnerable, as it has been ever since, to modish as well as seriously influential currents of thought in the West. Orientalism has been subjected to imperialism, positivism, utopianism, historicism, Darwinism, racism, Freudianism, Marxism, Spenglerism. But Orientalism, like many of the natural and social sciences, has had "paradigms" of research, its own learned societies, its own Establishment. During the nineteenth century the field increased enormously in prestige, as did also the reputation and influence of

---

[15]Edgar Quinet, *Le Génie des religions*, in *Oeuvres complètes* (Paris: Paguerre, 1857), pp. 55–74.

such institutions as the Société asiatique,[16] the Royal Asiatic Society, the Deutsche Morgenländische Gesellschaft,[17] and the American Oriental Society. With the growth of these societies went also an increase, all across Europe, in the number of professorships in Oriental studies; consequently there was an expansion in the available means for disseminating Orientalism. Orientalist periodicals, beginning with the *Fundgraben des Orients* (1809),[18] multiplied the quantity of knowledge as well as the number of specialties.

Yet little of this activity and very few of these institutions existed and flourished freely, for in a third form in which it existed, Orientalism imposed limits upon thought about the Orient. Even the most imaginative writers of an age, men like Flaubert, Nerval, or Scott,[19] were constrained in what they could either experience of or say about the Orient. For Orientalism was ultimately a political vision of reality whose structure promoted the difference between the familiar (Europe, the West, "us") and the strange (the Orient, the East, "them"). This vision in a sense created and then served the two worlds thus conceived. Orientals lived in their world, "we" lived in ours. The vision and material reality propped each other up, kept each other going. A certain freedom of intercourse was always the Westerner's privilege; because his was the stronger culture, he could penetrate, he could wrestle with, he could give shape and meaning to the great Asiatic mystery, as Disraeli[20] once called it. Yet what has, I think, been previously overlooked is the constricted vocabulary of such a privilege, and the comparative limitations of such a vision. My argument takes it that the Orientalist reality is both antihuman and persistent. Its scope, as much as its institutions and all-pervasive influence, lasts up to the present.

But how did and does Orientalism work? How can one describe it all together as a historical phenomenon, a way of thought, a contemporary problem, and a material reality? Consider Cromer again, an accomplished technician of empire but also a beneficiary of Orientalism. He can furnish us with a rudimentary answer. In "The Government of Subject Races" he wrestles with the problem of how Britain, a nation of individuals, is to administer a wide-flung empire according to a number of central principles. He contrasts the

---

[16]French: Asiatic Society. [Ed. note.]

[17]German: German Oriental Society. [Ed. note.]

[18]The periodical's title is actually *Fundgruben des Orients*, or *Storehouses of the Orient*, founded by German Orientalist scholar Joseph von Hammer-Purgstall. [Ed. note.]

[19]Gustave Flaubert (1821–1880), French novelist; Gérard de Nerval (1808–1855), French poet; Sir Walter Scott (1771–1832), Scottish novelist and poet.

[20]Benjamin Disraeli (1804–1881), British novelist and Prime Minister of England.

"local agent," who has both a specialist's knowledge of the native and an Anglo-Saxon individuality, with the central authority at home in London. The former may "treat subjects of local interest in a manner calculated to damage, or even to jeopardize, Imperial interests. The central authority is in a position to obviate any danger arising from this cause." Why? Because this authority can "ensure the harmonious working of the different parts of the machine" and "should endeavour, so far as is possible, to realise the circumstances attendant on the government of the dependency."[21] The language is vague and unattractive, but the point is not hard to grasp. Cromer envisions a seat of power in the West, and radiating out from it towards the East a great embracing machine, sustaining the central authority yet commanded by it. What the machine's branches feed into it in the East—human material, material wealth, knowledge, what have you—is processed by the machine, then converted into more power. The specialist does the immediate translation of mere Oriental matter into useful substance: the Oriental becomes, for example, a subject race, an example of an "Oriental" mentality, all for the enhancement of the "authority" at home. "Local interests" are Orientalist special interests, the "central authority" is the general interest of the imperial society as a whole. What Cromer quite accurately sees is the management of knowledge by society, the fact that knowledge—no matter how special—is regulated first by the local concerns of a specialist, later by the general concerns of a social system of authority. The interplay between local and central interests is intricate, but by no means indiscriminate.

In Cromer's own case as an imperial administrator the "proper study is also man," he says. When Pope[22] proclaimed the proper study of mankind to be man, he meant all men, including "the poor Indian"; whereas Cromer's "also" reminds us that certain men, such as Orientals, can be singled out as the subject for *proper* study. The proper study—in this sense—of Orientals is Orientalism, properly separate from other forms of knowledge, but finally useful (because finite) for the material and social reality enclosing all knowledge at any time, supporting knowledge, providing it with uses. An order of sovereignty is set up from East to West, a mock chain of being whose clearest form was given once by Kipling:[23]

> Mule, horse, elephant, or bullock, he obeys his driver, and the driver his sergeant,
> and the sergeant his lieutenant, and the lieutenant his captain, and the captain his

---

[21]Cromer, *Political and Literary Essays*, p. 35.

[22]Alexander Pope (1688–1744), English poet; the quote is from his *Essay on Man* (1733).

[23]Rudyard Kipling (1865–1936), English novelist and poet, primarily remembered for his glorification of the British Empire. The quote is from his *The Jungle Book* (1894).

major, and the major his colonel, and the colonel his brigadier commanding three regiments, and the brigadier his general, who obeys the Viceroy, who is the servant of the Empress.[24]

As deeply forged as is this monstrous chain of command, as strongly managed as is Cromer's "harmonious working," Orientalism can also express the strength of the West and the Orient's weakness—as seen by the West. Such strength and such weakness are as intrinsic to Orientalism as they are to any view that divides the world into large general divisions, entities that coexist in a state of tension produced by what is believed to be radical difference.

For that is the main intellectual issue raised by Orientalism. Can one divide human reality, as indeed human reality seems to be genuinely divided, into clearly different cultures, histories, traditions, societies, even races, and survive the consequences humanly? By surviving the consequences humanly, I mean to ask whether there is any way of avoiding the hostility expressed by the division, say, of men into "us" (Westerners) and "they" (Orientals). For such divisions are generalities whose use historically and actually has been to press the importance of the distinction between some men and some other men, usually towards not especially admirable ends. When one uses categories like Oriental and Western as both the starting and the end points of analysis, research, public policy (as the categories were used by Balfour and Cromer), the result is usually to polarize the distinction—the Oriental becomes more Oriental, the Westerner more Western—and limit the human encounter between different cultures, traditions, and societies. In short, from its earliest modern history to the present, Orientalism as a form of thought for dealing with the foreign has typically shown the altogether regrettable tendency of any knowledge based on such hard-and-fast distinctions as "East" and "West": to channel thought into a West or an East compartment. Because this tendency is right at the center of Orientalist theory, practice, and values found in the West, the sense of Western power over the Orient is taken for granted as having the status of scientific truth.

A contemporary illustration or two should clarify this observation perfectly. It is natural for men in power to survey from time to time the world with which they must deal. Balfour did it frequently. Our contemporary Henry Kissinger[25] does it also, rarely with more express frankness than in his essay "Domestic Structure and Foreign Policy." The drama he depicts is a real one, in which the United States must manage its behavior in the world under

---

[24]See Jonah Raskin, *The Mythology of Imperialism* (New York: Random House, 1971), p. 40.

[25]Henry Kissinger (1923–), Secretary of State of the United States, 1973–1977; Assitant to the President for National Security Affairs, 1969–1975; winner of the Nobel Peace Prize, 1973.

the pressures of domestic forces on the one hand and of foreign realities on the other. Kissinger's discourse must for that reason alone establish a polarity between the United States and the world; in addition, of course, he speaks consciously as an authoritative voice for the major Western power, whose recent history and present reality have placed it before a world that does not easily accept its power and dominance. Kissinger feels that the United States can deal less problematically with the industrial, developed West than it can with the developing world. Again, the contemporary actuality of relations between the United States and the so-called Third World (which includes China, Indochina, the Near East, Africa, and Latin America) is manifestly a thorny set of problems, which even Kissinger cannot hide.

Kissinger's method in the essay proceeds according to what linguists call binary opposition: that is, he shows that there are two styles in foreign policy (the prophetic and the political), two types of technique, two periods, and so forth. When at the end of the historical part of his argument he is brought face to face with the contemporary world, he divides it accordingly into two halves, the developed and the developing countries. The first half, which is the West, "is deeply committed to the notion that the real world is external to the observer, that knowledge consists of recording and classifying data—the more accurately the better." Kissinger's proof for this is the Newtonian revolution, which has not taken place in the developing world: "Cultures which escaped the early impact of Newtonian thinking have retained the essentially pre-Newtonian view that the real world is almost completely *internal* to the observer." Consequently, he adds, "empirical reality has a much different significance for many of the new countries than for the West because in a certain sense they never went through the process of discovering it."[26]

Unlike Cromer, Kissinger does not need to quote Sir Alfred Lyall on the Oriental's inability to be accurate; the point he makes is sufficiently unarguable to require no special validation. We had our Newtonian revolution; they didn't. As thinkers we are better off than they are. Good: the lines are drawn in much the same way, finally, as Balfour and Cromer drew them. Yet sixty or more years have intervened between Kissinger and the British imperialists. Numerous wars and revolutions have proved conclusively that the pre-Newtonian prophetic style, which Kissinger associates both with "inaccurate" developing countries and with Europe before the Congress of Vienna, is not entirely without its successes. Again unlike Balfour and Cromer, Kissinger therefore feels obliged to respect this pre-Newtonian perspective, since "it offers great flexibility with respect to the contemporary revolutionary turmoil."

---

[26]Henry A. Kissinger, *American Foreign Policy* (New York: W. W. Norton & Co., 1974), pp. 48–9.

Thus the duty of men in the post-Newtonian (real) world is to "construct an international order *before* a crisis imposes it as a necessity": in other words, *we* must still find a way by which the developing world can be contained. Is this not similar to Cromer's vision of a harmoniously working machine designed ultimately to benefit some central authority, which opposes the developing world?

Kissinger may not have known on what fund of pedigreed knowledge he was drawing when he cut the world up into pre-Newtonian and post-Newtonian conceptions of reality. But his distinction is identical with the orthodox one made by Orientalists, who separate Orientals from Westerners. And like Orientalism's distinction Kissinger's is not value-free, despite the apparent neutrality of his tone. Thus such words as "prophetic," "accuracy," "internal," "empirical reality," and "order" are scattered throughout his description, and they characterize either attractive, familiar, desirable virtues or menacing, peculiar, disorderly defects. Both the traditional Orientalist, as we shall see, and Kissinger conceive of the difference between cultures, first, as creating a battlefront that separates them, and second, as inviting the West to control, contain, and otherwise govern (through superior knowledge and accommodating power) the Other. With what effect and at what considerable expense such militant divisions have been maintained, no one at present needs to be reminded.

Another illustration dovetails neatly—perhaps too neatly—with Kissinger's analysis. In its February 1972 issue, the *American Journal of Psychiatry* printed an essay by Harold W. Glidden, who is identified as a retired member of the Bureau of Intelligence and Research, United States Department of State; the essay's title ("The Arab World"), its tone, and its content argue a highly characteristic Orientalist bent of mind. Thus for his four-page, double-columned psychological portrait of over 100 million people, considered for a period of 1,300 years, Glidden cites exactly four sources for his views: a recent book on Tripoli, one issue of the Egyptian newspaper *Al-Ahram*, the periodical *Oriente Moderno*, and a book by Majid Khadduri, a well-known Orientalist. The article itself purports to uncover "the inner workings of Arab behavior," which from *our* point of view is "aberrant" but for Arabs is "normal." After this auspicious start, we are told that Arabs stress conformity; that Arabs inhabit a shame culture whose "prestige system" involves the ability to attract followers and clients (as an aside we are told that "Arab society is and always has been based on a system of client-patron relationships"); that Arabs can function only in conflict situations; that prestige is based solely on the ability to dominate others; that a shame culture—and therefore Islam itself—makes a virtue of revenge (here Glidden triumphantly cites the June 29, 1970 *Ahram* to show that "in 1969 [in Egypt] in 1070 cases of murder where the perpetrators were apprehended, it was found that 20 percent of the murders were based on a desire to wipe out shame, 30 percent on a desire to satisfy real or imaginary wrongs, and 31 percent on a desire for blood revenge"); that if from a Western point of view "the only rational thing for the Arabs to do is to make peace . . . for the Arabs the situation is not governed by this kind of logic, for objectivity is not a value in the Arab system."

Glidden continues, now more enthusiastically: "it is a notable fact that while the Arab value system demands absolute solidarity within the group, it at the same time encourages among its members a kind of rivalry that is destructive of that very solidarity"; in Arab society only "success counts" and "the end justifies the means"; Arabs live "naturally" in a world "characterized by anxiety expressed in generalized suspicion and distrust, which has been labelled free-floating hostility"; "the art of subterfuge is highly developed in Arab life, as well as in Islam itself"; the Arab need for vengeance overrides everything, otherwise the Arab would feel "ego-destroying" shame. Therefore, if "Westerners consider peace to be high on the scale of values" and if "we have a highly developed consciousness of the value of time," this is not true of Arabs. "In fact," we are told, "in Arab tribal society (where Arab values originated), strife, not peace, was the normal state of affairs because raiding was one of the two main supports of the economy." The purpose of this learned disquisition is merely to show how on the Western and Oriental scale of values "the relative position of the elements is quite different." QED.[27]

This is the apogee of Orientalist confidence. No merely asserted generality is denied the dignity of truth; no theoretical list of Oriental attributes is without application to the behavior of Orientals in the real world. On the one hand there are Westerners, and on the other there are Arab-Orientals; the former are (in no particular order) rational, peaceful, liberal, logical, capable of holding real values, without natural suspicion; the latter are none of these things. Out of what collective and yet particularized view of the Orient do these statements emerge? What specialized skills, what imaginative pressures, what institutions and traditions, what cultural forces produce such similarity in the descriptions of the Orient to be found in Cromer, Balfour, and our contemporary statesmen?

[1978]

---

[27]Harold W. Glidden, "The Arab World," *American Journal of Psychiatry* 128, no. 8 (February 1972): 984–8.

Amy Tan
[1952–   ]

Acclaimed author of The Joy Luck Club *and several other books,* AMY TAN *was born in San Francisco to Chinese immigrant parents. Her father worked as a minister and electrical engineer; her mother was a vocational nurse who really did belong to a Joy Luck Club in China. After her father and brother died of brain cancer within six months of each other, Tan's mother brought the family to Europe, where the young Amy, according to her own accounts, ran wild. On returning to the United States, she defied her mother's wishes that she become a neurosurgeon and concert pianist, and earned a bachelor's degree in English and linguistics (1973) and a master's degree in linguistics (1974) from San Jose State. Tan has been married since 1974 to Lou DeMattei, a tax attorney. She began her creative writing career as therapy to distract her from her ninety-hour work weeks as a freelance technical writer.*

Tan's first novel, The Joy Luck Club *(1989), intertwines the stories of four aging Chinese immigrant women and their four Americanized daughters. Made into a feature film in 1993, the novel explores not only mother-daughter relationships, but the cultural conflict between immigrant parents and their American children. This novel, along with others including* The Kitchen God's Wife *(1991),* The Hundred Secret Senses *(1995), and* The Bonesetter's Daughter *(2001), draws heavily from stories Tan's mother recounted about her life in China. In 1992 Tan adapted one of the stories from* The Joy Luck Club *for a children's book,* The Moon Lady; *her second children's book,* The Chinese Siamese Cat, *was published in 1994 and is the basis for a long-running PBS cartoon.*

Often compared to fellow Chinese-American writer Maxine Hong Kingston, Amy Tan populates her novels with strong, conflicted, oppressed, but often triumphant women, undercutting the powerful patriarchal structure of Chinese society. Critics compare her fiction to the work of Victorian novelist Jane Austen, noting her acute sense of the complex relationships within families strained by cultural clashes. Of The Joy Luck Club, *critic Carolyn See observes, the mothers' "deepest wish is to pass their knowledge, their tales, on to their children, especially to their daughters, but those young women are undergoing a slow death of their own; drowning in American culture at the same time they starve for a past they can never fully understand." This novel remains her most acclaimed work, receiving the Commonwealth Club Gold Award; the Bay Area Book Reviewers Award; the American Library Association's best book for young adults award; and nominations for the National Book Critics Circle and the* Los Angeles Times *book awards.*

Tan's mother died in 1999 of complications from Alzheimer's disease. In the dedication for The Bonesetter's Daughter, *the author writes, "On the last day that my mother spent on earth, I learned her real name, as well as that of my grandmother. This book is dedicated to them." This dedication reflects what Tan once told a reporter for the* Seattle Times, *"My books have amounted to taking [my mother's] stories—a gift to me—and giving them back to her. To me, it was the ultimate thing I ever could have done for myself and my mother."*

Two Kinds from The Joy Luck Club

AMY TAN

MY MOTHER BELIEVED YOU could be anything you wanted to be in America. You could open a restaurant. You could work for the government and get good retirement. You could buy a house with almost no money down. You could become rich. You could become instantly famous.

"Of course you can be prodigy, too," my mother told me when I was nine. "You can be best anything. What does Auntie Lindo know? Her daughter, she is only best tricky."

America was where all my mother's hopes lay. She had come here in 1949 after losing everything in China: her mother and father, her family home, her first husband, and two daughters, twin baby girls. But she never looked back with regret. There were so many ways for thing to get better.

We didn't immediately pick the right kind of prodigy. At first my mother thought I could be a Chinese Shirley Temple. We'd watch Shirley's old movies on TV as though they were training films. My mother would poke my arm and say, "*Ni kan*"—You watch. And I would see Shirley tapping her feet, or singing a sailor song, or pursing her lips into a very round O while saying, "Oh my goodness."

"*Ni kan*," said my mother as Shirley's eyes flooded with tears. "You already know how. Don't need talent for crying!"

Soon after my mother got this idea about Shirley Temple, she took me to a beauty training school in the Mission district and put me in the hands of a student who could barely hold the scissors without shaking. Instead of getting big fat curls, I emerged with an uneven mass of crinkly black fuzz. My mother dragged me off to the bathroom and tried to wet down my hair.

"You look like Negro Chinese," she lamented, as if I had done this on purpose.

The instructor of the beauty training school had to lop off these soggy clumps to make my hair even again. "Peter Pan is very popular these days," the instructor assured my mother. I now had hair the length of a boy's, with

Reprinted from *The Joy Luck Club*. Copyright © 1989 by Amy Tan. Reprinted by permission of the author, Sandra Dijkstra Literary Agency, and Penguin Group (USA) Inc.

straight-across bangs that hung at a slant two inches above my eyebrows. I liked the haircut and it made me actually look forward to my future fame.

In fact, in the beginning, I was just as excited as my mother, maybe even more so. I pictured this prodigy part of me as many different images, trying each one on for size. I was a dainty ballerina girl standing by the curtains, waiting to hear the right music that would send me floating on my tiptoes. I was like the Christ child lifted out of the straw manger, crying with holy indignity. I was Cinderella stepping from her pumpkin carriage with sparkly cartoon music filling the air.

In all of my imaginings, I was filled with a sense that I would soon become *perfect*. My mother and father would adore me. I would be beyond reproach. I would never feel the need to sulk for anything.

But sometimes the prodigy in me became impatient. "If you don't hurry up and get me out of here, I'm disappearing for good," it warned. "And then you'll always be nothing."

Every night after dinner, my mother and I would sit at the Formica kitchen table. She would present new tests, taking her examples from stories of amazing children she had read in *Ripley's Believe It or Not,* or *Good Housekeeping, Reader's Digest,* and a dozen other magazines she kept in a pile in our bathroom. My mother got these magazines from people whose houses she cleaned. And since she cleaned many houses each week, we had a great assortment. She would look through them all, searching for stories about remarkable children.

The first night she brought out a story about a three-year-old boy who knew the capitals of all the states and even most of the European countries. A teacher was quoted as saying the little boy could also pronounce the names of the foreign cities correctly.

"What's the capital of Finland?" my mother asked me, looking at the magazine story.

All I knew was the capital of California, because Sacramento was the name of the street we lived on in Chinatown. "Nairobi!" I guessed, saying the most foreign word I could think of. She checked to see if that was possibly one way to pronounce "Helsinki" before showing me the answer.

The tests got harder—multiplying numbers in my head, finding the queen of hearts in a deck of cards, trying to stand on my head without using my hands, predicting the daily temperatures in Los Angeles, New York, and London.

One night I had to look at a page from the Bible for three minutes and then report everything I could remember. "Now Jehoshaphat had riches and honor in abundance and . . . that's all I remember, Ma," I said.

And after seeing my mother's disappointed face once again, something inside of me began to die. I hated the tests, the raised hopes and failed expectations. Before going to bed that night, I looked in the mirror above the bathroom sink and when I saw only my face staring back—and that it would always be this ordinary face—I began to cry. Such a sad, ugly girl! I made highpitched noises like a crazed animal, trying to scratch out the face in the mirror.

And then I saw what seemed to be the prodigy side of me—because I had never seen that face before. I looked at my reflection, blinking so I could see more clearly. The girl staring back at me was angry, powerful. This girl and I were the same. I had new thoughts, willful thoughts, or rather thoughts filled with lots of won'ts. I won't let her change me, I promised myself. I won't be what I'm not.

So now on nights when my mother presented her tests, I performed listlessly, my head propped on one arm. I pretended to be bored. And I was. I got so bored I started counting the bellows of the foghorns out on the bay while my mother drilled me in other areas. The sound was comforting and reminded me of the cow jumping over the moon. And the next day, I played a game with myself, seeing if my mother would give up on me before eight bellows. After a while I usually counted only one, maybe two bellows at most. At last she was beginning to give up hope.

Two or three months had gone by without any mention of my being a prodigy again. And then one day my mother was watching *The Ed Sullivan Show* on TV. The TV was old and the sound kept shorting out. Every time my mother got halfway up from the sofa to adjust the set, the sound would go back on and Ed would be talking. As soon as she sat down, Ed would go silent again. She got up, the TV broke into loud piano music. She sat down. Silence. Up and down, back and forth, quiet and loud. It was like a stiff embraceless dance between her and the TV set. Finally she stood by the set with her hand on the sound dial.

She seemed entranced by the music, a little frenzied piano piece with this mesmerizing quality, sort of quick passages and then teasing lilting ones before it returned to the quick playful parts.

"*Ni kan*," my mother said, calling me over with hurried hand gestures, "Look here."

I could see why my mother was fascinated by the music. It was being pounded out by a little Chinese girl, about nine years old, with a Peter Pan haircut. The girl had the sauciness of a Shirley Temple. She was proudly modest like a proper Chinese child. And she also did this fancy sweep of a curtsy, so that the fluffy skirt of her white dress cascaded slowly to the floor like the petals of a large carnation.

In spite of these warning signs, I wasn't worried. Our family had no piano and we couldn't afford to buy one, let alone reams of sheet music and piano lessons. So I could be generous in my comments when my mother bad-mouthed the little girl on TV.

"Play note right, but doesn't sound good! No singing sound," complained my mother.

"What are you picking on her for?" I said carelessly. "She's pretty good. Maybe she's not the best, but she's trying hard." I knew almost immediately I would be sorry I said that.

"Just like you," she said. "Not the best. Because you not trying." She gave a little huff as she let go of the sound dial and sat down on the sofa.

The little Chinese girl sat down also to play an encore of "Anitra's Dance" by Grieg. I remember the song, because later on I had to learn how to play it.

Three days after watching *The Ed Sullivan Show*, my mother told me what my schedule would be for piano lessons and piano practice. She had talked to Mr. Chong, who lived on the first floor of our apartment building. Mr. Chong was a retired piano teacher and my mother had traded housecleaning services for weekly lessons and a piano for me to practice on every day, two hours a day, from four until six.

When my mother told me this, I felt as though I had been sent to hell. I whined and then kicked my foot a little when I couldn't stand it anymore.

"Why don't you like me the way I am? I'm *not* a genius! I can't play the piano. And even if I could, I wouldn't go on TV if you paid me a million dollars!" I cried.

My mother slapped me. "Who ask you be genius?" she shouted. "Only ask you be your best. For you sake. You think I want you be genius? Hnnh! What for! Who ask you!"

"So ungrateful," I heard her mutter in Chinese. "If she had as much talent as she had temper, she would be famous now."

Mr. Chong, whom I secretly nicknamed Old Chong, was very strange, always tapping his fingers to the silent music of an invisible orchestra. He looked ancient in my eyes. He had lost most of the hair on top of his head and he wore thick glasses and had eyes that always looked tired and sleepy. But he must have been younger than I thought, since he lived with his mother and was not yet married.

I met Old Lady Chong once and that was enough. She had this peculiar smell like a baby that had done something in his pants. And her fingers felt like a dead person's, like an old peach I once found in the back of the refrigerator; the skin just slid off the meat when I picked it up.

I soon found out why Old Chong had retired from teaching piano. He was deaf. "Like Beethoven!" he shouted to me. "We're both listening only in our head!" And he would start to conduct his frantic silent sonatas.

Our lessons went like this. He would open the book and point to different things, explaining their purpose: "Key! Treble! Bass! No sharps or flats! So this is C major! Listen now and play after me!"

And then he would play the C scale a few times, a simple chord, and then, as if inspired by an old, unreachable itch, he gradually added more notes and running trills and a pounding bass until the music was really something quite grand.

I would play after him, the simple scale, the simple chord, and then I just played some nonsense that sounded like a cat running up and down on top of garbage cans. Old Chong smiled and applauded and then said, "Very good! But now you must learn to keep time!"

So that's how I discovered that Old Chong's eyes were too slow to keep up with the wrong notes I was playing. He went through the motions in halftime. To help me keep rhythm, he stood behind me, pushing down on my right shoulder for every beat. He balanced pennies on top of my wrists so I would keep them still as I slowly played scales and arpeggios. He had me curve my hand around an apple and keep that shape when playing chords. He marched stiffly to show me how to make each finger dance up and down, staccato like an obedient little soldier.

He taught me all these things, and that was how I also learned I could be lazy and get away with mistakes, lots of mistakes. If I hit the wrong notes because I hadn't practiced enough, I never corrected myself. I just kept playing in rhythm. And Old Chong kept conducting his own private reverie.

So maybe I never really gave myself a fair chance. I did pick up the basics pretty quickly, and I might have become a good pianist at that young age. But I was so determined not to try, not to be anybody different that I learned to play only the most ear-splitting preludes, the most discordant hymns.

Over the next year, I practiced like this, dutifully in my own way. And then one day I heard my mother and her friend Lindo Jong both talking in a loud bragging tone of voice so others could hear. It was after church, and I was leaning against the brick wall wearing a dress with stiff white petticoats. Auntie Lindo's daughter, Waverly, who was about my age, was standing farther down the wall about five feet away. We had grown up together and shared all the closeness of two sisters squabbling over crayons and dolls. In other words, for the most part, we hated each other. I thought she was snotty. Waverly Jong had gained a certain amount of fame as "Chinatown's Littlest Chinese Chess Champion."

"She bring home too many trophy," lamented Auntie Lindo that Sunday. "All day she play chess. All day I have no time do nothing but dust off her winnings." She threw a scolding look at Waverly, who pretended not to see her.

"You lucky you don't have this problem," said Auntie Lindo with a sigh to my mother.

And my mother squared her shoulders and bragged: "Our problem worser than yours. If we ask Jing-mei wash dish, she hear nothing but music. It's like you can't stop this natural talent."

And right then, I was determined to put a stop to her foolish pride.

A few weeks later, Old Chong and my mother conspired to have me play in a talent show which would be held in the church hall. By then, my parents had saved up enough to buy me a secondhand piano, a black Wurlitzer spinet with a scarred bench. It was the showpiece of our living room.

For the talent show, I was to play a piece called "Pleading Child" from Schumann's *Scenes from Childhood*. It was a simple, moody piece that sounded more difficult than it was. I was supposed to memorize the whole thing, playing the repeat parts twice to make the piece sound longer. But I dawdled over it, playing a few bars and then cheating, looking up to see what notes followed. I never really listened to what I was playing. I daydreamed about being somewhere else, about being someone else.

The part I liked to practice best was the fancy curtsy: right foot out, touch the rose on the carpet with a pointed foot, sweep to the side, left leg bends, look up and smile.

My parents invited all the couples from the Joy Luck Club to witness my debut. Auntie Lindo and Uncle Tin were there. Waverly and her two older brothers had also come. The first two rows were filled with children both younger and older than I was. The littlest ones got to go first. They recited simple nursery rhymes, squawked out tunes on miniature violins, twirled Hula Hoops, pranced in pink ballet tutus, and when they bowed or curtsied, the audience would sigh in unison, "Awww," and then clap enthusiastically.

When my turn came, I was very confident. I remember my childish excitement. It was as if I knew, without a doubt, that the prodigy side of me really did exist. I had no fear whatsoever, no nervousness. I remember thinking to myself, This is it! This is it! I looked out over the audience, at my mother's blank face, my father's yawn, Auntie Lindo's stiff-lipped smile, Waverly's sulky expression. I had on a white dress layered with sheets of lace, and a pink bow in my Peter Pan haircut. As I sat down I envisioned people jumping to their feet and Ed Sullivan rushing up to introduce me to everyone on TV.

And I started to play. It was so beautiful. I was so caught up in how lovely I looked at first I didn't worry how I would sound. So it was a surprise to me when I hit the first wrong note and I realized something didn't sound quite right. And then I hit another and another followed that. A chill started at the top of my head and began to trickle down. Yet I couldn't stop playing, as though my hands were bewitched. I kept thinking my fingers would adjust themselves back, like a train switching to the right track. I played this strange jumble through two repeats, the sour notes staying with me all the way to the end.

When I stood up, I discovered my legs were shaking. Maybe I had just been nervous and the audience, like Old Chong, had seen me go through the right motions and had not heard anything wrong at all. I swept my right foot out, went down on my knee, looked up and smiled. The room was quiet, except for Old Chong, who was beaming and shouting, "Bravo! Bravo! Well done!" But then I saw my mother's face, her stricken face. The audience clapped weakly, and as I walked back to my chair, with my whole face quivering as I tried not to cry, I heard a little boy whisper loudly to his mother, "That was awful," and the mother whispered back, "Well, she certainly tried."

And now I realized how many people were in the audience, the whole world it seemed. I was aware of eyes burning into my back. I felt the shame of my mother and father as they sat stiffly throughout the rest of the show.

We could have escaped during intermission. Pride and some strange sense of honor must have anchored my parents to their chairs. And so we watched it all: the eighteen-year-old boy with a fake mustache who did a magic show and juggled flaming hoops while riding a unicycle. The breasted girl with white makeup who sang from *Madama Butterfly* and got honorable mention. And the eleven-year-old boy who won first prize playing a tricky violin song that sounded like a busy bee.

After the show, the Hsus, the Jongs, and the St. Clairs from the Joy Luck Club came up to my mother and father.

"Lots of talented kids," Auntie Lindo said vaguely, smiling broadly.

"That was somethin' else," said my father, and I wondered if he was referring to me in a humorous way, or whether he even remembered what I had done.

Waverly looked at me and shrugged her shoulders. "You aren't a genius like me," she said matter-of-factly. And if I hadn't felt so bad, I would have pulled her braids and punched her stomach.

But my mother's expression was what devastated me: a quiet, blank look that said she had lost everything. I felt the same way, and it seemed as if everybody were now coming up, like gawkers at the scene of an accident, to see what parts were actually missing. When we got on the bus to go home, my father was humming the busy-bee tune and my mother was silent. I kept thinking she wanted to wait until we got home before shouting at me. But when my father unlocked the door to our apartment, my mother walked in and then went to the back, into the bedroom. No accusations. No blame. And in a way, I felt disappointed. I had been waiting for her to start shouting, so I could shout back and cry and blame her for all my misery.

I assumed my talent-show fiasco meant I never had to play the piano again. But two days later, after school, my mother came out of the kitchen and saw me watching TV.

"Four clock," she reminded me as if it were any other day. I was stunned, as though she were asking me to go through the talent-show torture again. I wedged myself more tightly in front of the TV.

"Turn off TV," she called from the kitchen five minutes later.

I didn't budge. And then I decided. I didn't have to do what my mother said anymore. I wasn't her slave. This wasn't China. I had listened to her before and look what happened. She was the stupid one.

She came out of the kitchen and stood in the arched entryway of the living room. "Four clock," she said once again, louder.

"I'm not going to play anymore," I said nonchalantly. "Why should I? I'm not a genius."

She walked over and stood in front of the TV. I saw her chest was heaving up and down in an angry way.

"No!" I said, and I now felt stronger, as if my true self had finally emerged. So this was what had been inside me all along.

"No! I won't!" I screamed.

She yanked me by the arm, pulled me off the floor, snapped off the TV. She was frighteningly strong, half pulling, half carrying me toward the piano as I kicked the throw rugs under my feet. She lifted me up and onto the hard bench. I was sobbing by now, looking at her bitterly. Her chest was heaving even more and her mouth was open, smiling crazily as if she were pleased I was crying.

"You want me to be someone that I'm not!" I sobbed. "I'll never be the kind of daughter you want me to be!"

"Only two kinds of daughters," she shouted in Chinese. "Those who are obedient and those who follow their own mind! Only one kind of daughter can live in this house. Obedient daughter!"

"Then I wish I wasn't your daughter. I wish you weren't my mother," I shouted. As I said these things I got scared. It felt like worms and toads and slimy things crawling out of my chest, but it also felt good, as if this awful side of me had surfaced, at last.

"Too late change this," said my mother shrilly.

And I could sense her anger rising to its breaking point. I wanted to see it spill over. And that's when I remembered the babies she had lost in China, the ones we never talked about. "Then I wish I'd never been born!" I shouted. "I wish I were dead! Like them."

It was as if I had said the magic words. Alakazam!—and her face went blank, her mouth closed, her arms went slack, and she backed out of the room, stunned, as if she were blowing away like a small brown leaf, thin, brittle, lifeless.

It was not the only disappointment my mother felt in me. In the years that followed, I failed her so many times, each time asserting my own will, my right to fall short of expectations. I didn't get straight As. I didn't become class president. I didn't get into Stanford. I dropped out of college.

For unlike my mother, I did not believe I could be anything I wanted to be. I could only be me.

And for all those years, we never talked about the disaster at the recital or my terrible accusations afterward at the piano bench. All that remained unchecked, like a betrayal that was now unspeakable. So I never found a way to ask her why she had hoped for something so large that failure was inevitable.

And even worse, I never asked her what frightened me the most: Why had she given up hope?

For after our struggle at the piano, she never mentioned my playing again. The lessons stopped. The lid to the piano was closed, shutting out the dust, my misery, and her dreams.

So she surprised me. A few years ago, she offered to give me the piano, for my thirtieth birthday. I had not played in all those years. I saw the offer as a sign of forgiveness, a tremendous burden removed.

"Are you sure?" I asked shyly. "I mean, won't you and Dad miss it?"

"No, this your piano," she said firmly. "Always your piano. You only one can play."

"Well, I probably can't play anymore," I said. "It's been years."

"You pick up fast," said my mother, as if she knew this was certain. "You have natural talent. You could been genius if you want to."

"No I couldn't."

"You just not trying," said my mother. And she was neither angry nor sad. She said it as if to announce a fact that could never be disproved. "Take it," she said.

But I didn't at first. It was enough that she had offered to me. And after that, every time I saw it in my parent's living room, standing in front of the bay windows, it made me feel proud, as if it were a shiny trophy I had won back.

Last week I sent a tuner over to my parents' apartment and had the piano reconditioned, for purely sentimental reasons. My mother had died a few months before and I had been getting things in order for my father, a little bit at a time. I put the jewelry in special silk pouches. The sweaters she had knitted in yellow, pink, bright orange—all the colors I hated—I put those in moth-proof boxes. I found some old Chinese silk dresses, the kind with little slits up the sides. I rubbed the old silk against my skin, then wrapped them in tissue and decided to take them home with me.

After I had the piano tuned, I opened the lid and touched the keys. It sounded even richer than I remembered. Really, it was a very good piano. Inside the bench were the same exercise notes with handwritten scales, the same secondhand music books with their covers held together with yellow tape.

I opened up the Schumann book to the dark little piece I had played at the recital. It was on the left-hand side of the page, "Pleading Child." It looked more difficult than I remembered. I played a few bars, surprised at how easily the notes came back to me.

And for the first time, or so it seemed, I noticed the piece on the right-hand side. It was called "Perfectly Contented." I tried to play this one as well. It had a lighter melody but the same flowing rhythm and turned out to be quite easy. "Pleading Child" was shorter but slower; "Perfectly Contented" was longer, but faster. And after I played them both a few times, I realized they were two halves of the same song.

[1989]

Hisaye Yamamoto
[1921–   ]

HISAYE YAMAMOTO *was born to Issei (Japanese immigrant) parents in Redondo Beach, California. She attended public schools and Japanese language schools in southern California and went on to study European languages at Compton Junior College near Los Angeles. With the advent of World War II, some 50,000 Issei and 70,000 Nisei (second generation Japanese-Americans) were interned in nine camps located throughout the western United States. Yamamoto and her family were sent to Arizona's Poston Relocation Center from 1942 to 1945. During this time, Yamamoto's brother was killed in action, fighting with the U.S. Army in Italy. Yamamoto began to write in her early teens, contributing regularly to Japanese-American newspapers (she received her first rejection slip from a local newspaper at the age of fourteen). While at Poston, Yamamoto served as a reporter and columnist for the camp newspaper; she also published a serialized mystery story titled "Death Rides the Rails to Poston." After her release from Poston in 1945, Yamamoto continued her journalistic career as a reporter for the* Los Angeles Tribune, *a small weekly that served the African-American community. In the postwar years, Yamamoto published a series of short stories that launched her career as a fictionist. Nineteen forty-eight was a momentous year for Yamamoto; she published "High-heeled Shoes," the first of several well-received short stories, and adopted a five-month-old infant named Paul. "High-Heeled Shoes" was followed by "Seventeen Syllables" (1949); "The Legend of Miss Sasagawara" (1950); "The Brown House" (1951); and "Yoneko's Earthquake" (1952). These acclaimed stories earned Yamamoto a John Hay Whitney Foundation Opportunity Fellowship in 1950 and a Stanford Writing Fellowship, which Yamamoto declined in order to volunteer in the Staten Island Catholic Workers rehabilitation farm, where she lived with her son from 1953 to 1955. In 1955, Yamamoto married Anthony DeSoto and returned to Los Angeles; the couple eventually raised four more children.*

Coming of age amid the virulent anti-Japanese sentiments of World War II and its aftermath, Yamamoto illuminates the lives of mid and late twentieth century Japanese Americans. Yamamoto's most widely read book is Seventeen Syllables, *a collection of short fiction published between 1948 and 1987. As seen in stories such as "Seventeen Syllables" and "Yoneko's Earthquake," one of the overriding themes of this book is the generation gap between Issei and Nisei in America. "The Legend of Miss Sasagawara," however, reflects the ways in which Yamamoto illuminates the traumatic legacy of Japanese-American internment. Both of these stories, along with "The High-Heeled Shoes" and "Underground Lady" (1986), exemplify Yamamoto's persistent concern with women's issues.*

Whether emphasizing sensual awakening, marital abuse, mental illness, or sexual harassment, Yamamoto is ever attentive to the difficulties of women living in the doubly patriarchal world of Japanese America. The Before Columbus Foundation has recognized Seventeen Syllables *with its American Book Award for Lifetime Achievement. The book's eponymous story, along with "Yoneko's Earthquake," was adapted for an American Playhouse/PBS film titled* Hot Summer Winds.

Seventeen Syllables

HISAYE YAMAMOTO

THE FIRST ROSIE KNEW that her mother had taken to writing poems was one evening when she finished one and read it aloud for her daughter's approval. It was about cats, and Rosie pretended to understand it thoroughly and appreciate it no end, partly because she hesitated to disillusion her mother about the quantity and quality of Japanese she had learned in all the years now that she had been going to Japanese school every Saturday (and Wednesday, too, in the summer). Even so, her mother must have been skeptical about the depth of Rosie's understanding, because she explained afterwards about the kind of poem she was trying to write.

See, Rosie, she said, it was a *haiku*,[1] a poem in which she must pack all her meaning into seventeen syllables only, which were divided into three lines of five, seven, and five syllables. In the one she had just read, she had tried to capture the charm of a kitten, as well as comment on the superstition that owning a cat of three colors meant good luck.

"Yes, yes, I understand. How utterly lovely," Rosie said, and her mother, either satisfied or seeing through the deception and resigned, went back to composing.

The truth was that Rosie was lazy: English lay ready on the tongue but Japanese had to be searched for and examined, and even then put forth tentatively (probably to meet with laughter). It was so much easier to say yes, yes, even when one meant no, no. Besides, this was what was in her mind to say: I was looking through one of your magazines from Japan last night, Mother, and towards the back I found some *haiku* in English that delighted me. There was one that made me giggle off and on until I fell asleep—

> It is morning, and lo!
> I lie awake, comme il faut,[2]
> sighing for some dough.

---

[1]In this Japanese poetic form, seventeen syllables must be arranged into three unrhymed lines of five, seven, and five syllables. Haiku often juxtapose images of nature with human emotions and experience, inviting the reader's comparisons.

[2]French: "as is done."

Reprinted from *Seventeen Syllables and Other Stories,* by permission of Rutgers University Press. Copyright © 1988 by Hisaye Yamamoto DeSoto.

Now, how to reach her mother, how to communicate the melancholy song? Rosie knew formal Japanese by fits and starts, her mother had even less English, no French. It was much more possible to say yes, yes.

It developed that her mother was writing the *haiku* for a daily newspaper, the *Mainichi Shimbun,* that was published in San Francisco. Los Angeles, to be sure, was closer to the farming community in which the Hayashi family lived and several Japanese vernaculars were printed there, but Rosie's parents said they preferred the tone of the northern paper. Once a week, the *Mainichi* would have a section devoted to *haiku,* and her mother became an extravagant contributor, taking for herself the blossoming pen name, Ume Hanazono.

So Rosie and her father lived for awhile with two women, her mother and Ume Hanazono. Her mother (Tome Hayashi by name) kept house, cooked, washed, and, along with her husband and the Carrascos, the Mexican family hired for the harvest, did her ample share of picking tomatoes out in the sweltering fields and boxing them in tidy strata in the cool packing shed. Ume Hanazono, who came to life after the dinner dishes were done, was an earnest, muttering stranger who often neglected speaking when spoken to and stayed busy at the parlor table as late as midnight scribbling with pencil on scratch paper or carefully copying characters on good paper with her fat, pale green Parker.[3]

The new interest had some repercussions on the household routine Before. Rosie had been accustomed to her parents and herself taking their hot baths early and going to bed almost immediately afterwards, unless her parents challenged each other to a game of flower cards or unless company dropped in. Now if her father wanted to play cards, he had to resort to solitaire (at which he always cheated fearlessly), and if a group of friends came over, it was bound to contain someone who was also writing *haiku,* and the small assemblage would be split in two, her father entertaining the non-literary members and her mother comparing ecstatic notes with the visiting poet.

If they went out, it was more of the same thing. But Ume Hanazono's life span, even for a poet's, was very brief—perhaps three months at most.

One night they went over to see the Hayano family in the neighboring town to the west, an adventure both painful and attractive to Rosie. It was attractive because there were four Hayano girls, all lovely and each one named after a season of the year (Haru, Natsu, Aki, Fuyu), painful because something had been wrong with Mrs. Hayano ever since the birth of her first child. Rosie would sometimes watch Mrs. Hayano, reputed to have been the belle of her

---

[3]Parker is a popular brand of ink-pens.

native village, making her way about a room, stooped, slowly shuffling, violently trembling (*always* trembling), and she would be reminded that this woman, in this same condition, had carried and given issue to three babies. She would look wonderingly at Mr. Hayano, handsome, tall, and strong, and she would look at her four pretty friends. But it was not a matter she could come to any decision about.

On this visit, however, Mrs. Hayano sat all evening in the rocker, as motionless and unobtrusive as it was possible for her to be, and Rosie found the greater part of the evening practically anaesthetic. Too, Rosie spent most of it in the girls' room, because Haru, the garrulous one, said almost as soon as the bows and other greetings were over, "Oh, you must see my new coat!"

It was a pale plaid of grey, sand, and blue, with an enormous collar, and Rosie, seeing nothing special in it, said, "Gee, how nice."

"Nice?" said Haru, indignantly. "Is that all you can say about it? It's gorgeous! And so cheap, too. Only seventeen ninety-eight, because it was a sale. The saleslady said it was twenty-five dollars regular."

"Gee," said Rosie. Natsu, who never said much and when she said anything said it shyly, fingered the coat covetously and Haru pulled it away.

"Mine," she said, putting it on. She minced in the aisle between the two large beds and smiled happily. "Let's see how your mother likes it."

She broke into the front room and the adult conversation and went to stand in front of Rosie's mother, while the rest watched from the door. Rosie's mother was properly envious. "May I inherit it when you're through with it?"

Haru, pleased, giggled and said yes, she could, but Natsu reminded gravely from the door. "You promised me, Haru."

Everyone laughed but Natsu, who shamefacedly retreated into the bedroom. Haru came in laughing, taking off the coat. "We were only kidding, Natsu," she said. "Here, you try it on now."

After Natsu buttoned herself into the coat, inspected herself solemnly in the bureau mirror, and reluctantly shed it, Rosie, Aki, and Fuyu got their turns, and Fuyu, who was eight, drowned in it while her sisters and Rosie doubled up in amusement. They all went into the front room later, because Haru's mother quaveringly called to her to fix the tea and rice cakes and open a can of sliced peaches for everybody. Rosie noticed that her mother and Mr. Hayano were talking together at the little table—they were discussing a *haiku* that Mr. Hayano was planning to send to the *Mainichi*, while her father was sitting at one end of the sofa looking through a copy of *Life*, the new picture magazine. Occasionally, her father would comment on a photograph, holding it toward Mrs. Hayano and speaking to her as he always did—loudly, as though he thought someone such as she must surely be at least a trifle deaf also.

The five girls had their refreshments at the kitchen table, and it was while Rosie was showing the sisters her trick of swallowing peach slices without chewing (she chased each slippery crescent down with a swig of tea) that her father brought his empty teacup and untouched saucer to the sink and said, "Come on, Rosie, we're going home now."

"Already?" asked Rosie.

"Work tomorrow," he said.

He sounded irritated, and Rosie, puzzled, gulped one last yellow slice and stood up to go, while the sisters began protesting, as was their wont.

"We have to get up at five-thirty," he told them, going into the front room quickly, so that they did not have their usual chance to hang onto his hands and plead for an extension of time.

Rosie, following, saw that her mother and Mr. Hayano were sipping tea and still talking together, while Mrs. Hayano concentrated, quivering, on raising the handleless Japanese cup to her lips with both her hands and lowering it back to her lap. Her father, saying nothing, went out the door, onto the bright porch, and down the steps. Her mother looked up and asked. "Where is he going?"

"Where is he going?" Rosie said. "He said we were going home now."

"Going home?" Her mother looked with embarrassment at Mr. Hayano and his absorbed wife and then forced a smile. "He must be tired." she said.

Haru was not giving up yet. "May Rosie stay overnight?" she asked, and Natsu, Aki, and Fuyu came to reinforce their sister's plea by helping her make a circle around Rosie's mother. Rosie, for once having no desire to stay, was relieved when her mother, apologizing to the perturbed Mr. and Mrs. Hayano for her father's abruptness at the same time, managed to shake her head no at the quartet, kindly but adamant, so that they broke their circle and let her go.

Rosie's father looked ahead into the windshield as the two joined him. "I'm sorry," her mother said. "You must be tired." Her father, stepping on the starter said nothing. "You know how I get when it's *haiku*," she continued, "I forget what time it is." He only grunted.

As they rode homeward silently, Rosie, sitting between, felt a rush of hate for both—for her mother for begging, for her father for denying her mother. I wish this old Ford would crash, right now, she thought, then immediately, no, no, I wish my father would laugh, but it was too late; already the vision had passed through her mind of the green pick-up crumpled in the dark against one of the mighty eucalyptus trees they were just riding past, of the three contorted, bleeding bodies, one of them hers.

Rosie ran between two patches of tomatoes, her heart working more rambunctiously than she had ever known it to. How lucky it was that Aunt Taka and Uncle Gimpachi had come tonight, though, how very lucky. Otherwise she might not have really kept her half-promise to meet Jesus Carrasco. Jesus was going to be a senior in September at the same school she went to, and his parents were the ones helping with the tomatoes this year. She and Jesus, who hardly remembered seeing each other at Cleveland High where there were so many other people and two whole grades between them, had become great friends this summer—he always had a joke for her when he periodically drove the loaded pick-up up from the fields to the shed where she was usually sorting while her mother and father did the packing, and they laughed a great deal together over infinitesimal repartee during the afternoon break for chilled watermelon or ice cream in the shade of the shed.

What she enjoyed most was racing him to see which could finish picking a double row first. He, who could work faster, would tease her by slowing down until she thought she would surely pass him this time, then speeding up furiously to leave her several sprawling vines behind. Once he had made her screech hideously by crossing over, while her back was turned, to place atop the tomatoes in her green stained bucket a truly monstrous, pale green worm (it had looked more like an infant snake). And it was when they had finished a contest this morning, after she had pantingly pointed a green finger at the immature tomatoes evident in the lugs at the end of his row and he had returned the accusation (with justice), that he had startlingly brought up the matter of their possibly meeting outside the range of both their parents' dubious eyes.

"What for?" she had asked.

"I've got a secret I want to tell you," he said.

"Tell me now," she demanded.

"It won't be ready till tonight," he said.

She laughed. "Tell me tomorrow then."

"It'll be gone tomorrow," he threatened.

"Well, for seven hakes, what is it?" she had asked, more than twice, and when he had suggested that the packing shed would be an appropriate place to find out, she had cautiously answered maybe. She had not been certain she was going to keep the appointment until the arrival of mother's sister and her husband. Their coming seemed a sort of signal of permission, of grace, and she had definitely made up her mind to lie and leave as she was bowing them welcome.

So as soon as everyone appeared settled back for the evening she announced loudly that she was going to the privy outside. "I'm going to the *benjo!*"[4] and slipped out the door. And now that she was actually on her way, her heart pumped in such an undisciplined way that she could hear it with her

---

[4]Japanese: A benjo is an outhouse or outdoor toilet.

ears. It's because I'm running, she told herself, slowing to a walk. The shed was up ahead, one more patch away, in the middle of the fields. Its bulk, looming in the dimness, took on a sinisterness that was funny when Rosie reminded herself that it was only a wooden frame with a canvas roof and three canvas walls that made a slapping noise on breezy days.

Jesus was sitting on the narrow plank that was the sorting platform and she went around to the other side and jumped backwards to seat herself on the rim of a packing stand. "Well, tell me," she said without greeting, thinking her voice sounded reassuringly familiar.

"I saw you coming out the door," Jesus said. "I heard you running part of the way, too."

"Uh-huh," Rosie said. "Now tell me the secret."

"I was afraid you wouldn't come," he said.

Rosie delved around on the chicken-wire bottom of the stall for number two tomatoes, ripe, which she was sitting beside, and came up with a left-over that felt edible. She bit into it and began sucking out the pulp and seeds. "I'm here," she pointed out.

"Rosie, are you sorry you came?"

"Sorry? What for?" she said. "You said you were going to tell me something."

"I will, I will," Jesus said, but his voice contained disappointment, and Rosie fleetingly felt the older of the two, realizing a brand-new power which vanished without category under her recognition.

"I have to go back in a minute," she said. "My aunt and uncle are here from Wintersburg. I told them I was going to the privy."

Jesus laughed. "You funny thing," he said. "You slay me!"

"Just because you have a bathroom *inside*." Rosie said. "Come on, tell me."

Chuckling, Jesus came around to lean on the stand facing her. They still could not see each other very clearly, but Rosie noticed that Jesus became very sober again as he took the hollow tomato from her hand and dropped it back into the stall. When he took hold of her empty hand, she could find no words to protest: her vocabulary had become distressingly constricted and she thought desperately that all that remained intact now was yes and no and oh, and even these few sounds would not easily out. Thus, kissed by Jesus, Rosie fell for the first time entirely victim to a helplessness delectable beyond speech. But the terrible, beautiful sensation lasted no more than a second, and the reality of Jesus' lips and tongue and teeth and hands made her pull away with such strength that she nearly tumbled.

Rosie stopped running as she approached the lights from the windows of home. How long since she had left? She could not guess, but gasping yet, she went to the privy in back and locked herself in. Her own breathing deafened her in the dark, close space, and she sat and waited until she could hear at last the nightly calling of the frogs and crickets. Even then, all she could think to say was oh, my, and the pressure of Jesus' face against her face would not leave.

No one had missed her in the parlor, however, and Rosie walked in and through quickly, announcing that she was next going to take a bath. "Your father's in the bathhouse," her mother said, and Rosie, in her room, recalled that she had not seen him when she entered. There had been only Aunt Taka and Uncle Gimpachi with her mother at the table, drinking tea. She got her robe and straw sandals and crossed the parlor again to go outside. Her mother was telling them about the *haiku* competition in the *Mainichi* and the poem she had entered.

Rosie met her father coming out of the bathhouse. "Are you through, Father?" she asked. "I was going to ask you to scrub my back."

"Scrub your own back," he said shortly, going toward the main house.

"What have I done now?" she yelled after him. She suddenly felt like doing a lot of yelling. But he did not answer, and she went into the bathhouse Turning on the dangling light, she removed her denims and T-shirt and threw them in the big carton for dirty clothes standing next to the washing machine. Her other things she took with her into the bath compartment to wash after her bath. After she had scooped a basin of hot water from the square wooden tub, she sat on the grey cement of the floor and soaped herself at exaggerated leisure singing "Red Sails in the Sunset" at the top of her voice and using da-da-da where she suspected her words. Then, standing up, still singing, for she was possessed by the notion that any attempt now to analyze would result in spoilage and she believed that the larger her volume the less she would be able to hear herself think, she obtained more hot water and poured it on until she was free of lather. Only then did she allow herself to step in to the steaming vat, one leg first, then the remainder of her body inch by inch until the water no longer stung and she could move around at will.

She took a long time soaking, afterwards remembering to go around outside to stoke the embers of the tin-lined fireplace beneath the tub and to throw on a few more sticks so that the water might keep its heat for her mother, and when she finally returned to the parlor, she found her mother still talking *haiku* with her aunt and uncle, the three of them on another round of tea. Her father was nowhere in sight.

At Japanese school the next day (Wednesday, it was), Rosie was grave and giddy by turns. Preoccupied at her desk in the row for students on Book Eight, she made up for it at recess by performing wild mimicry for the benefit of her friend Chizuko. She held her nose and whined a witticism or two in what she considered was the manner of Fred Allen; she assumed intoxication and a British accent to go over the climax of the Rudy Vallee recording of the pub conversation about William Ewart Gladstone; she was the child Shirley Temple piping, "On the Good Ship Lollipop"; she was the gentleman soprano of the Four Inkspots[5] trilling. "If I Didn't Care." And she felt reasonably satisfied when Chizuko wept and gasped. "Oh, Rosie, you ought to be in the movies!"

Her father came after her at noon, bringing her sandwiches of minced ham and two nectarines to eat while she rode, so that she could pitch right into the sorting when they got home. The lugs were piling up, he said, and the ripe tomatoes in them would probably have to be taken to the cannery tomorrow if they were not ready for the produce haulers tonight. "This heat's not doing them any good. And we've got no time for a break today."

It *was* hot, probably the hottest day of the year, and Rosie's blouse stuck damply to her back even under the protection of the canvas. But she worked as efficiently as a flawless machine and kept the stalls heaped, with one part of her mind listening in to the parental murmuring about the heat and the tomatoes and with another part planning the exact words she would say to Jesus when he drove up with the first load of the afternoon. But when at last she saw that the pick-up was coming, her hands went berserk and the tomatoes started falling in the wrong stalls, and her father said. "Hey, hey! Rosie, watch what you're doing!"

"Well, I have to go to the *benjo*," she said, hiding panic.

"Go in the weeds over there," he said, only half-joking.

"Oh, Father!" she protested.

"Oh, go on home," her mother said. "We'll make out for awhile."

In the privy Rosie peered through a knothole toward the fields, watching as much as she could of Jesus. Happily she thought she saw him look in the direction of the house from time to time before he finished unloading and went back toward the patch where his mother and father worked. As she was heading for the shed, a very presentable black car purred up the dirt driveway to the house and its driver motioned to her. Was this the Hayashi home, he wanted to know. She nodded. Was she a Hayashi? Yes, she said, thinking that he was a good-looking man. He got out of the car with a huge, flat package and she saw that he warmly wore a business suit. "I have something here for your mother then," he said, in a more elegant Japanese than she was used to.

---

[5]Each of these celebrities was a popular entertainer of the 1940s.

She told him where her mother was and he came along with her, patting his face with an immaculate white handkerchief and saying something about the coolness of San Francisco. To her surprised mother and father, he bowed and introduced himself as, among other things, the *haiku* editor of the *Mainichi Shimbun*, saying that since he had been coming as far as Los Angeles anyway, he had decided to bring her the first prize she had won in the recent contest.

"First prize?" her mother echoed, believing and not believing, pleased and overwhelmed. Handed the package with a bow, she bobbed her head up and down numerous times to express her utter gratitude.

"It is nothing much," he added, "but I hope it will serve as a token of our great appreciation for your contributions and our great admiration of your considerable talent."

"I am not worthy," she said, falling easily into his style. "It is I who should make some sign of my humble thanks for being permitted to contribute."

"No, no, to the contrary," he said bowing again.

But Rosie's mother insisted, and then saying that she knew she was being unorthodox, she asked if she might open the package because her curiosity was so great. Certainly she might. In fact, he would like her reaction to it, for personally, it was one of his favorite *Hiroshiges*.[6]

Rosie thought it was a pleasant picture, which looked to have been sketched with delicate quickness. There were pink clouds, containing some graceful calligraphy, and a sea that was a pale blue except at the edges, containing four sampans with indications of people in them. Pines edged the water and on the far-off beach there was a cluster of thatched huts towered over by pine-dotted mountains of grey and blue. The frame was scalloped and gilt.

After Rosie's mother pronounced it without peer and somewhat prodded her father into nodding agreement, she said Mr. Kuroda must at least have a cup of tea after coming all this way, and although Mr. Kuroda did not want to impose, he soon agreed that a cup of tea would be refreshing and went along with her to the house, carrying the picture for her.

"Ha, your mother's crazy!" Rosie's father said, and Rosie laughed uneasily as she resumed judgment on the tomatoes. She had emptied six lugs when he broke into an imaginary conversation with Jesus to tell her to go and remind her mother of the tomatoes, and she went slowly.

Mr. Kuroda was in his shirtsleeves expounding some *haiku* theory as he munched a rice cake, and her mother was rapt. Abashed in the great man's presence, Rosie stood next to her mother's chair until her mother looked up inquiringly, and then she started to whisper the message, but her mother

---

[6]Ando Hiroshige (1797–1858), Japanese painter and printmaker known for landscapes.

pushed her gently away and reproached. "You are not being very polite to our guest."

"Father says the tomatoes . . ." Rosie said aloud, smiling foolishly.

"Tell him I shall only be a minute," her mother said, speaking the language of Mr. Kuroda.

When Rosie carried the reply to her father, he did not seem to hear and she said again. "Mother says she'll be back in a minute."

"All right, all right," he nodded, and they worked again in silence. But suddenly, her father uttered an incredible noise, exactly like the cork of a bottle popping, and the next Rosie knew, he was stalking angrily toward the house, almost running in fact, and she chased after him crying. "Father! Father! What are you going to do?"

He stopped long enough to order her back to the shed. "Never mind" he shouted. "Get on with the sorting!"

And from the place in the fields where she stood, frightened and vacillating, Rosie saw her father enter the house. Soon Mr. Kuroda came out alone, putting on his coat. Mr. Kuroda got into his car and backed out down the driveway onto the highway. Next her father emerged, also alone, something in his arms (it was the picture, she realized), and, going over to the bathhouse woodpile, he threw the picture on the ground and picked up the axe. Smashing the picture, glass and all (she heard the explosion faintly), he reached over for the kerosene that was used to encourage the bath fire and poured it over the wreckage. I am dreaming, Rosie said to herself, I am dreaming, but her father, having made sure that his act of cremation was irrevocable, was even then returning to the fields.

Rosie ran past him and toward the house. What had become of her mother? She burst into the parlor and found her mother at the back window watching the dying fire. They watched together until there remained only a feeble smoke under the blazing sun. Her mother was very calm.

"Do you know why I married your father?" she said without turning.

"No," said Rosie. It was the most frightening question she had ever been called upon to answer. Don't tell me now, she wanted to say, tell me tomorrow, tell me next week, don't tell me today. But she knew she would be told now, that the telling would combine with the other violence of the hot afternoon to level her life, her world to the very ground.

It was like a story out of the magazines illustrated in sepia,[7] which she had consumed so greedily for a period until the information had somehow reached her that those wretchedly unhappy autobiographies, offered to her as

---

[7]Magazine photographs were often colored with sepia, a brownish toning agent.

the testimonials of living men and women, were largely inventions: Her mother, at nineteen, had come to America and married her father as an alternative to suicide.

At eighteen she had been in love with the first son of one of the well-to-do families in her village. The two had met whenever and wherever they could, secretly, because it would not have done for his family to see him favor her—her father had no money; he was a drunkard and a gambler besides. She had learned she was with child; an excellent match had already been arranged for her lover. Despised by her family, she had given premature birth to a stillborn son, who would be seventeen now. Her family did not turn her out, but she could no longer project herself in any direction without refreshing in them the memory of her indiscretion. She wrote to Aunt Taka, her favorite sister in America, threatening to kill herself if Aunt Taka would not send for her. Aunt Taka hastily arranged a marriage with a young man of whom she knew, but lately arrived from Japan, a young man of simple mind, it was said, but of kindly heart. The young man was never told why his unseen betrothed was so eager to hasten the day of meeting.

The story was told perfectly, with neither groping for words nor untoward passion. It was as though her mother had memorized it by heart, reciting it to herself so many times over that its nagging vileness had long since gone.

"I had a brother then?" Rosie asked, for this was what seemed to matter now; she would think about the other later, she assured herself, pushing back the illumination which threatened all that darkness that had hitherto been merely mysterious or even glamorous. "A half-brother?"

"Yes."

"I would have liked a brother," she said.

Suddenly, her mother knelt on the floor and took her by the wrists. "Rosie," she said urgently. "Promise me you will never marry!" Shocked more by the request than the revelation, Rosie stared at her mother's face. Jesus, Jesus, she called silently, not certain whether she was invoking the help of the son of the Carrascos or of God, until there returned sweetly the memory of Jesus' hand, how it had touched her and where. Still her mother waited for an answer, holding her wrists so tightly that her hands were going numb. She tried to pull free. Promise, her mother whispered fiercely, promise. Yes, yes, I promise. Rosie said. But for an instant she turned away, and her mother, hearing the familiar glib agreement, released her. Oh, you, you, you, her eyes and twisted mouth said, you fool. Rosie, covering her face, began at last to cry, and the embrace and consoling hand came much later than she expected.

[1949]

Julia Alvarez
[1950–   ]

JULIA ALVAREZ *once told an interviewer, "I am a Dominican, hyphen, American. As a fiction writer, I find that the most exciting things happen in the realm of that hyphen—the place where two worlds collide or blend together." That collision, or blending, occurred frequently during Alvarez's early years. Her parents returned to their native Dominican Republic three months after her birth, and she spent the next ten years living in her mother's family compound. It was this family's close ties to the United States that kept them safe during the brutal Trujillo dictatorship, despite her father's activity in the underground resistance. Alvarez recalls growing up in an American-influenced household, attending American schools, eating American food, and wearing American clothes. Thus when the family fled the Dominican Republic for New York City in 1960, she thought she was fulfilling her every dream. In reality, however, she and her sisters endured ridicule for their imperfect English and discrimination because of their background. "The watershed experience of coming to this country," according to Alvarez, coupled with her childhood love of storytelling, led to her becoming a writer: "Not understanding the language, I had to pay close attention to each word—great training for a writer. I also discovered the welcoming world of the imagination and books."*

Alvarez went on to study literature and writing, graduating summa cum laude from Middlebury College, attending the Bread Loaf School of English, and earning a master of fine arts in creative writing from Syracuse University. She has worked in the Poet-in-the-Schools program in several states, and has taught English and writing at Phillips Andover Academy, the University of Vermont, the University of Illinois, and George Washington University. At present she is Writer-in-Residence at Middlebury College.

Although she has been writing since she was a child, Alvarez's first novel, How the García Girls Lost Their Accents *(1991), was not published until she was forty-one years old. Like her contemporary Sandra Cisneros's* The House on Mango Street, García Girls *is a collection of stories focusing on a young girl's struggles with adolescence, family, and culture clash. The four Garcia girls experience, as does Cisneros's Esperanza, "the realm of [the] hyphen," desperately trying to construct an identity amid conflicting cultural expectations. In her second novel,* In the Time of the Butterflies *(1994), Alvarez returned to her Dominican roots to tell the story of the Mirabal sisters, revolutionary leaders who were murdered by Trujillo's troops in 1960. She wrote this historical novel in part, she says, because "being a survivor placed a responsibility on me to tell the story of these brave young women who did not survive the dictatorship."*

In addition to these works, Alvarez has also published another novel, ¡Yo! (1997), as well as several collections of poetry, essay collections, and children's books. She has been awarded a Robert Frost Poetry fellowship from Bread Loaf Writers' Conference, a grant from National Endowment for the Arts, and a PEN Oakland/Josephine Miles Award for excellence in multicultural literature. Several of her works have been selected by the American Library Association as Notable Books.

Queens, 1963

JULIA ALVAREZ

Everyone seemed more American
than we, newly arrived,
foreign dirt still on our soles.
By year's end, a sprinkler waving
like a flag on our mowed lawn,   5
we were melted into the block,
owned our own mock Tudor house.
Then the house across the street
sold to a black family.
Cop cars patrolled our block   10
from the Castellucci's at one end
to the Balakian's on the other.
We heard rumors of bomb threats,
a burning cross on their lawn.
(It turned out to be a sprinkler.)   15
Still the neighborhood buzzed.
The barber's family, Haralambides,
our left side neighbors, didn't want trouble.
They'd come a long way to be free!
Mr. Scott, the retired plumber,   20
and his plump midwestern wife,
considered moving back home
where white and black got along
by staying where they belonged.
They had cultivated our street   25
like the garden she'd given up
on account of her ailing back,
bad knees, poor eyes, arthritic hands.
She went through her litany daily.
Politely, my mother listened—   30
¡Ay, Mrs. Scott, qué pena!

Reprinted from *The Other Side/El Otro Lado*, by permission of Susan Bergholz Literary Services. Copyright © 1995 by Julia Alvarez.

—her Dominican good manners
still running on automatic.
The Jewish counselor next door,
had a practice in her house;   35
clients hurried up her walk
ashamed to be seen needing.
(I watched from my upstairs window,
gloomy with adolescence,
and guessed how they too must have   40
hypocritical old world parents.)
Mrs. Bernstein said it was time
the neighborhood opened up.
As the first Jew on the block,
she remembered the snubbing she got   45
a few years back from Mrs. Scott.
But real estate worried her,
our houses' plummeting value.
She shook her head as she might
at a client's grim disclosures.   50
Too bad the world works this way.
The German girl playing the piano
down the street abruptly stopped
in the middle of a note.
I completed the tune in my head   55
as I watched *their* front door open.
A dark man in a suit
with a girl about my age
walked quickly into a car.
My hand lifted but fell   60
before I made a welcoming gesture.
On her face I had seen a look
from the days before we had melted
into the United States of America.
It was hardness mixed with hurt.   65
It was knowing she never could be
the right kind of American.
A police car followed their car.
Down the street, curtains fell back.
Mrs. Scott swept her walk   70
as if it had just been dirtied.
Then the German piano commenced

downward scales as if tracking
the plummeting real estate.
One by one I imagined the houses   *75*
sinking into their lawns,
the grass grown wild and tall
in the past tense of this continent
before the first foreigners owned
any of this free country.   *80*

[1995]

Trespass

JULIA ALVAREZ

THE DAY THE GARCÍAS were one American year old, they had a celebration at dinner. Mami had baked a nice flan and stuck a candle in the center. "Guess what day it is today?" She looked around the table at her daughters' baffled faces. "One year ago today," Papi began orating, "we came to the shores of this great country." When he was done misquoting the poem on the Statue of Liberty, the youngest, Fifi, asked if she could blow out the candle, and Mami said only after everyone had made a wish.

What do you wish for on the first celebration of the day you lost everything? Carla wondered. Everyone else around the table had their eyes closed as if they had no trouble deciding. Carla closed her eyes too. She should make an effort and not wish for what she always wished for in her homesickness. But just this last time, she would let herself. "Dear God," she began. She could not get used to this American wish-making without bringing God into it. "Let us please go back home, please," she half prayed and half wished. It seemed a less and less likely prospect. In fact, her parents were sinking roots here. Only a month ago, they had moved out of the city to a neighborhood on Long Island so that the girls could have a yard to play in, so Mami said. The little green squares around each look-alike house seemed more like carpeting that had to be kept clean than yards to play in. The trees were no taller than little Fifi. Carla thought yearningly of the lush grasses and thick-limbed, vine-ladened trees around the compound back home. Under the *amapola* tree her best-friend cousin, Lucinda, and she had told each other what each knew about how babies were made. What is Lucinda doing right this moment? Carla wondered.

Down the block the neighborhood dead-ended in abandoned farmland that Mami read in the local paper the developers were negotiating to buy. Grasses and real trees and real bushes still grew beyond the barbed-wire fence posted with a big sign: PRIVATE, NO TRESPASSING. The sign had surprised Carla since "forgive us our trespasses" was the only other context in which she had heard the word. She pointed the sign out to Mami on one of their first walks

Reprinted from *How the García Girls Lost Their Accents*, by permission of Susan Bergholz Literary Services. Copyright © 1991 by Julia Alvarez.

to the bus stop. "Isn't that funny, Mami? A sign that you have to be good." Her mother did not understand at first until Carla explained about the Lord's Prayer. Mami laughed. Words sometimes meant two things in English too. This trespass meant that no one must go inside the property because it was not public like a park, but private. Carla nodded, disappointed. She would never get the hang of this new country.

Mami walked her to the bus stop for her first month at her new school over in the next parish. The first week, Mami even rode the buses with her, transferring, going and coming, twice a day, until Carla learned the way. Her sisters had all been enrolled at the neighborhood Catholic school only one block away from the house the Garcías had rented at the end of the summer. But by then, Carla's seventh grade was full. The nun who was the principal had suggested that Carla stay back a year in sixth grade, where they still had two spaces left. At twelve, though, Carla was at least a year older than most sixth graders, and she felt mortified at the thought of having to repeat yet another year. All four girls had been put back a year when they arrived in the country. Sure, Carla could use the practice with her English, but that also meant she would be in the same grade as her younger sister, Sandi. That she could not bear. "Please," she pleaded with her mother, "let me go to the other school!" The public school was a mere two blocks beyond the Catholic school, but Laura García would not hear of it. Public schools, she had learned from other Catholic parents, were where juvenile delinquents went and where teachers taught those new crazy ideas about how we all came from monkeys. No child of hers was going to forget her family name and think she was nothing but a kissing cousin to an orangutan.

Carla soon knew her school route *by heart*, an expression she used for weeks after she learned it. First, she walked down the block by heart, noting the infinitesimal differences between the look-alike houses: different color drapes, an azalea bush on the left side of the door instead of on the right, a mailbox or door with a doodad of some kind. Then by heart, she walked the long mile by the deserted farmland lot with the funny sign. Finally, a sharp right down the service road into the main thoroughfare, where by heart she boarded the bus. "A young lady señorita," her mother pronounced the first morning Carla set out by herself, her heart drumming in her chest. It was a long and scary trek, but she was too grateful to have escaped the embarrassment of being put back a year to complain.

And as the months went by, she neglected to complain about an even scarier development. Every day on the playground and in the halls of her new school, a gang of boys chased after her, calling her names, some of which she had heard before from the old lady neighbor in the apartment they had rented in the city. Out of sight of the nuns, the boys pelted Carla with stones, aiming them at her feet so there would be no bruises. "Go back to where you came from, you dirty spic!" One of them, standing behind her in line, pulled her blouse out of her skirt where it was tucked in and lifted it high. "No titties," he snickered. Another yanked down her socks, displaying her legs, which had begun growing soft, dark hairs. "Monkey legs!" he yelled to his pals.

"Stop!" Carla cried. "Please stop."

"Eh-stop!" they mimicked her. "Plees eh-stop."

They were disclosing her secret shame: her body was changing. The girl she had been back home in Spanish was being shed. In her place—almost as if the boys' ugly words and taunts had the power of spells—was a hairy, breast-budding grownup no one would ever love.

Every day, Carla set out on her long journey to school with a host of confused feelings. First of all, there was this body whose daily changes she noted behind the closed bathroom door until one of her sisters knocked that Carla's turn was over. How she wished she could wrap her body up the way she'd heard Chinese girls had their feet bound so they wouldn't grow big. She would stay herself, a quick, skinny girl with brown eyes and a braid down her back, a girl she had just begun to feel could get things in this world.

But then, too, Carla felt relieved to be setting out towards her very own school in her proper grade away from the crowding that was her family of four girls too close in age. She could come home with stories of what had happened that day and not have a chorus of three naysayers to correct her. But she also felt dread. There, in the playground, they would be waiting for her—the gang of four or five boys, blond, snotty-nosed, freckled-faced. They looked bland and unknowable, the way all Americans did. Their faces betrayed no sign of human warmth. Their eyes were too clear for cleaving, intimate looks. Their pale bodies did not seem real but were like costumes they were wearing as they played the part of her persecutors.

She watched them. In the classroom, they bent over workbooks or wore scared faces when Sister Beatrice, their beefy, no-nonsense teacher, scolded them for missing their homework. Sometimes Carla spied them in the playground, looking through the chain link fence and talking about the cars parked on the sidewalk. To Carla's bafflement, those cars had names beyond the names of their color or size. All she knew of their family car, for instance, was that it was a big black car where all four sisters could ride in the back, though Fifi always made a fuss and was allowed up front. Carla could also identify Volkswagens because that had been the car (in black) of the secret police back home; every time Mami saw one she made the sign of the cross and said a prayer for Tío Mundo, who had not been allowed to leave the Island. Beyond Volkswagens and medium blue cars or big black cars, Carla could not tell one car from the other.

But the boys at the fence talked excitedly about Fords and Falcons and Corvairs and Plymouth Valiants. They argued over how fast each car could go and what models were better than others. Carla sometimes imagined herself being driven to school in a flashy red car the boys would admire. Except there was no one *to* drive her. Her immigrant father with his thick mustache and accent and three-piece suit would only bring her more ridicule. Her mother did not yet know how to drive. Even though Carla could imagine owning a very expensive car, she could not imagine her parents as different from what they were. They were, like this new body she was growing into, givens.

One day when she had been attending Sacred Heart about a month, she was followed by a car on her mile walk home from the bus stop. It was a lime green car, sort of medium sized, and with a kind of long snout, so had it been a person, Carla would have described it as having a long nose. A long-nosed, lime-green car. It drove slowly, trailing her. Carla figured the driver was looking for an address, just as Papi drove slowly and got honked at when he was reading the signs of shops before stopping at a particular one.

A blat from the horn made Carla jump and turn to the car, now fully stopped just a little ahead of her. She could see the driver clearly, from the shoulders up, a man in a red shirt about the age of her parents—though it was hard for Carla to tell with Americans how old they were. They were like cars to her, identifiable by the color of their clothes and a general age group—a little kid younger than herself, a kid her same age, a teenager in high school, and then the vast indistinguishable group of American grownups.

This grownup American man about her parents' age beckoned for her to come up to the window. Carla dreaded being asked directions since she had just moved into this area right before school started, and all she knew for sure was the route home from the bus stop. Besides, her English was still just classroom English, a foreign language. She knew the neutral bland things: how to ask for a glass of water, how to say good morning and good afternoon and good night. How to thank someone and say they were welcomed. But if a grownup American of indeterminable age asked her for directions, invariably speaking too quickly, she merely shrugged and smiled an inane smile. "I don't speak very much English," she would say in a small voice by way of apology. She hated having to admit this since such an admission proved, no doubt, the boy gang's point that she didn't belong here.

As Carla drew closer, the driver leaned over and rolled down the passenger door window. Carla bent down as if she were about to speak to a little kid and peeked in. The man smiled a friendly smile, but there was something wrong with it that Carla couldn't put her finger on: this smile had a bruised, sorry quality as if the man were someone who'd been picked on all his life, and so his smiles were appeasing, not friendly. He was wearing his red shirt unbuttoned, which seemed normal given the warm Indian-summer day. In fact, if Carla's legs hadn't begun to grow hairs, she would have taken off her school-green knee socks and walked home bare-legged.

The man spoke up. "Whereyagoin?" he asked, running all his words together the way the Americans always did. Carla was, as usual, not quite sure if she had heard right.

"Excuse me?" she asked politely, leaning into the car to hear the man's whispery voice better. Something caught her eye. She looked down and stared, aghast.

The man had tied his two shirtends just above his waist and was naked from there on down. String encircled his waist, the loose ends knotted in front and then looped around his penis. As Carla watched, his big blunt-headed thing grew so that it filled and strained at the lasso it was caught in.

"Where ya' going?" His voice had slowed down when he spoke this time, so that Carla definitely understood him. Her eyes snapped back up to his eyes.

"Excuse me?" she said again dumbly.

He leaned towards the passenger door and clicked it open. "C'moninere." He nodded towards the seat beside him. "C'm'on," he moaned. He cupped his hand over his thing as if it were a flame that might blow out.

Carla clutched her bookbag tighter in her hand. Her mouth hung open. Not one word, English or Spanish, occurred to her. She backed away from the big green car, all the while keeping her eyes on the man. A pained, urgent expression was deepening on his face like a plea that Carla did not know how to answer. His arm pumped at something Carla could not see, and then after much agitation, he was still. The face relaxed into something like peacefulness. The man bowed his head as if in prayer. Carla turned and fled down the street, her bookbag banging against her leg like a whip she was using to make herself go faster, faster.

Her mother called the police after piecing together the breathless, frantic story Carla told. The enormity of what she had seen was now topped by the further enormity of involving the police. Carla and her sisters feared the American police almost as much as the SIM[1] back home. Their father, too, seemed uneasy around policemen; whenever a cop car was behind them in traffic, he kept looking at the rearview mirror and insisting on silence in the car so he could think. If officers stood on the sidewalk as he walked by, he bowed ingratiatingly at them. Back home, he had been tailed by the secret police for months and the family had only narrowly escaped capture their last day on the Island. Of course, Carla knew American policemen were "nice guys," but still she felt uneasy around them.

---

[1] Servicio de Inteligencia Militar, the much-feared military police in the Dominican Republic.

The doorbell rang only minutes after Carla's mother had called the station. This was a law-abiding family neighborhood, and no one wanted a creep like this on the loose among so many children, least of all the police. As her mother answered the door, Carla stayed behind in the kitchen, listening with a racing heart to her mother's explanation. Mami's voice was high and hesitant and slightly apologetic—a small, accented woman's voice among the booming, impersonal American male voices that interrogated her.

"My daughter, she was walking home—"

"Where exactly?" a male voice demanded.

"That street, you know?" Carla's mother must have pointed. "The one that comes up the avenue, I don't know the name of it."

"Must be the service road," a nicer male voice offered.

"Yes, yes, the service road." Her mother's jubilant voice seemed to conclude whatever had been the problem.

"Please go on, ma'am."

"Well, my daughter, she said this, this crazy man in this car—" Her voice lowered. Carla heard snatches: something, something "to come in the car—"

"Where's your daughter, ma'am?" the male voice with authority asked.

Carla cringed behind the kitchen door. Her mother had promised that she would not involve Carla with the police but would do all the talking herself.

"She is just a young girl," her mother excused Carla.

"Well, ma'am, if you want to file charges, we have to talk to her."

"File charges? What does that mean, file charges?"

There was a sigh of exasperation. A too-patient voice with dividers between each word explained the legal procedures as if repeating a history lesson Carla's mother should have learned long before she had troubled the police or moved into this neighborhood.

"I don't want any trouble," her mother protested. "I just think this is a crazy man who should not be allowed on the streets."

"You're absolutely right, ma'am, but our hands are tied unless you, as a responsible citizen, help us out."

Oh no, Carla groaned, now she was in for it. The magic words had been uttered. The Garcías were only legal residents, not citizens, but for the police to mistake Mami for a citizen was a compliment too great to spare a child discomfort "Carla!" her mother called from the door.

"What's the girl's name?" the officer with the voice in charge asked.

Her mother repeated Carla's full name and spelled it for the officer, then called out again in her voice of authority, "Carla Antonia!"

Slowly, sullenly, Carla wrapped herself around the kitchen door, only her head poking out and into the hallway. "¿Sí, Mami?" she answered in a polite, law-abiding voice to impress the cops.

"Come here," her mother said, motioning. "These very nice officers need for you to explain what you saw." There was an apologetic look on her face. "Come on, Cuca, don't be afraid."

"There's nothing to be afraid of," the policeman said in his gruff, scary voice.

Carla kept her head down as she approached the front door, glancing up briefly when the two officers introduced themselves. One was an embarrassingly young man with a face no older than the boys' faces at school on top of a large, muscular man's body. The other man, also big and fair-skinned, looked older because of his meaner, sharp-featured face like an animal's in a beast fable a child knows by looking at the picture not to trust. Belts were slung around both their hips, guns poking out of the holsters. Their very masculinity offended and threatened. They were so big, so strong, so male, so American.

After a few facts about her had been established, the meanfaced cop with the big voice and the pad asked her if she would answer a few questions. Not knowing she could refuse, Carla nodded meekly, on the verge of tears.

"Could you describe the vehicle the suspect was driving?"

She wasn't sure what a vehicle was or a suspect, for that matter. Her mother translated into simpler English, "What car was the man driving, Carla?"

"A big green car," Carla mumbled.

As if she hadn't answered in English, her mother repeated for the officers, "A big green car."

"What make?" the officer wanted to know.

"Make?" Carla asked.

"You know, Ford, Chrysler, Plymouth." The man ended his catalogue with a sigh. Carla and her mother were wasting his time.

"*¿Qué clase de carro?*" her mother asked in Spanish, but of course she knew Carla wouldn't know the make of a car. Carla shook her head, and her mother explained to the officer, helping her save face, "She doesn't remember."

"Can't she talk?" the gruff cop snapped. The boyish-looking one now asked Carla a question. "Carla," he began, pronouncing her name so that Carla felt herself coated all over with something warm and too sweet. "Carla," he coaxed, "can you please describe the man you saw?"

All memory of the man's face fled. She remembered only the bruised smile and a few strands of dirty blond hair laid carefully over a bald pate. But she could not remember the word for bald and so she said, "He had almost nothing on his head."

"You mean no hat?" the gentle cop suggested.

"Almost no hair," Carla explained, looking up as if she had taken a guess and wanted to know if she was wrong or right.

"Bald?" The gruff cop pointed first to a hairy stretch of wrist beyond his uniform's cuff, then to his pink, hairless palm.

"Bald, yes." Carla nodded. The sight of the man's few dark hairs had disgusted her. She thought of her own legs sprouting dark hairs, of the changes going on in secret in her body, turning her into one of these grownup persons. No wonder the high-voiced boys with smooth, hairless cheeks hated her. They could see that her body was already betraying her.

The interrogation proceeded through a description of the man's appearance, and then the dreaded question came.

"What did you see?" the boy-faced cop asked.

Carla looked down at the cops' feet. The black tips of their shoes poked out from under their cuffs like the snouts of wily animals. "The man was naked all down here." She gestured with her hand. "And he had a string around his waist."

"A string?" The man's voice was like a hand trying to lift her chin to make her look up, which is precisely what her mother did when the man repeated, "A string?"

Carla was forced to confront the cop's face. It was indeed an adult version of the sickly white faces of the boys in the playground. This is what they would look like once they grew up. There was no meanness in this face, no kindness either. No recognition of the difficulty she was having in trying to describe what she had seen with her tiny English vocabulary. It was the face of someone in a movie Carla was watching ask her, "What was he doing with the string?"

She shrugged, tears peeping at the corners of her eyes.

Her mother intervened. "The string was holding up this man's—"

"Please, ma'am," the cop who was writing said. "Let your daughter describe what she saw."

Carla thought hard for what could be the name of a man's genitals. They had come to this country before she had reached puberty in Spanish, so a lot of the key words she would have been picking up in the last year, she had missed. Now, she was learning English in a Catholic classroom, where no nun had ever mentioned the words she was needing. "He had a string around his waist," Carla explained. By the ease with which the man was writing, she could tell she was now making perfect sense.

"And it came up to the front"—she showed on herself—"and here it was tied in a—" She held up her fingers and made the sign for zero.

"A noose?" the gentle cop offered.

"A noose, and his thing—" Carla pointed to the policeman's crotch. The cop writing scowled. "His thing was inside that noose and it got bigger and bigger," she blurted, her voice wobbling.

The friendly cop lifted his eyebrows and pushed his cap back on his head. His big hand wiped the small beads of sweat that had accumulated on his brow.

Carla prayed without prayer that this interview would stop now. What she had begun fearing was that her picture—but who was there to take a picture?—would appear in the paper the next day and the gang of mean boys would torment her with what she had seen. She wondered if she could report them now to these young officers. "By the way," she could say, and the gruff one would begin to take notes. She would have the words to describe them: their mean, snickering faces she knew by heart. Their pale look-alike sickly bodies. Their high voices squealing with delight when Carla mispronounced some word they coaxed her to repeat.

But soon after her description of the incident, the interview ended. The cop snapped his pad closed, and each officer gave Carla and her mother a salute of farewell. They drove off in their squad car, and all down the block, drapes fell back to rest, half-opened shades closed like eyes that saw no evil.

For the next two months before Carla's mother moved her to the public school close to home for the second half of her seventh grade, she took Carla on the bus to school and was there at the end of the day to pick her up. The tauntings and chasings stopped. The boys must have thought Carla had complained, and so her mother was along to defend her. Even during class times, when her mother was not around, they now ignored her, their sharp, clear eyes roaming the classroom for another victim, someone too fat, too ugly, too poor, too different. Carla had faded into the walls.

But their faces did not fade as fast from Carla's life. They trespassed in her dreams and in her waking moments. Sometimes when she woke in the dark, they were perched at the foot of her bed, a grim chorus of urchin faces, boys without bodies, chanting without words, "Go back! Go back!"

So as not to see them, Carla would close her eyes and wish them gone. In that dark she created by keeping her eyes shut, she would pray, beginning with the names of her own sisters, for all those she wanted God to especially care for, here and back home. The seemingly endless list of familiar names would coax her back to sleep with a feeling of safety, of a world still peopled by those who loved her.

[1991]

Aaron Abeyta
[1971–   ]

AARON ABEYTA *was born and raised in the San Luis Valley in southern Colorado, and received a master of fine arts in creative writing from Colorado State University. Abeyta was the recipient of the Colorado Council on the Arts Fellowship for Poetry in 1998, and his poem "Colcha" received a Grand Prize from the Academy of American Poets. The volume in which that poem was published, also titled* Colcha, *won the American Book Award in 2002. The titles of both poem and collection refer to a kind of embroidery done in the San Luis Valley; in this style of needlework, the artist embroiders scenes from memory that develop into a quilt-like story of his or her life. This kind of local cultural reference bears great significance in Abeyta's writing; reporter Ruth Heide wrote that Abeyta's poetry works "to preserve a culture and way of life." Moreover, Abeyta is, as George Sibley has pointed out, "deeply immersed in the multigenerational continuity (and he stresses that continuity) of a place-based Chicano culture." His poems embroider both a personal and a cultural history, revealing the intimate details of a life while connecting those details to the social, political, and familial histories from which they spring.*

thirteen ways of looking at a tortilla

AARON ABEYTA

i.
among twenty different tortillas
the only thing moving
was the mouth of the niño[1]

ii.
i was of three cultures
like a tortilla   5
for which there are three bolios[2]

iii.
the tortilla grew on the wooden table
it was a small part of the earth

iv.
a house and a tortilla
are one   10
a man a woman and a tortilla
are one

v.
i do not know which to prefer
the beauty of the red wall
or the beauty of the green wall   15
the tortilla fresh
or just after

---

[1]Spanish: boy.

[2]A Mexican bread or roll.

Reprinted by permission from *Colcha*. Copyright © 2000 by the University of Colorado.

vi.
tortillas filled the small kitchen
with ancient shadows
the shadow of Maclovia   *20*
cooking long ago
the tortilla
rolled from the shadow
the innate roundness

vii.
o thin viejos of chimayo[3]   *25*
why do you imagine biscuits
do you not see how the tortilla
lives with the hands
of the women about you

viii.
i know soft corn   *30*
and beautiful inescapable sopapillas
but i know too
that the tortilla
has taught me what I know

ix.
when the tortilla is gone   *35*
it marks the end
of one of many tortillas

x.
at the sight of tortillas
browning on a black comal[4]
even the pachucos of española[5]   *40*
would cry out sharply

---

[3]Spanish: old ones from Chimayo. Chimayo is a town in northern New Mexico, between Taos and
Española (see line 40).

[4]A thick metal or earthen plate for cooking tortillas.

[5]"Pachuco" is a slang term for a Mexican-American youth or teenager, particularly one who belongs
to a local gang; Española is a town in northern New Mexico.

xi.
he rode over new mexico
in a pearl low rider
once he got a flat
in that he mistook   45
the shadow of his spare
for a tortilla

xii.
the abuelitas[6] are moving
the tortilla must be baking

xiii.
it was cinco de mayo all year   50
it was warm
and it was going to get warmer
the tortilla sat
on the frijolito[7] plate

[2001]

---

[6]Spanish: grandmothers.

[7]Spanish: literally, "little bean."

Jimmy Santiago Baca
[1952–   ]

JIMMY SANTIAGO BACA *was born in Santa Fe, New Mexico, and is of Chicano and Apache descent. His parents divorced when Baca was two; he lived with a grandparent until he was five, when he was placed in an orphanage. After running away from the orphanage at age eleven, Baca lived on the streets, and was convicted of drug possession at age twenty. Sentenced to a maximum security prison in Arizona, Baca served four of his six years in prison in isolation, and was given electric shock treatments due to his "combativeness." Despite this, Baca found a way to stay intellectually and emotionally alive. While he was in prison, he taught himself to read and write, and began writing poetry. Unlike the stereotypical poetry written in prison, filled with rage and despair, Baca's poems focus on rebirth and spiritual triumph; as he told Bath Ann Krier in the* Los Angeles Times, *in prison, "The only way of transcending was through language and understanding. Had I not found the language, I would have been a guerrilla in the mountains. It was language that saved [me]." Urged on by a fellow inmate, Baca sent some of his early poems to poet Denise Levertov, then poetry editor of* Mother Jones *magazine, who printed his poems and eventually helped Baca find a publisher for his first book, titled* Immigrants in Our Own Land *(1979). He has published numerous books of poetry since then, including the novel-in-verse,* Martin and Meditations on the South Valley *(1987), for which he received the* American Book Award. *Baca has also received the National Endowment for the Arts award in poetry; the National Hispanic Heritage Award; the Wallace Stevens Poetry fellowship from Yale University; and the Vogelstein Foundation Award in poetry. Baca's more recent poetry celebrates the new phases his life has gone through since prison, including marriage and fatherhood, the life that he has built in his working class Chicano neighborhood, and the power of language to change lives. As Baca has said of his work with troubled and underprivileged kids, "If you don't get the language down, you're not going to have access to a tool that people use as a weapon against you. The only reason I was never taught to read and write was because it was easier for them to lead me. But the second I learned to read and write, I began to lead myself." Baca's autobiography,* A Place to Stand, *was published in 2001.*

So Mexicans Are Taking Jobs from Americans

JIMMY SANTIAGO BACA

O Yes? Do they come on horses
with rifles, and say,
   Ese gringo,[1] gimmee your job?
And do you, gringo, take off your ring,
drop your wallet into a blanket   5
spread over the ground, and walk away?

I hear Mexicans are taking your jobs away.
Do they sneak into town at night,
and as you're walking home with a whore,
do they mug you, a knife at your throat,   10
saying, I want your job?

Even on TV, an asthmatic leader
crawls turtle heavy, leaning on an assistant,
and from a nest of wrinkles on his face,
a tongue paddles through flashing waves   15
of lightbulbs, of cameramen, rasping
"They're taking our jobs away."

Well, I've gone about trying to find them,
asking just where the hell are these fighters.

The rifles I hear sound in the night   20
are white farmers shooting blacks and browns
whose ribs I see jutting out
and starving children,

---

[1] "Hey, whitey."

Reprinted from *Immigrants in Our Own Lands,* by permission from New Directions
Publishing Corp. Copyright © 1982 by Jimmy Santiago Baca.

I see the poor marching for a little work,
I see small white farmers selling out   *25*
to clean-suited farmers living in New York,
who've never been on a farm,
don't know the look of a hoof or the smell
of a woman's body bending all day long in fields.

I see this, and I hear only a few people   *30*
got all the money in this world, the rest
count their pennies to buy bread and butter.

Below that cool green sea of money,
millions and millions of people fight to live,
search for pearls in the darkest depths   *35*
of their dreams, hold their breath for years
trying to cross poverty to just having something.

The children are dead already. We are killing them,
that is what America should be saying;
on TV, in the streets, in offices, should be saying,   *40*
    "We aren't giving the children a chance to live."
Mexicans are taking our jobs, they say instead.
What they really say is, let them die,
and the children too.

[1979]

Gloria Anzaldúa
[1942–2004]

Among GLORIA ANZALDÚA'S *major accomplishments must be counted the revolution that she inspired in the feminist movement in the United States. By calling attention to the ways that experiences of women of color had been marginalized in mainstream feminism, she expanded the scope of feminism's critique to include questions not simply of gender, but of race, of class, and of sexuality as well. In* This Bridge Called My Back: Writings by Radical Women of Color *(1981), co-edited with Cherríe Moraga, Anzaldúa began her life-long project of exploring the intersections and divisions in the personal experiences of women of color, particularly Chicanas, who must struggle against multiple forces silencing them, including the oppressive patriarchal structures of both Chicano and European-American cultures. Anzaldúa dramatically opens up the means of self-expression for women of color in her best-known text,* Borderlands/La Frontera: The New Mestiza *(1987), which puts forward a series of daring experiments in its very form, through a blending of the genres of essay and poetry, and through a representation of the code-switching so integral to the bilingual experience. Throughout her writing, she has explored the metaphors of the bridge and the borderland, each representing the divisions between contemporary cultures and the intersections that join them. In focusing on the crossing of cultures experienced by Chicanas, Anzaldúa introduced to American literary scholarship the notion of* mestizaje, *or hybridity: the complexity of the experiences of those who inhabit the borderlands.*

How to Tame a Wild Tongue

GLORIA ANZALDÚA

"WE'RE GOING TO HAVE to control your tongue," the dentist says, pulling out all the metal from my mouth. Silver bits plop and tinkle into the basin. My mouth is a motherlode.

The dentist is cleaning out my roots. I get a whiff of the stench when I gasp. "I can't cap that tooth yet, you're still draining," he says.

"We're going to have to do something about your tongue," I hear the anger rising in his voice. My tongue keeps pushing out the wads of cotton, pushing back the drills, the long thin needles. "I've never seen anything as strong or as stubborn," he says. And I think, how do you tame a wild tongue, train it to be quiet, how do you bridle and saddle it? How do you make it lie down?

> "Who is to say that robbing a people of
> its language is less violent than war?"
>
> —RAY GWYN SMITH[1]

I remember being caught speaking Spanish at recess—that was good for three licks on the knuckles with a sharp ruler. I remember being sent to the corner of the classroom for "talking back" to the Anglo teacher when all I was trying to do was tell her how to pronounce my name. "If you want to be American, speak 'American.' If you don't like it, go back to Mexico where you belong."

"I want you to speak English. *Pa' hallar buen trabajo tienes que saber hablar el inglés bien. Qué vale toda tu educación si todavía hables inglés con un* 'accent,' " my mother would say, mortified that I spoke English like a Mexican. At Pan American University, I, and all Chicano students, were required to take two speech classes. Their purpose: to get rid of our accents.

Attacks on one's form of expression with the intent to censor are a violation of the First Amendment. *El Anglo con cara de inocente nos arrancó la lengua.* Wild tongues can't be tamed, they can only be cut out.

---

[1]Ray Gwyn Smith, *Moorland Is Cold Country*, unpublished book.

Reprinted from *Borderlands/La Frontera: The New Mestiza*, by permission of Aunt Lute Books for the Estate of Gloria Anzaldúa.

Overcoming the Tradition of Silence

Ahogadas, escupimos el oscuro.
Peleando con nuestra propia sombra
el silencio nos sepulta.

En boca cerrada no entran moscas. "Flies don't enter a closed mouth" is a saying I kept hearing when I was a child. *Ser habladora* was to be a gossip and a liar, to talk too much. *Muchachitas bien criadas,* well-bred girls, don't answer back. *Es una falta de respeto* to talk back to one's mother or father. I remember one of the sins I'd recite to the priest in the confession box the few times I went to confession: talking back to my mother, *hablar pa' 'tras, replar.* *Hocicona, repelona, chismosa,* having a big mouth, questioning, carrying tales are all signs of being *mal criada.* In my culture they are all words that are derogatory if applied to women—I've never heard them applied to men.

The first time I heard two women, a Puerto Rican and a Cuban, say the word "*nosotras,*" I was shocked. I had not known the word existed. Chicanos use *nosotros* whether we're male or female. We are robbed of our female being by the masculine plural. Language is a male discourse.

> *And our tongues have become dry*
> *the wilderness has*
> *dried out our tongues*
> *and we have forgotten speech.*
>
> —IRENA KLEPFISZ[2]

Even our own people, other Spanish speakers *nos quieren poner candados en la boca.* They would hold us back with their bag of *reglas de academia.*

Oyé como ladra: el lenguaje de la frontera

Quien tiene boca se equivoca.
                                                    —MEXICAN SAYING

"*Pocho,* cultural traitor, you're speaking the oppressor's language by speaking English, you're ruining the Spanish language," I have been accused by

---

[2]Irena Klepfisz, "*Di rayze aheym*/The Journey Home," in *The Tribe of Dina: A Jewish Women's Anthology,* Melanie Kaye/Kantrowitz and Irena Klepfisz, eds. (Montpelier, VT: Sinister Wisdom Books, 1986), 49.

various Latinos and Latinas. Chicano Spanish is considered by the purist and by most Latinos deficient, a mutilation of Spanish.

But Chicano Spanish is a border tongue which developed naturally. Change, *evolución, enriquecimiento de palabras nuevas por invención o adopción* have created variants of Chicano Spanish, *un nuevo lenguaje. Un lenguaje que corresponds a un modo de vivir.* Chicano Spanish is not incorrect; it is a living language.

For a people who are neither Spanish nor live in a country in which Spanish is the first language; for a people who live in a country in which English is the reigning tongue but who are not Anglo; for a people who cannot identify with either standard (formal, Castilian) Spanish nor standard English, what recourse is left to them but to create their own language? A language which they can connect their identity to, one capable of communicating the realities and values true to themselves—a language with terms that are neither *español ni inglés*, but both. We speak a *patois*, a forked tongue, a variation of two languages.

Chicano Spanish sprang out of the Chicanos' need to identify ourselves as a distinct people. We needed a language with which we could communicate with ourselves, a secret language. For some of us, language is a homeland closer than the Southwest—for many Chicanos today live in the Midwest and the East. And because we are a complex, heterogeneous people, we speak many languages. Some of the languages we speak are:

1. Standard English
2. Working class and slang English
3. Standard Spanish
4. Standard Mexican Spanish
5. North Mexican Spanish dialect
6. Chicano Spanish (Texas, New Mexico, Arizona and California have regional variations)
7. Tex-Mex
8. *Pachuco* (called *caló*)

My "home" tongues are the languages I speak with my sister and brothers, with my friends. They are the last five listed, with 6 and 7 being closest to my heart. From school, the media and job situations, I've picked up standard and working class English. From Mamagrande Locha and from reading Spanish and Mexican literature, I've picked up Standard Spanish and Standard Mexican Spanish. From *los recién llegados*, Mexican immigrants, and *braceros*, I learned the North Mexican dialect. With Mexicans I'll try to speak either Standard Mexican Spanish or the North Mexican dialect. From my parents and Chicanos living in the Valley, I picked up Chicano Texas Spanish, and I speak it with my mom, younger brother (who married a Mexican and who rarely mixes Spanish with English), and aunts and older relatives.

With Chicanas from *Nuevo México* or *Arizona* I will speak Chicano Spanish a little, but often they don't understand what I'm saying. With most California Chicanas I speak entirely in English (unless I forget). When I first moved to San Francisco, I'd rattle off something in Spanish, unintentionally embarrassing them. Often it is only with another Chicana *tejana* that I can talk freely.

Words distorted by English are known as anglicisms or *pochismos*. The *pocho* is an anglicized Mexican or American of Mexican origin who speaks Spanish with an accent characteristic of North Americans and who distorts and reconstructs the language according to the influence of English.[3] Tex-Mex, or Spanglish, comes most naturally to me. I may switch back and forth from English to Spanish in the same sentence or in the same word. With my sister and my brother Nune and with Chicano *tejano* contemporaries I speak in Tex-Mex.

From kids and people my own age I picked up *Pachuco*. *Pachuco* (the language of the zoot suiters) is a language of rebellion, both against Standard Spanish and Standard English. It is a secret language. Adults of the culture and outsiders cannot understand it. It is made up of slang words from both English and Spanish. *Ruca* means girl or woman, *vato* means guy or dude, *chale* means no, *simón* means yes, *churro* is sure, talk is *periquiar,* *pigionear* means petting, *qué gacho* means how nerdy, *ponte áquila* means watch out, death is called *la pelona*. Through lack of practice and not having others who can speak it, I've lost most of the *Pachuco* tongue.

Chicano Spanish

Chicanos, after 250 years of Spanish/Anglo colonization, have developed significant differences in the Spanish we speak. We collapse two adjacent vowels into a single syllable and sometimes shift the stress in certain words such as *maíz/maiz, cohete/cuete*. We leave out certain consonants when they appear between vowels: *lado/lao, mojado/mojao*. Chicanos from South Texas pronounce *f* as *j* as in *jue (fue)*. Chicanos use "archaisms," words that are no longer in the Spanish language, words that have been evolved out. We say *semos, truje, haiga, ansina,* and *naiden*. We retain the "archaic" *j*, as in *jalar*, that derives from an earlier *h*, (the French *halar* or the Germanic *halon* which was lost to standard

---

[3] R. C. Ortega, *Dialectología Del Barrio*, trans. Hortencia S. Alwan (Los Angeles, CA: R. C. Ortega Publisher & Bookseller, 1977), 132.

Spanish in the 16th century), but which is still found in several regional dialects such as the one spoken in South Texas. (Due to geography, Chicanos from the Valley of South Texas were cut off linguistically from other Spanish speakers. We tend to use words that the Spaniards brought over from Medieval Spain. The majority of the Spanish colonizers in Mexico and the Southwest came from Extremadura—Hernán Cortés was one of them—and Andalucía. Andalucians pronounce *ll* like a *y*, and their *d*'s tend to be absorbed by adjacent vowels: *tirado* becomes *tirao*. They brought *el lenguaje popular, dialectos y regionalismos*.[4])

Chicanos and other Spanish speakers also shift *ll* to *y* and *z* to *s*.[5] We leave out initial syllables, saying *tar* for *estar*, *toy* for *estoy*, *hora* for *ahora* (*cubanos* and *puertorriqueños* also leave out initial letters of some words.) We also leave out the final syllable such as *pa* for *para*. The intervocalic *y*, the *ll* as in *tortilla*, *ella, botella*, gets replaced by *tortia* or *tortiya, ea, botea*. We add an additional syllable at the beginning of certain words: *atocar* for *tocar*, *agastar* for *gastar*. Sometimes we'll say *lavaste las vacijas*, other times *lavates* (substituting the *ates* verb endings for the *aste*).

We use anglicisms, words borrowed from English: *bola* from ball, *carpeta* from carpet, *máchina de lavar* (instead of *lavadora*) from washing machine. Tex-Mex argot, created by adding a Spanish sound at the beginning or end of an English word such as *cookiar* for cook, *watchiar* for watch, *parkiar* for park, and *rapiar* for rape, is the result of the pressures on Spanish speakers to adapt to English.

We don't use the word *vosotros/as* or its accompanying verb form. We don't say *claro* (to mean yes), *imagínate*, or *me emociona*, unless we picked up Spanish from Latinas, out of a book, or in a classroom. Other Spanish-speaking groups are going through the same, or similar, development in their Spanish.

Linguistic Terrorism

Deslenguadas. Somos los del español deficiente. We are
your linguistic nightmare, your linguistic aberration,
your linguistic *mestisaje*, the subject of your *burla*.
Because we speak with tongues of fire we are culturally
crucified. Racially, culturally and linguistically *somos
huérfanos*—we speak an orphan tongue.

---

[4]Eduardo Hernández-Chávez, Andrew D. Cohen, and Anthony F. Beltramo, *El Lenguaje de los Chicanos: Regional and Social Characteristics Used By Mexican Americans* (Arlington, VA: Center for Applied Linguistics, 1975), 39.

[5]Hernández-Chávez, xvii.

Chicanas who grew up speaking Chicano Spanish have internalized the belief that we speak poor Spanish. It is illegitimate, a bastard language. And because we internalize how our language has been used against us by the dominant culture, we use our language differences against each other.

Chicana feminists often skirt around each other with suspicion and hesitation. For the longest time I couldn't figure it out. Then it dawned on me. To be close to another Chicana is like looking into the mirror. We are afraid of what we'll see there. *Pena*. Shame. Low estimation of self. In childhood we are told that our language is wrong. Repeated attacks on our native tongue diminish our sense of self. The attacks continue throughout our lives.

Chicanas feel uncomfortable talking in Spanish to Latinas, afraid of their censure. Their language was not outlawed in their countries. They had a whole lifetime of being immersed in their native tongue; generations, centuries in which Spanish was a first language, taught in school, heard on radio and TV, and read in the newspaper.

If a person, Chicana or Latina, has a low estimation of my native tongue, she also has a low estimation of me. Often with *mexicanas y latinas* we'll speak English as a neutral language. Even among Chicanas we tend to speak English at parties or conferences. Yet, at the same time, we're afraid the other will think we're *agringadas* because we don't speak Chicano Spanish. We oppress each other trying to out-Chicano each other, vying to be the "real" Chicanas, to speak like Chicanos. There is no one Chicano language just as there is no one Chicano experience. A monolingual Chicana whose first language is English or Spanish is just as much a Chicana as one who speaks several variants of Spanish. A Chicana from Michigan or Chicago or Detroit is just as much a Chicana as one from the Southwest. Chicano Spanish is as diverse linguistically as it is regionally.

By the end of this century, Spanish speakers will comprise the biggest minority group in the U.S., a country where students in high schools and colleges are encouraged to take French classes because French is considered more "cultured." But for a language to remain alive it must be used.[6] By the end of this century English, and not Spanish, will be the mother tongue of most Chicanos and Latinos.

So, if you want to really hurt me, talk badly about my language. Ethnic identity is twin skin to linguistic identity—I am my language. Until I can take pride in my language, I cannot take pride in myself. Until I can accept as legitimate Chicano Texas Spanish, Tex-Mex and all the other languages I speak, I cannot accept the legitimacy of myself. Until I am free to write bilingually and

---

[6]Irena Klepfisz, "Secular Jewish Identity: Yidishkayt in American," in *The Tribe of Dina*, Kaye/Kantrowitz and Klepfisz, eds., 43.

to switch codes without having always to translate, while I still have to speak English or Spanish when I would rather speak Spanglish, and as long as I have to accommodate the English speakers rather than having them accommodate me, my tongue will be illegitimate.

I will no longer be made to feel ashamed of existing. I will have my voice: Indian, Spanish, white. I will have my serpent's tongue—my woman's voice, my sexual voice, my poet's voice. I will overcome the tradition of silence.

> *My fingers*
> *move sly against your palm*
> *Like women everywhere, we speak in code. . . .*
> —MELANIE KAYE/KANTROWITZ[7]

"Vistas," corridos, y comida: My Native Tongue

In the 1960s, I read my first Chicano novel. It was *City of Night* by John Rechy, a gay Texan, son of a Scottish father and a Mexican mother. For days I walked around in stunned amazement that a Chicano could write and could get published. When I read *I Am Joaquín*[8] I was surprised to see a bilingual book by a Chicano in print. When I saw poetry written in Tex-Mex for the first time, a feeling of pure joy flashed through me. I felt like we really existed as a people. In 1971, when I started teaching High School English to Chicano students, I tried to supplement required texts with works by Chicanos, only to be reprimanded and forbidden to do so by the principal. He claimed that I was supposed to teach "American" and English literature. At the risk of being fired, I swore my students to secrecy and slipped in Chicano short stories, poems, a play. In graduate school, while working toward a Ph.D., I had to "argue" with one advisor after the other, semester after semester, before I was allowed to make Chicano literature an area of focus.

Even before I read books by Chicanos or Mexicans, it was the Mexican movies I saw at the drive-in—the Thursday night specials of $1.00 a carload—that gave me a sense of belonging. "Vámonos a las vistas," my mother would call out and we'd all—grandmother, brothers, sister and cousins—squeeze into the car. We'd wolf down cheese and bologna white bread sandwiches while watching Pedro Infante in melodramatic tearjerkers like *Nosotros los pobres*, the first "real" Mexican movie (that was not an imitation of European

---

[7]Melanie Kaye/Kantrowitz, "Sign," in *We Speak in Code: Poems and other Writings* (Pittsburgh, PA: Motheroot Publications, Inc., 1980), 85.

[8]Rodolfo Gonzales, *I Am Joaquín/Yo Soy Joaquín* (New York, NY: Bantam Books, 1972). It was first published in 1967.

movies). I remember seeing *Cuando los hijos se van* and surmising that all Mexican movies played up the love a mother has for her children and what ungrateful sons and daughters suffer when they are not devoted to their mothers. I remember the singing-type "westerns" of Jorge Negrete and Miquel Aceves Mejía. When watching Mexican movies, I felt a sense of homecoming as well as alienation. People who were to amount to something didn't go to Mexican movies, or *bailes* or tune their radios to *bolero, rancherita,* and *corrido* music.

The whole time I was growing up, there was *norteño* music, sometimes called North Mexican border music, or Tex-Mex music, or Chicano music, or *cantina* (bar) music. I grew up listening to *conjuntos,* three- or four-piece bands made up of folk musicians playing guitar, *bajo sexto,* drums and button accordion, which Chicanos had borrowed from the German immigrants who had come to Central Texas and Mexico to farm and build breweries. In the Rio Grande Valley, Steve Jordan and Little Joe Hernández were popular, and Flaco Jiménez was the accordion king. The rhythms of Tex-Mex music are those of the polka, also adapted from the Germans, who in turn had borrowed the polka from the Czechs and Bohemians.

I remember the hot, sultry evenings when *corridos*—songs of love and death on the Texas-Mexican borderlands—reverberated out of cheap amplifiers from the local *cantinas* and wafted in through my bedroom window.

Corridos first became widely used along the South Texas/Mexican border during the early conflict between Chicanos and Anglos. The *corridos* are usually about Mexican heroes who do valiant deeds against the Anglo oppressors. Pancho Villa's song, "*La cucaracha,*" is the most famous one. *Corridos* of John F. Kennedy and his death are still very popular in the Valley. Older Chicanos remember Lydia Mendoza, one of the great border corrido singers who was called *la Gloria de Tejas.* Her "*El tango negro,*" sung during the Great Depression, made her a singer of the people. The everpresent *corridos* narrated one hundred years of border history, bringing news of events as well as entertaining. These folk musicians and folk songs are our chief cultural mythmakers, and they made our hard lives seem bearable.

I grew up feeling ambivalent about our music. Country-western and rock-and-roll had more status. In the 50s and 60s, for the slightly educated and *agringado* Chicanos, there existed a sense of shame at being caught listening to our music. Yet I couldn't stop my feet from thumping to the music, could not stop humming the words, nor hide from myself the exhilaration I felt when I heard it.

There are more subtle ways that we internalize identification, especially in the forms of images and emotions. For me food and certain smells are tied to my identity, to my homeland. Woodsmoke curling up to an immense blue sky; woodsmoke perfuming my grandmother's clothes, her skin. The stench of cow manure and the yellow patches on the ground; the crack of a .22 rifle and the reek of cordite. Homemade white cheese sizzling in a pan, melting inside a folded *tortilla*. My sister Hilda's hot, spicy *menudo, chile colorado* making it deep red, pieces of *panza* and hominy floating on top. My brother Carito barbecuing *fajitas* in the backyard. Even now and 3,000 miles away, I can see my mother spicing the ground beef, pork and venison with *chile*. My mouth salivates at the thought of the hot steaming *tamales* I would be eating if I were home.

Si le preguntas a mi mamá, "¿Qué eres?"

> "Identity is the essential core of who
> we are as individuals, the conscious
> experience of the self inside."
>
> —KUFMAN[9]

Nosotros los Chicanos straddle the borderlands. On one side of us, we are constantly exposed to the Spanish of the Mexicans, on the other side we hear the Anglos' incessant clamoring so that we forget our language. Among ourselves we don't say *nosotros los americanos, o nosotros los españoles, o nosotros los hispanos*. We say *nosotros los mexicanos* (by *mexicanos* we do not mean citizens of Mexico; we do not mean a national identity, but a racial one). We distinguish between *mexicanos del otro lado* and *mexicanos de este lado*. Deep in our hearts we believe that being Mexican has nothing to do with which country one lives in. Being Mexican is a state of soul—not one of mind, not one of citizenship. Neither eagle nor serpent, but both. And like the ocean, neither animal respects borders.

> *Dime con quien andas y te diré quien eres.*
> (Tell me who your friends are and I'll tell you who you
> are.)
>
> —MEXICAN SAYING

Si le preguntas a mi mamá, "¿Qué eres?" te dirá, "Soy mexicana." My brothers and sisters say the same. I sometimes will answer "*soy mexicana*" and at others will say "*soy Chicana*" o "*soy tejana*." But I identified as "*Raza*" before I ever identified as "*mexicana*" or "*Chicana*".

As a culture, we call ourselves Spanish when referring to ourselves as a linguistic group and when copping out. It is then that we forget our predominant

---

[9]Kaufman, 68.

Indian genes. We are 70–80% Indian.[10] We call ourselves Hispanic[11] or Spanish-American or Latin-American or Latin when linking ourselves to other Spanish-speaking peoples of the Western hemisphere and when copping out. We call ourselves Mexican-American[12] to signify we are neither Mexican nor American, but more the noun "American" than the adjective "Mexican" (and when copping out).

Chicanos and other people of color suffer economically for not acculturating. This voluntary (yet forced) alienation makes for psychological conflict, a kind of dual identity—we don't identify with the Anglo-American cultural values and we don't totally identify with the Mexican cultural values. We are a synergy of the two cultures with various degrees of Mexicanness or Angloness. I have so internalized the borderland conflict that sometimes I feel like one cancels out the other and we are zero, nothing, no one. *A veces no soy nada ni nadie. Pero hasta cuando no lo soy, lo soy.*

When not copping out, when we know we are more than nothing, we call ourselves Mexican, referring to race and ancestry; *mestizo* when affirming both our Indian and Spanish (but we hardly ever own our Black ancestry); Chicano when referring to a politically aware people born and/or raised in the U.S.; *Raza* when referring to Chicanos; *tejanos* when we are Chicanos from Texas.

Chicanos did not know we were a people until 1965 when César Chávez and the farmworkers united and *I Am Joaquín* was published and *la Raza Unida* party was formed in Texas. With that recognition, we became a distinct people. Something momentous happened to the Chicano soul—we became aware of our reality and acquired a name and a language (Chicano Spanish) that reflected that reality. Now that we had a name, some of the fragmented pieces began to fall together—who we were, what we were, how we had evolved. We began to get glimpses of what we might eventually become.

Yet the struggle of identities continues, the struggle of borders is our reality still. One day the inner struggle will cease and a true integration take place. In the meantime, *tenémos que hacer la lucha. ¿Quién está protegiendo los ranchos de mi gente? ¿Quién está tratando de cerrar la fisura entre la india y el blanco en nuestra sangre? El Chicano, si, el Chicano que anda como un ladrón en su propia casa.*

---

[10]Hernández-Chávez, 88–90.

[11]"Hispanic" is derived from *Hispania (España)*, a name given to the Iberian Peninsula in ancient times when it was part of the Roman Empire, and is a term designated by the U.S. government to make it easier to handle us on paper.

[12]The Treaty of Guadalupe Hidalgo created the Mexican-American in 1848.

Los Chicanos, how patient we seem, how very patient. There is the quiet of the Indian about us.[13] We know how to survive. When other races have given up their tongue, we've kept ours. We know what it is to live under the hammer blow of the dominant *norteamericano* culture. But more than we count the blows, we count the days the weeks the years the centuries the eons until the white laws and commerce and customs will rot in the deserts they've created, lie bleached. *Humildes* yet proud, *quietos* yet wild, *nosotros los mexicanos-Chicanos* will walk by the crumbling ashes as we go about our business. Stubborn, persevering, impenetrable as stone, yet possessing a malleability that renders us unbreakable, we, the *mestizas* and *mestizos,* will remain.

[1987]

---

[13]Anglos, in order to alleviate their guilt for dispossessing the Chicano, stressed the Spanish part of us and perpetuated the myth of the Spanish Southwest. We have accepted the fiction that we are Hispanic, that is Spanish, in order to accommodate ourselves to the dominant culture and its abhorrence of Indians. Hernández-Chávez, 88–91.

To live in the Borderlands means you

GLORIA ANZALDÚA

To live in the Borderlands means you
   are neither *hispana india negra española*
   ni gabacha, eres mestiza, mulata, half-breed
   caught in the crossfire between camps
   while carrying all five races on your back   5
   not knowing which side to turn to, run from;

To live in the Borderlands means knowing
   that the *india* in you, betrayed for 500 years,
   is no longer speaking to you,
   that *mexicanas* call you *rajetas,*   10
   that denying the Anglo inside you
   is as bad as having denied the Indian or Black;

Cuando vives en la frontera
   people walk through you, the wind steals your voice,
   you're a *burra, buey,* scapegoat,   15
   forerunner of a new race,
   half and half—both woman and man, neither—
   a new gender;

To live in the Borderlands means to
   put *chile* in the borscht,   20
   eat whole wheat *tortillas,*
   speak Tex-Mex with a Brooklyn accent;
   be stopped by *la migra* at the border checkpoints;

Living in the Borderlands means you fight hard to   25
   resist the gold elixer beckoning from the bottle,
   the pull of the gun barrel,
   the rope crushing the hollow of your throat;

Reprinted from *Borderlands/La Frontera: The New Mestiza,* by permission of Aunt Lute Books for the Estate of Gloria Anzaldúa.

In the Borderlands
    you are the battleground
    where enemies are kin to each other;   *30*
    you are at home, a stranger,
    the border disputes have been settled
    the volley of shots have shattered the truce
    you are wounded, lost in action
    dead, fighting back;   *35*

To live in the Borderlands means
    the mill with the razor white teeth wants to shred off
    your olive-red skin, crush out the kernel, your heart
    pound you pinch you roll you out
    smelling like white bread but dead;   *40*

To survive the Borderlands
    you must live *sin fronteras*
    be a crossroads.

                         [1987]

Sandra Cisneros
[1954–   ]

One of the most popular and critically acclaimed Latina writers of the past twenty years, SANDRA CISNEROS *has created a body of work that clearly reflects her cultural background. As she says in a* New York Times *interview: "I am a woman and I am a Latina. Those are the things that make my writing distinctive. Those are the things that give my writing power. They are the things that give it sabor [flavor], the things that give it picante [spice]."*

Born in Chicago in 1954 to a Mexican father and a Chicana mother, Cisneros spent much of her childhood moving from the United States to Mexico and back. The sense of displacement she felt as a result of these frequent moves was offset by the tight control exercised by her father and six brothers. Her desire for stability and control over her own life led her to read avidly and to write poems and stories even as a child. Her writing ability earned her admission to the prestigious University of Iowa Writers Workshop, an experience that revealed to her the vast difference between her life and that of her classmates. She says she knew nothing of the suburban houses and gardens about which they wrote; her experience was of "third-floor flats" in economically depressed and ethnically segregated Chicago neighborhoods. It was at Iowa that the metaphor of the house came to represent to Cisneros a freedom and independence that she never enjoyed as a child.

After earning a master of fine arts degree from Iowa, Cisneros went on to teach in high school and college and to write—first poetry and later fiction. Her first collection of poetry, Bad Boys, *was published in 1980, followed in 1983 by the fiction collection* The House on Mango Street. *Other work followed, including the poetry collection* My Wicked Wicked Ways *(1987) and the fiction collection* Woman Hollering Creek *(1991). Her most recent novel,* Caramelo *(2002), intersperses lyrics and prose with extensive footnotes on family and Mexican history. Cisneros has won a number of literary prizes, including the Before Columbus Foundation American Book Award for* The House on Mango Street, *the PEN Center West Best Fiction Award for* Woman Hollering Creek, *and a MacArthur Foundation grant.*

Cisneros believes that a good deal of her intensity comes from the influence of her mother, whom she describes as "a fierce woman who was brave enough to raise her daughter in a nontraditional way, who fought for my right to be a person of letters." Calling her work "fiercely political," Cisneros writes about gender, culture, and class. In her work she focuses on people whose lives have been marginalized, whose "stories don't get told—my mother's stories, my students" stories, the stories

of women in the neighborhood, the stories of all of those people who don't have
the ability to document their lives." Cisneros currently lives—to the chagrin of
many of her neighbors—in a bright purple house in the historic King William
neighborhood in San Antonio. She remains, as she stated in a biographical sketch
for The House on Mango Street, *"nobody's mother and nobody's wife."*

The House on Mango Street

SANDRA CISNEROS

WE DIDN'T ALWAYS LIVE on Mango Street. Before that we lived on Loomis on the third floor, and before that we lived on Keeler. Before Keeler it was Paulina, and before that I can't remember. But what I remember most is moving a lot. Each time it seemed there'd be one more of us. By the time we got to Mango Street we were six—Mama, Papa, Carlos, Kiki, my sister Nenny and me.

The house on Mango Street is ours, and we don't have to pay rent to anybody, or share the yard with the people downstairs, or be careful not to make too much noise, and there isn't a landlord banging on the ceiling with a broom. But even so, it's not the house we'd thought we'd get.

We had to leave the flat on Loomis quick. The water pipes broke and the landlord wouldn't fix them because the house was too old. We had to leave fast. We were using the washroom next door and carrying water over in empty milk gallons. That's why Mama and Papa looked for a house, and that's why we moved into the house on Mango Street, far away, on the other side of town.

They always told us that one day we would move into a house, a real house that would be ours for always so we wouldn't have to move each year. And our house would have running water and pipes that worked. And inside it would have real stairs, not hall-way stairs, but stairs inside like the houses on TV. And we'd have a basement and at least three washrooms so when we took a bath we wouldn't have to tell everybody. Our house would be white with trees around it, a great big yard and grass growing without a fence. This was the house Papa talked about when he held a lottery ticket and this was the house Mama dreamed up in the stories she told us before we went to bed.

But the house on Mango Street is not the way they told it at all. It's small and red with tight steps in front and windows so small you'd think they were holding their breath. Bricks are crumbling in places, and the front door is so swollen you have to push hard to get in. There is no front yard, only four little elms the city planted by the curb. Out back is a small garage for the car we don't own yet and a small yard that looks smaller between the two buildings on either side. There are stairs in our house, but they're ordinary hallway stairs, and the house has only one washroom. Everybody has to share a bedroom—Mama and Papa, Carlos and Kiki, me and Nenny.

Reprinted from *The House on Mango Street,* by permission of Susan Bergholz Literary Services. Copyright © 1984 by Sandra Cisneros.

Once when we were living on Loomis, a nun from my school passed by and saw me playing out front. The laundromat downstairs had been boarded up because it had been robbed two days before and the owner had painted on the wood YES WE'RE OPEN so as not to lose business.

Where do you live? she asked.

There, I said pointing up to the third floor.

You live *there?*

There. I had to look to where she pointed—the third floor, the paint peeling, wooden bars Papa had nailed on the windows so we wouldn't fall out. You live *there?* The way she said it made me feel like nothing. *There.* I lived *there.* I nodded.

I knew then I had to have a house. A real house. One I could point to. But this isn't it. The house on Mango Street isn't it. For the time being, Mama says. Temporary, says Papa. But I know how those things go.

[1983]

Octavio Paz

[1914–1998]

Born in 1914 in Mexico City, OCTAVIO PAZ is at the center of a strong tradition of twentieth century Latin American literature. While Paz's work is firmly rooted in Mexican culture and history, it also blurs lines between genres, traditions, and critical categories. Often characterized as a modernist, a postmodernist, and a surrealist writer, Paz experiments with the boundaries of language in his poetry and prose. His writing plays with the relationship between space and time, and between the self and a larger culture—in fluid works that demonstrate the possibilities of language, of poetry as a medium for exploration and discovery.

As the first Mexican writer to win the Nobel Prize in Literature (1990), Paz represents the significance of a Latin American literary tradition. As such, his work is often read in terms of its representation of Mexican art, culture, and even politics. While attending the National Autonomous University (1932–1937), Paz published his first collection of poetry, Sylvan Moon (1933). The 1930s and 1940s, for Paz, marked a time of exploration and discovery. Paz's travels to Spain, France, and the United States informed his sense of politics and aesthetics and became the foundation for his works during that period and throughout his later career. And throughout his career, from the 1940s up to his Nobel Prize in 1990, Paz's critical reception is represented by prestigious international praise: the Guggenheim fellowship (1944); Grand Prix International de Poesie (1963); Jerusalem Prize, Critics Prize and National Prize for Letters (1977); Grand Aigle d'Or (1979); Premio Ollin Yoliztli (1980); Miguel de Cervantes Prize (1982); Neustadt International Prize for Literature (1982); Wilheim Heinse Medal (1984); German Book Trade Peace prize (1984); T. S. Eliot Award for Creative Writing (1987); Tocqueville Prize (1989); Nobel Prize for Literature (1990).

In the second half of the twentieth century, Paz's collections of poetry mark each decade, reflecting the historical contexts of the time as well as the development of ideas about poetic language and form. Sun Stone (1958); The Violent Season (1958); Salamander (1962); Blanco (1966); Eastern Rampart (1968); and Renga (1971) reflect Paz's development as a poet as well as his consistency in focus and style. Complementing his poetry, The Labyrinth of Solitude reflects, in prose, Paz's commitment to his politics. Both his poetry and his prose reflect the political climate of Mexico—its larger history and current politics in the context of the massacres of students in 1968. The publication of Collected Poems, 1957–1987 (1987) demonstrates the centrality of Paz's work and the significance of his poetry toward the end of the century. Throughout his poetry, Paz experiments with magical realism—the ways in which time and space can be altered by an individual's perception. Between surrealism and existentialism, Paz's poetry questions the individual's role in the larger world and in history, and complicates notions of the self as autonomous.

Paz was appointed ambassador to India in 1962, but resigned in 1968 after the massacres in Mexico. He went on to become a visiting professor of Spanish-American Literature at the University of Texas at Austin and the University of Pittsburgh (1968–1970) and a professor at Cambridge University (1970–1971) and Harvard University (1971–1972; 1973–1980). In 1995, Paz published his last book, In Light of India (1997), representing, in part, a final development in his work but also a return to origins. His death in 1998 marks the end of an era; a twentieth century Latin American literature that is well grounded in a cultural tradition and is open to (and animated by) experimentation.

—Lisa Perdigao, *Florida Institute of Technology*

With Our Eyes Shut

OCTAVIO PAZ
TRANSLATED BY JOHN FELSTINER

Con los ojos cerrados
Te iluminas por dentro
Ertes la piedra ciega

Noche a noche te labro
Con los ojos cerrados
Eres la piedra franca

Nos volvemos inmensos
Solo por conocernos
Con los ojos cerrados

With your eyes shut
You light up from within
You are blind stone

Night by night I carve you
With my eyes shut   5
You are clear stone

We become immense
Just knowing each other
With our eyes shut

[1958]

Reprinted from *Collected Poems 1957-1987*, by permission of New Directions Publishing Corp. Copyright © 1986 by Octavio Paz and Eliot Weinberger.

Ana Castillo
[1953–   ]

ANA CASTILLO *was born and raised in Chicago, where she credits the rich storytelling heritage of her Mexican family as the inspiration for her writing. She wrote her first poems at age nine, following the death of her grandmother. Castillo is among the most significant and prolific authors of what has been considered the Chicano literary renaissance. She received a bachelor's degree in art from Northeastern Illinois University, after which she spent several years teaching Ethnic Studies at a junior college in California. Her interest in Latin American issues drew her back into graduate school, and she went on to receive a master of arts in Latin American and Caribbean Studies from the University of Chicago and a doctorate in American Studies from the University of Bremen.*

Her earliest published books were volumes of poetry, including Otro Canto *(chapbook, 1977),* Women Are Not Roses *(1984), and* My Father Was a Toltec *(1988). These often-anthologized and critically acclaimed poems helped create Castillo's reputation as a social protest poet; she has, however, become most famous as a novelist. Her first novel,* The Mixquiahuala Letters *(1986), traces the relationship between Teresa, a California poet, and Alicia, a New York artist, and explores the shifting roles of Latinas and Chicanas in the culture of the United States. Castillo gives the reader three possible versions of the story by presenting the reader with three possible orders in which to read the letters; one "Conformist," one "Cynic," and one "Quixotic."* The Mixquiahuala Letters *was awarded the Before Columbus Foundation's American Book Award in 1987. Castillo's next novel,* Sapogonia *(1990), tells a complex story of the destructive possibilities in relationships between men and women.* So Far From God *(1993), Castillo's third novel, received both the Carl Sandburg Literary Award in Fiction and the Mountains and Plains Bookseller Award, and is perhaps Castillo's most widely read book, following the lives of a Latina woman and her four daughters in a style that draws on the Latin American "magical realist" authors. Castillo has since released a volume of short stories,* Loverboys *(1996) and another novel,* Peel My Love Like an Onion *(1999).*

Castillo has also published a volume of nonfiction, titled Massacre of the Dreamers: Reflections on Mexican-Indian Women in the United States 500 Years After the Conquest *(1992), in which she argues for what was described by one critic as "a new, aggressive brand of feminism she calls Xicanisma, to win brown women a place in a black-and-white country." She is, moreover, the cofounder of the literary magazine* Third Woman, *and the coeditor of the landmark volume of feminist literature,* This Bridge Called My Back *(1988), translated as* Esta Puente, Mi Espalda. *All of Castillo's work explores the intersections of race, gender, and sexuality in American culture. All of it, as one reviewer said, "sizzles with equal measures of passion and intelligence."*

Loverboys

ANA CASTILLO

TWO BOYS ARE MAKING out in the booth across from me. I ain't got nothing else to do, so I watch them. I drink the not-so-aged house brandy and I watch two boys make out. It's more like they're in the throes of passion, as they say. And they're not boys, really. I think I've seen them around before, somewhere on campus maybe. Not making out though.

One gets up, to get them each another drink I guess, and he and I check each other out briefly as he passes me up on his way to the bar. He's a white boy wearing a T-shirt with a graphic of Malcolm X[1] on it.

This is the way my life is these days or maybe it's a sign of the nineties: a white boy with a picture of Malcolm X on his T-shirt and me, sitting here in a gay bar trying to forget a man.

Well, okay. He must not have been just any man and I'm sure not just any woman. Before him there were only women. Puras mujeres (¡sino mujeres puras)![2] A cast of thousands. Women's music festivals, feminist symposiums, women of color retreats and camp-outs, women's healing rituals under a full moon, ceremonies of union and not-so-ceremonious reunions, women-only panels and caucuses at conferences, en fin, women ad infinitum.

And then one day a boy—not much older than either of these two loving it up in front of me, nor the half-dozen other clientele here on a dead Monday night for that matter—comes into my store asking for a copy of *The Rebel*.[3] I point in the direction of Albert—whom once I was so fond of we were on a first-name basis—and he, the boy in my store, kind of casually goes over to check out what we got on the shelf. We're always stocked up on the existentialists, so I didn't bother to offer assistance.

---

[1]Malcolm X (1925–1965), black nationalist leader during the Civil Rights movement and spokesperson for the Nation of Islam.

[2]Spanish: purely women (but no pure women)!

[3]A collection of essays by French-Algerian existentialist author Albert Camus (1913–1960), published in 1951.

Reprinted from *Loverboys*, by permission of W.W. Norton & Company. Copyright © 1996 by Ana Castillo.

My partner—who used to be my partner in all senses of the word and whom I bought out a year ago—and I opened up the store about ten years ago. We thought about making it a woman's bookstore, a lesbian bookstore, a gay and lesbian bookstore, a "Third World" bookstore, or even an exclusively Latina bookstore. Heaven knows, any town could use at least one of each of those kind of bookshops—stocked up on alternative-press publications that inform you about what's going on with the majority of the population when you sure don't hear it from the mass media. You know? But no, spirituality won out—since all roads eventually lead to one place, we reasoned.

So along with Camus, Sartre, and Kierkegaard,[4] we . . . I carry almost anything you can imagine that comes out of the East and Native imaginations and ancient practices.

I sat back and picked up the book I was reading. I let the boy browse. I saw him leafing through some other things and, finally, he came over with a copy of *The Stranger*.[5]

"Didn't you see *The Rebel* up on the shelf?" I asked, not really looking at him, just taking the book and ringing it up.

"Yeah. But I don't think I'm ready for it," he answered. "I read this in high school. I think I'll read it again . . . I really like this translation anyway," he said, referring to the edition he had chosen.

I rang it up. But he didn't pick up his package right away. Just kept looking at me. I looked back and smiled, a little cockily. I'm a mirror that way. You look at me a certain way and I respond in kind. Just like with this white guy here who just passed me by again with two Coronas. He looks. He doesn't smile. He just looks like I don't belong here. *I* don't belong here? I helped start this joint about twelve years ago when you couldn't find a gay bar within ten miles of this town.

Me and Rosie and her compadre, who's over there tending bar—the big guy with the Pancho Villa[6] charm and beer belly. He looks like someone's father, right? Not the kind of bartender you would expect to find in a gay bar. Well, just for the record, he *is* somebody's father. His oldest son enlisted in the air force—overcompensating for his dad's dubious machismo or patriotism, if you ask me. He just got shipped off to the Middle East last week. His daughter, Belinda, Rosie's godchild, got married last summer.

That's the way it goes.

---

[4] Jean-Paul Sartre (1905–1980), French existentialist author; Soren Kierkegaard (1813–1855), Danish philosopher generally thought to be the first existentialist.

[5] A novel by Albert Camus, published in 1942.

[6] Pancho Villa (1878–1923), the foremost general of the Mexican Revolution.

Yeah. His wife knows he owns this bar. And she knows all the rest, too. But she's pretty religious and would never have thought to divorce him. Besides, Rosie told me that his wife really doesn't find the men in her husband's life a threat to her marriage. He's got it pretty good, huh?

Anyway, I say to this young man with Indian smooth skin like glazed clay, and the offhanded manner of a chile alegre[7] if I ever saw one, after he's been staring at me for a good minute or so without saying anything, "Is there anything else I can help you with?"

His dark face got darker when he blushed, and he laughed a little, "Naw, naw . . .," he said, shaking his head. "Actually, I *did* wanna get that one of his, too, but I can't afford it till payday," he admitted, referring to *The Rebel.*

Liking his white, uneven teeth, although I'm not very good with quotes, except to massacre them usually, I said, " 'I was placed halfway between poverty and the sun.' " With that he got this expression like I had just done a wondrous thing by quoting Albert spontaneously. I was ready to part the sea if I could continue to elicit that gaze of a devotee from those obsidian eyes, so I dared to continue quoting: " 'Poverty kept me from thinking all was well under the sun and in history; the sun taught me that history was not everything . . .' "

He laughed out loud. He laughed like he had just discovered he was in the presence of Camus himself and he slapped his thigh, as if to say, "What a kick!" He stared at me some more and then he left, still laughing.

After that it was all out of our hands. He came back a few more times that week and finally one evening just before I closed. He wasn't buying anything, just browsing and talking with me when I had a minute between customers. By this time we were old chums—talking about all kinds of things, literature mostly. He likes poetry. He writes poetry. Well, at least he says he does. He never showed me anything. But who am I to question or to judge?

So we went to get a taco down the street at my favorite taco joint. I'm really a creature of habit, no doubt about it. There's only one place where I go for tacos and only one place where I go to get loaded. And there's my store. In between is home and sleep.

Anyway, then we came here, as you might have guessed, to have a drink. I used to come just on weekends but since about the time when we stopped hanging out I am here just about every night of the week, it seems.

That night we got pretty "hammered," his favorite word for what we used to do very well together—besides make love. We made love anytime, anyplace, as often as we could—like a happy pair of rabbits—with the one big difference that I don't reproduce—never did when I could and now I never will.

---

[7] Literally, a happy pepper. Spanish slang for a promiscuous man, a stud, or "ladies' man."

He's really gonna hate me for telling you all this (and I don't doubt that he'll find out someday that I have, since it was the very fact that I'm kind of a public person that scared him off), but little by little, his PMS started to get the better of him. You know, his "Pure Macho Shit." Maybe it's not fair to call what he started to feel towards me that, but I don't know what else it was. I can't explain none of it. I don't know why he's gone, why I'm here worrying about it . . . Why *you're* here, for that matter . . .

Except to drink. And we know how far that will get you. It's just like that Mexican joke with the two drunks just barely hanging on to their bar stools. "Well, why do *you* drink?" one asks the other. "I drink to forget," the other guy replies. "And what's it you're trying to forget?" the first guy asks. The other looks up, kind of thinking for a bit, then says, "I dunno. I forgot."

Well, it's a lot funnier in Spanish. Or maybe you have to be Mexican. But for sure, you have to be a drunk to get it . . . or maybe just drunk.

I went over to the pay phone when I first got here and tried to call him. Although I promised myself never to look for him again, I broke down finally—because between books and drinks, there's only him in my head, like one of those melodies where you only know half the words. I called him without thinking about it, like I had done so many times before, and him always on the other end, and pretty soon, he would be with me.

I called the gas station where he *used* to work 'cause I can't call his house, but apparently he's not gigging there anymore. The guy that answered couldn't tell me anything. High turnover in those places is all the consolation he could give me.

Where do you think my boy went? Fired, most likely. Left town, maybe? I doubt it. He's not ready for that kind of wandering, the kind of wandering his soul takes when he's alone and the kind of wandering loving me gave his imagination. Unless I really underestimated him.

Well, see, in the beginning he seemed very cool about my life. The fact that I had not been with a man since college, just women . . . one woman mostly. Considering himself a sensitive progressive politically conscious self-defined young male of color—*of course* he was cool about my life, he said. How could he not be, he insisted.

But that didn't stop him from jumping on top of me the first night we were alone, did it?—when he came over to my place with the excuse to drop off a copy of Neruda's *Veinte poemas de amor y una canción desesperada*[8] that he bought in Mexico where he lived for a semester as an exchange student.

---

[8]Pablo Neruda (1904–1973), Chilean poet considered to be among the most significant literary figures in twentieth century Latin America; his *Veinte poemas de amor y una cancion desesperada* was published in 1924 (translated as *Twenty Poems of Love and a Song of Desperation* in 1969). Neruda received the Nobel Prize for Literature in 1971.

A bright young man, he was. Is. A bright splendid ray in my life. But like Picasso[9] said, "When you come right down to it, all you have is your self. Your self is a sun with a thousand rays in your belly. The rest is nothing." But for a while, he was all mine. Mio. Mio. Mio.

Then his brothers started ragging him about running around with a lesbian—or worse, a bisexual, nothing more shady or untrustworthy (except for a liberal)—who plays soccer and who knows how to do her own tune-ups and oil change. And his mother, about me being a woman with a past. And his father, about me being an independent businesswoman, and what could he teach an older woman?

As if my loverboy were not tormenting himself well enough on his own day and night over all this as it was. Once he was reading a book by a male psychologist that talked about the history of goddess worship and said that in early times the pig and cow represented the female and were considered powerful deities. So one night we were sleeping and his body gave a great jerk and we both woke up. He told me, "I was dreaming that I was at home in the kitchen and I was telling my brothers that a pig was after me . . . and suddenly this huge pig leaped right through the window at me . . . and I jumped!"

Well, of course it didn't take a genius to figure out who the pig was but I was pretty impressed by his metaphorical interpretation of what I was in his life. He was cool about us for a while, as I said, although he did spend the first months doing some hard drinking over it. Then he sobered up so that he could sort it all out with a clear head, he said.

And then he left.

I went on with my business without missing a beat. You know, I got the store to run. And I spoke at a pro-choice rally last weekend. I started dating a woman I met some time back who had asked me to go out with her before, but I was too busy being in love with an existentialist Catholic pseudo-poet manito[10] fifteen years younger than me to have noticed even Queen Nefertiti[11] herself gliding by on the shoulders of two eunuchs. ¡Jijola![12] Was I cruisin' for a bruisin'—¿o qué?[13]

I stopped drinking too. You know? For about a week. I couldn't take the hangovers, I told my new friend, who was already frowning pretty seriously on

---

[9]Pablo Picasso (1881–1973), Spanish artist recognized among the masters of twentieth century painting.

[10]Literally, little man. Spanish slang for buddy, friend.

[11]The wife of a fourteenth century B.C.E. Egyptian pharaoh, known for her beauty.

[12]An exclamation of pleasant surprise.

[13]Spanish: "Or what?"

the extent of my alcohol consumption. "You drink too much," she told me at the end of our first date as she walked me to my door. Then she turned around and left me standing there feeling bare-assed with my drunkenness showing and my broken heart, which I would not admit to no matter what. Like everybody, she comes from a dysfunctional family and all that brings up too much stuff for her, she said.

But the funny thing was that when I stopped drinking, I didn't feel any better about him, but I did feel worse about *her*. I just took a good, hard, sober look at her one day and thought, who wants someone around who's gonna be telling you about yourself all the time? Especially when you haven't asked her for her opinion in the first place.

So I told her last Sunday that we were gonna have to be just friends and we talked about it for a while on the phone (I didn't have it in me to tell her to her face) and she said, "Fine, I understand."

Yeah, yeah, yeah. After we hung up I went out. I came here, naturally, and around closing time I made it back home, seeing cross-eyed and hardly able to find the keyhole to get my key in the door when I jumped back and would have screamed like a banshee except that nothing came out of my mouth I was so scared by something moving suddenly out of the darkness coming right at me. And there she was. She had been sitting on the front porch all night waiting for me.

Now, I ask you: Is there justice to this life at all? Or maybe the question should be: Is life even supposed to make sense? Or maybe we shouldn't bother trying to figure it out, just go about our business tripping over it like that crack in the sidewalk that sends you flying in an embarrassing way and when you look back to see what tripped you, and everybody's looking at you, there's nothing there.

I mean, I have been half out of my mind since I said goodbye to my loverboy and I ain't heard nor seen hide nor hair of him since; and meanwhile this woman, whom I forgot the moment I hung up the phone saying goodbye, is convinced that God has put her on this planet for the sole purpose of rescuing me from myself!

Yeah, you heard right just now. I know I said earlier that he left me. But it was me who suggested we not see each other anymore. I mean, it was just a suggestion, right? A damn good one I thought at the time, driven by my self-respect as I am, since he had just told me that he was gonna take a trip and travel around South America with a college friend of his, and didn't know exactly when we'd see each other again. So I decided to give him a head start on feeling what it was to not see me anymore and said I was gonna be pretty busy myself and as of that moment didn't know when *I* could see *him*.

Well, let me tell you how it was with us. We had done all the hokey things people in love do. We stayed up in bed for hours after making love, just talking, confessing all our childhood traumas to each other; we cried together about a lot of things. We went to the zoo, the movies; we took walks and had picnics. We even kissed in the rain, making out in the downpour like nobody's business.

Which of course, it wasn't. He said to me once, "You are the kind of woman who deserves to be kissed in front of everybody."

We had only one fight in all those months. I don't remember what stupid thing started it, but the next thing I know I threw a cushion at him that must've been tearing already because it hardly had an impact and there was fluff all over the place like it was snowing in the room. Well then, he throws a cushion at me. And before you know it, we're laughing and pounding each other with almohadas destripas[14], a flurry of feathers and fluff all over the room.

That's the way it was with us. A lot of laughs. A lot of good times. It's real hard to find someone to laugh with, you know?

Like, you see those two guys still sitting there in the dark? Now they're not smooching anymore. In fact, it looks like they're a little pissed off at each other. Who knows why? I was sitting here since before they came in and never once did those two laugh with each other. They came in, sat down without a word, and as soon as the one got the other a drink, they started making out. Now, they're mad at each other.

But those two will probably grow old together because they really know how to be mad at each other, while me and my loverboy who didn't have a bad moment together have already gone up in smoke—with the force of burning copal[15] and all the professed tragedy of La Noche Triste[16]—succumbing to our destiny. Between the sun and poverty there was us for a little while.

Well, someone had to take my lunch away. I don't mind admitting it. I hurt Rosie pretty bad after being with her all our adult lives, practically. I just fell out of love with her and even out of like, since we fought so much toward the end. Actually, I know by then that she was seeing that woman who she ran off to Las Cruces[17] with. But she would never admit to that. I couldn't prove it, but I knew it in my heart—the little emaciated excuse for a heart I had left

---

[14]Spanish: gutted pillows.

[15]A form of resinous incense.

[16]Literally, "the sad night"; used to refer to the night in 1520 when, as legend has it, the Spanish conquistador Cortez sat under a tree and wept after a defeat by the Aztecs.

[17]A town in New Mexico, northwest of El Paso, Texas.

when she took off. But I can't say I blame her for leaving since it wasn't happening with us anymore.

Anyway, I don't really know why I'm telling you about Rosie. That's all over with. But it's like the one who matters is too hard to talk about. I can't talk about it without thinking I look ridiculous—like the classic jilted older woman. Of course it wasn't going to work out. *I* knew that. *He* knew that. And his family didn't help it any either. But even so. Somewhere in the middle of all its fatality, *we*, me, him, even his mother, who was busy having Masses said for her son's salvation—and I'm not putting down his mother either, in case you ever run into him and tell him any of this—*she* knew that what we had was indelible.

I'm gonna stop drinking. This time not because someone is shaming me out of it. And not because I can stand to go to bed at night thinking of him or waking up alone remembering waking up with him. But because it doesn't help anymore.

I'm gonna stop torturing myself in all the ways that I've been doing; I'll even stop playing all those Agustín Lara[18] records he brought over—for us to make love to. And we did, over and over again.

I saw Agustín Lara perform in Mexico City when I was a kid. Did you know that? He was gaunt and very elegant. My mother was swooning. I was just a little kid, so I was just there. But when I mentioned it to my loverboy, he gave me the sign of la bendición[19]—implying that I was among the blessed to have laid eyes on the late, great, inimitable saint of Mexican music:

Santa, santa mía, mujer que brilla en mi existencia[20] . . . His saint he called me, his saint and his treasure. His first and only love.

I've been thinking about renting the storefront next to my bookstore and extending my business to include a café. You know, café latte, avocado-and-sprout croissant sandwiches, and natural fruit drinks. I think this town is ready for a place like that. Maybe I'll exhibit local artists there, not that there are too many good ones around. But there are a few who are going places—I'll get them to show in my establishment before they do . . .

I think he already split town with his friend; he's probably somewhere in Veracruz[21] at Carnival at this very moment—having a great old time. Well, at least for his sake, I hope so.

You think that maybe he misses me a little bit?

---

[18]Agustin Lara (1897–1970), seminal songwriter and musician of pre-World War II Mexico.

[19]Spanish: blessing

[20]Spanish: "My saint, woman who shines in my life . . .".

[21]State on the east coast of Mexico.

Probably the saddest boy in Mexico right now, you say?

I hope so.

Let me tell el compadre over there to send those two unhappy lovers a couple of beers, on me. There's something insupportable about being pissed with the one person on this planet that sends your adrenaline flowing to remind you that you're alive. It's almost like we're mad because we've been shocked out of our usual comatose state of being by feeling something for someone, for ourselves, for just a moment.

He made me feel alive, cliché or not. Drunk or sober. If he ever finds out I told you all this, he'll really be furious. I guess he felt like he was living in a glass bowl with me. Not that I'm not discreet, but everyone in town seems to know me, or at least think that they do. But I like my privacy, too, you know? Mis cosas son mis cosas.[22] I just had to talk to somebody about it. Been carrying it around inside me like a sin, a crime, like that guy in *Crime and Punishment*.[23] And it wasn't like that at all—far from it.

Anyway, I haven't used any names, in case you didn't notice, not even yours—even though people'll figure it out soon enough. And everybody already knows who I am. I run the only bookstore in town that deals with the question of the soul. All roads sooner or later will lead you there.

[1996]

---

[22]Spanish: "My things are my things".

[23]A novel by Russian author Fyodor Dostoyevsky (1821–1881), published in 1866, which tells the story of a destitute student's murder of a pawnbroker and the psychological effects of his actions.

Louise Erdich
[1954–   ]

Born in Little Falls, Minnesota to a Chippewa mother and a German-American father, LOUISE ERDRICH *was the eldest of seven children. Her parents taught at the Wahpeton Indian School, an institution run by the Bureau of Indian Affairs. Although Erdrich was raised a Roman Catholic, she was also introduced to Native American spirituality while growing up; both traditions inform her writing, which was encouraged by both her parents. As she told* Contemporary Authors, *"My father used to give me a nickel for every story I wrote, and my mother wove strips of construction paper together and stapled them into book covers. So at an early age I felt myself to be a published author earning substantial royalties." Erdrich was one of the first women to be admitted to Dartmouth College, where she graduated in 1976 with a degree in English and Native American Studies. She received a master's degree in creative writing from Johns Hopkins University in 1979, compiling a collection of poetry for her thesis.*

Despite her immersion in poetry during her years at Johns Hopkins, Erdrich's early career focused on publication of short fiction and editing the Boston Indian Council newspaper The Circle. *Returning to Dartmouth as a writer-in-residence, she married Michael Dorris, founder of the university's Native American Studies program and her former teacher. Until Dorris's death in 1997, the two wrote together and raised their six children in New Hampshire. Erdrich's first novel,* Love Medicine *(1984), won the National Book Critics' Circle Award for fiction. This novel was followed by* Beet Queen *(1986),* Tracks *(1988),* Bingo Palace *(1994),* Tales of Burning Love *(1996),* The Antelope Wife *(1999),* The Last Report on the Miracles at Little No Horse *(2002),* The Master Butchers Singing Club *(2004), and* Four Souls *(2004). In addition to these fictional explorations of Native American and immigrant life in North Dakota, Erdrich has also published poetry, essays, children's books, and a memoir. She and Dorris co-authored* The Crown of Columbus *in 1991 to commemorate the landing of Columbus in the New World.*

Erdrich currently lives in Minneapolis, where she opened the independent bookstore BirchBark Books in 2000. The shop features lesser-known writers—particlarly Native Americans—as well as children's books, public readings, and Native American craft demonstrations and classes.

Erdrich's work has been compared to William Faulkner's in that she has created an entire community, populating it with generations of characters whose struggles reflect a unique facet of American experience. Her stories, like

Faulkner's, are also told from multiple perspectives, with narrative lines drifting across borders of time and place. Considered a master of humor, irony, and vivid imagery, Louise Erdrich has established herself as one of the most American accomplished writers of the late twentieth and early twenty-first century.

Indian Boarding School: The Runaways

LOUISE ERDRICH

Home's the place we head for in our sleep.
Boxcars stumbling north in dreams
don't wait for us. We catch them on the run.
The rails, old lacerations that we love,
shoot parallel across the face and break   5
just under Turtle Mountains. Riding scars
you can't get lost. Home is the place they cross.

The lame guard strikes a match and makes the dark
less tolerant. We watch through cracks in boards
as the land starts rolling, rolling till it hurts   10
to be here, cold in regulation clothes.
We know the sheriff's waiting at midrun
to take us back. His car is dumb and warm.
The highway doesn't rock, it only hums
like a wing of long insults. The worn-down welts   15
of ancient punishments lead back and forth.
All runaways wear dresses, long green ones,
the color you would think shame was. We scrub
the sidewalks down because it's shameful work.
Our brushes cut the stone in watered arcs   20
and in the soak frail outlines shiver clear
a moment, things us kids pressed on the dark
face before it hardened, pale, remembering
delicate old injuries, the spines of names and leaves.

[1984]

Reprinted from *Jacklight*, by permission of The Wylie Agency, Inc. Copyright © 1984 by
Louise Erdrich.

Wendy Rose
[1948–   ]

WENDY ROSE *was born in Oakland, California in 1948 under the name Bronwen Elizabeth Edwards. The fact that she changed her birth name, and later wrote under the pseudonym Chiron Khanshendel, reflects the feelings of divided- ness that have pervaded Rose's life and work. While Rose's father is Hopi, her mother is of Miwok, Scottish, Irish, and German descent. As a Fourth World per- son (an aboriginal person living within a colonial "settler" nation), Rose suffered a profound sense of alienation. In her teens, she became estranged from her father and dropped out of high school to join the countercultural milieu of 1960s San Francisco. Resuming her schooling in 1966, Rose attended Cabrillo and Contra Costa Junior Colleges and ultimately completed a bachelor of arts, master of arts and a doctorate in cultural anthropology at the University of California, Berkeley. Rose went on to achieve a distinguished academic career: She wrote the monograph* Aboriginal Tattooing in California *(1979)—the only full-length study of the subject—and continues compilation of an exhaustive bibliography of Native American writing. She has held several faculty positions, including that of coordinator of the American Indian Studies Program at Fresno City College in Fresno, California. Rose also served as editor of* American Indian Quarterly *and as a facilitator of for the Association of Non-Federally Recognized California Tribes.*

As suggested by the title of her 1977 book Academic Squaw: Reports to the World From the Ivory Tower *(1977), Rose has been ambivalent about the world of higher education subject to the same Eurocentric prejudices as American soci- ety at large. Since the early 1970s, she has devoted most of her creative energy to poetry rather than to conventional scholarship. Rose has written eleven volumes of poetry, including* Long Division: A Tribal History *(1977);* Lost Cropper *(1980);* The Halfbreed Chronicles and Other Poems *(1985);* Going to War with All My Relations *(1993); and* Now Proof She Is Gone *(1994). These titles suggest the themes of loss, alienation, and "division" that run throughout Rose's poetry. Whether lamenting the loss of native ecology in "Alien Seeds" or drawing attention to the indignities inflicted on the aboriginal body in "Truganinny" and "Julia," Rose directs much of her writing toward a critique of First World devas- tations of Fourth World peoples and cultures. In collections such as* Hopi Roadrunner Dancing *(1973) and* Builder Kachina: A Home-Going Cycle *(1979), however, Rose balances her pessimistic themes with celebrations of com- munity and solidarity. The latter book treats the poet's journey toward of recon- ciliation with her father and, by extension, confidence in her cultural identity.*

For the White Poets Who Would be Indian

WENDY ROSE

just once
just long enough
to snap up the words
fish-hooked
from our tongues.   5
You think of us now
when you kneel
on the earth,
turn holy
in a temporary tourism   10
of our souls.
With words
you paint your faces,
chew your doeskin,
touch breast to tree   15
as if sharing a mother
were all it takes,
could bring
instant and primal
of knowledge.   20
You think of us only
when your voice
wants for roots,
when you have sat back
on your heels   25
and become primitive.
You finish your poem
and go back.

[1977]

Reprinted from *Lost Copper*, by permission of the Malki Museum/Malki Museum Press.
Copyright © 1980 by Wendy Rose.

Sherman Alexie
[1966–   ]

SHERMAN ALEXIE, *a Spokane/Coeur d'Alene Indian, grew up on the Spokane Indian Reservation in Wellpinit, Washington. He was born hydrocephalic and had to undergo an operation on his brain at six months of age; he was not expected to survive, or at least not to survive without suffering permanent mental disabilities. Though he made a remarkable recovery, his childhood was marked by severe side-effects, including seizures; this, combined with his bookishness, served to ostracize Alexie from his peers. When, in the reservation's school, Alexie found his mother's name written in the textbook he'd been assigned, he made the decision to attend a white high school, hoping for a better education. As he has said, he was "the only Indian" in his high school, "except for the school mascot." Alexie was a star basketball player, and he received a scholarship to attend Gonzaga University in Spokane, Washington; after two years at Gonzaga, Alexie transferred to Washington State University, where he first began to study poetry. Alexie received the Washington State Arts Commission Poetry Fellowship in 1991, and the National Endowment for the Arts Poetry Fellowship in 1992, the same year his first two collections of poetry,* The Business of Fancydancing *and* I Would Steal Horses, *were published.*

The publication of these books coincided with the beginning of Alexie's recovery from a bout with active alcoholism; this disease, which has devastated Indian communities, is a recurring theme in his writing. Alexie has published sixteen books, among which are included two novels, Reservation Blues *(1995; winner, American Book Award) and* Indian Killer *(1996), and three short story collections,* The Lone Ranger and Tonto Fistfight in Heaven *(1993; winner, PEN/Hemingway Award for Best First Book of Fiction, and the Lila Wallace-Reader's Digest Writer's Award),* The Toughest Indian in the World *(2000), and* Ten Little Indians *(2003). Alexie has also collaborated in the adaptation of his short story, "This Is What It Means to Say Phoenix, Arizona," for the screen, writing the script for the film* Smoke Signals *(1998), for which he won the 1999 Independent Spirit Award for Best First Screenplay.*

Alexie's writing blends a matter-of-fact exploration of the issues facing contemporary Indian communities—among them racism, poverty, violence, and alcoholism—with a fine-tuned sense of humor, the humor that has, he suggests, been a key means of cultural and spiritual survival for Indians in the United States. Alexie resists exoticizing Native American life, avoiding stereotypical representations of traditional Indian culture, and instead focuses on the day-to-day experiences of average Indians, experiences that are highly affected by mainstream popular culture. As Alexie writes in The Lone Ranger and Tonto

Fistfight in Heaven, *"It's almost like Indians can easily survive the big stuff. Mass murder, loss of language and land rights. It's the small things that hurt the most. The white waitress who wouldn't take an order, Tonto, the Washington Redskins."* These seemingly mundane elements of U.S. culture color Alexie's work by creating a textured sense of the world through which his characters move, the world they must survive every day.

The Lone Ranger and Tonto Fistfight in Heaven

SHERMAN ALEXIE

TOO HOT TO SLEEP so I walked down to the Third Avenue 7-11 for a Creamsicle and the company of a graveyard-shift cashier. I know that game. I worked graveyard for a Seattle 7-11 and got robbed once too often. The last time the bastard locked me in the cooler. He even took my money and basketball shoes.

The graveyard-shift worker in the Third Avenue 7-11 looked like they all do. Acne scars and a bad haircut, work pants that showed off his white socks, and those cheap black shoes that have no support. My arches still ache from my year at the Seattle 7-11.

"Hello," he asked when I walked into his store. "How you doing?"

I gave him a half-wave as I headed back to the freezer. He looked me over so he could describe me to the police later. I knew the look. One of my old girlfriends said I started to look at her that way, too. She left me not long after that. No, I left her and don't blame her for anything. That's how it happened. When one person starts to look at another like a criminal, then the love is over. It's logical.

"I don't trust you," she said to me. "You get too angry."

She was white and I lived with her in Seattle. Some nights we fought so bad that I would just get in my car and drive all night, only stop to fill up on gas. In fact, I worked the graveyard shift to spend as much time away from her as possible. But I learned all about Seattle that way, driving its back ways and dirty alleys.

Sometimes, though, I would forget where I was and get lost. I'd drive for hours, searching for something familiar. Seems like I'd spent my whole life that way, looking for anything I recognized. Once, I ended up in a nice residential neighborhood and somebody must have been worried because the police showed up and pulled me over.

Reprinted from *The Lone Ranger and Tonto Fistfight in Heaven*, by permission of Grove/Atlantic, Inc. Copyright © 1994 by Sherman Alexie.

"What are you doing out here?" the police officer asked me as he looked over my license and registration.

"I'm lost."

"Well, where are you supposed to be?" he asked me, and I knew there were plenty of places I wanted to be, but none where I was supposed to be.

"I got in a fight with my girlfriend," I said. "I was just driving around, blowing off steam, you know?"

"Well, you should be more careful where you drive," the officer said. "You're making people nervous. You don't fit the profile of the neighborhood."

I wanted to tell him that I didn't really fit the profile of the country but I knew it would just get me into trouble.

"Can I help you?" the 7-11 clerk asked me loudly, searching for some response that would reassure him that I wasn't an armed robber. He knew this dark skin and long, black hair of mine was dangerous. I had potential.

"Just getting a Creamsicle," I said after a long interval. It was a sick twist to pull on the guy, but it was late and I was bored. I grabbed my Creamsicle and walked back to the counter slowly, scanned the aisles for effect. I wanted to whistle low and menacingly but I never learned to whistle.

"Pretty hot out tonight?" he asked, that old rhetorical weather bullshit question designed to put us both at ease.

"Hot enough to make you go crazy," I said and smiled. He swallowed hard like a white man does in those situations. I looked him over. Same old green, red, and white 7-11 jacket and thick glasses. But he wasn't ugly, just misplaced and marked by loneliness. If he wasn't working there that night, he'd be at home alone, flipping through channels and wishing he could afford HBO or Showtime.

"Will this be all?" he asked me, in that company effort to make me do some impulse shopping. Like adding a clause onto a treaty. *We'll take Washington and Oregon and you get six pine trees and a brand-new Chrysler Cordoba.* I knew how to make and break promises.

"No," I said and paused. "Give me a Cherry Slushie, too."

"What size?" he asked, relieved.

"Large," I said, and he turned his back to me to make the drink. He realized his mistake but it was too late. He stiffened, ready for the gunshot or the blow behind the ear. When it didn't come, he turned back to me.

"I'm sorry," he said. "What size did you say?"

"Small," I said and changed the story.

"But I thought you said large."

"If you knew I wanted a large, then why did you ask me again?" I asked him and laughed. He looked at me, couldn't decide if I was giving him serious shit or just goofing. There was something about him I liked, even if it was three in the morning and he was white.

"Hey," I said. "Forget the Slushie. What I want to know is if you know all the words to the theme from 'The Brady Bunch'?"

He looked at me, confused at first, then laughed.

"Shit," he said. "I was hoping you weren't crazy. You were scaring me."

"Well, I'm going to get crazy if you don't know the words."

He laughed loudly then, told me to take the Creamsicle for free. He was the graveyard-shift manager and those little demonstrations of power tickled him. All seventy-five cents of it. I knew how much everything cost.

"Thanks," I said to him and walked out the door. I took my time walking home, let the heat of the night melt the Cream-sicle all over my hand. At three in the morning I could act just as young as I wanted to act. There was no one around to ask me to grow up.

In Seattle, I broke lamps. She and I would argue and I'd break a lamp, just pick it up and throw it down. At first she'd buy replacement lamps, expensive and beautiful. But after a while she'd buy lamps from Goodwill or garage sales. Then she just gave up the idea entirely and we'd argue in the dark.

"You're just like your brother," she'd yell. "Drunk all the time and stupid."

"My brother don't drink that much."

She and I never tried to hurt each other physically. I did love her, after all, and she loved me. But those arguments were just as damaging as a fist. Words can be like that, you know? Whenever I get into arguments now, I remember her and I also remember Muhammad Ali. He knew the power of his fists but, more importantly, he knew the power of his words, too. Even though he only had an IQ of 80 or so, Ali was a genius. And she was a genius, too. She knew exactly what to say to cause me the most pain.

But don't get me wrong. I walked through that relationship with an executioner's hood. Or more appropriately, with war paint and sharp arrows. She was a kindergarten teacher and I continually insulted her for that.

"Hey, schoolmarm," I asked. "Did your kids teach you anything new today?"

And I always had crazy dreams. I always have had them, but it seemed they became nightmares more often in Seattle.

In one dream, she was a missionary's wife and I was a minor war chief. We fell in love and tried to keep it secret. But the missionary caught us fucking in the barn and shot me. As I lay dying, my tribe learned of the shooting and attacked the whites all across the reservation. I died and my soul drifted above the reservation.

Disembodied, I could see everything that was happening. Whites killing Indians and Indians killing whites. At first it was small, just my tribe and the few whites who lived there. But my dream grew, intensified. Other tribes arrived on horseback to continue the slaughter of whites, and the United States Cavalry rode into battle.

The most vivid image of that dream stays with me. Three mounted soldiers played polo with a dead Indian woman's head. When I first dreamed it, I thought it was just a product of my anger and imagination. But since then, I've read similar accounts of that kind of evil in the old West. Even more terrifying, though, is the fact that those kinds of brutal things are happening today in places like El Salvador.

All I know for sure, though, is that I woke from that dream in terror, packed up all my possessions, and left Seattle in the middle of the night.

"I love you," she said as I left her. "And don't ever come back."

I drove through the night, over the Cascades, down into the plains of central Washington, and back home to the Spokane Indian Reservation.

When I finished the Creamsicle that the 7-11 clerk gave me, I held the wooden stick up into the air and shouted out very loudly. A couple lights flashed on in windows and a police car cruised by me a few minutes later. I waved to the men in blue and they waved back accidentally. When I got home it was still too hot to sleep so I picked up a week-old newspaper from the floor and read.

There was another civil war, another terrorist bomb exploded, and one more plane crashed and all aboard were presumed dead. The crime rate was rising in every city with populations larger than 100,000, and a farmer in Iowa shot his banker after foreclosure on his 1,000 acres.

A kid from Spokane won the local spelling bee by spelling the word *rhinoceros*.

When I got back to the reservation, my family wasn't surprised to see me. They'd been expecting me back since the day I left for Seattle. There's an old Indian poet who said that Indians can reside in the city, but they can never live there. That's as close to truth as any of us can get.

Mostly I watched television. For weeks I flipped through channels, searched for answers in the game shows and soap operas. My mother would circle the want ads in red and hand the paper to me.

"What are you going to do with the rest of your life?" she asked.

"Don't know," I said, and normally, for almost any other Indian in the country, that would have been a perfectly fine answer. But I was special, a former college student, a smart kid. I was one of those Indians who was supposed to make it, to rise above the rest of the reservation like a fucking eagle or something. I was the new kind of warrior.

For a few months I didn't even look at the want ads my mother circled, just left the newspaper where she had set it down. After a while, though, I got tired of television and started to play basketball again. I'd been a good player in high school, nearly great, and almost played at the college I attended for a couple years. But I'd been too out of shape from drinking and sadness to ever be good again. Still, I liked the way the ball felt in my hands and the way my feet felt inside my shoes.

At first I just shot baskets by myself. It was selfish, and I also wanted to learn the game again before I played against anybody else. Since I had been good before and embarrassed fellow tribal members, I knew they would want to take revenge on me. Forget about the cowboys versus Indians business. The most intense competition on any reservation is Indians versus Indians.

But on the night I was ready to play for real, there was this white guy at the gym, playing with all the Indians.

"Who is that?" I asked Jimmy Seyler.

"He's the new BIA[1] chief's kid."

"Can he play?"

"Oh, yeah."

And he could play. He played Indian ball, fast and loose, better than all the Indians there.

"How long's he been playing here?" I asked.

"Long enough."

I stretched my muscles, and everybody watched me. All these Indians watched one of their old and dusty heroes. Even though I had played most of my ball at the white high school I went to, I was still all Indian, you know? I was Indian when it counted, and this BIA kid needed to be beaten by an Indian, any Indian.

I jumped into the game and played well for a little while. It felt good. I hit a few shots, grabbed a rebound or two, played enough defense to keep the other team honest. Then that white kid took over the game. He was too good. Later, he'd play college ball back East and would nearly make the Knicks team a couple years on. But we didn't know any of that would happen. We just knew he was better that day and every other day.

---

[1]Bureau of Indian Affairs.

The next morning I woke up tired and hungry, so I grabbed the want ads, found a job I wanted, and drove to Spokane to get it. I've been working at the high school exchange program ever since, typing and answering phones. Sometimes I wonder if the people on the other end of the line know that I'm Indian and if their voices would change if they did know.

One day I picked up the phone and it was her, calling from Seattle.

"I got your number from your mom," she said. "I'm glad you're working."

"Yeah, nothing like a regular paycheck."

"Are you drinking?"

"No, I've been on the wagon for almost a year."

"Good."

The connection was good. I could hear her breathing in the spaces between our words. How do you talk to the real person whose ghost has haunted you? How do you tell the difference between the two?

"Listen," I said. "I'm sorry for everything."

"Me, too."

"What's going to happen to us?" I asked her and wished I had the answer for myself.

"I don't know," she said. "I want to change the world."

These days, living alone in Spokane, I wish I lived closer to the river, to the falls where ghosts of salmon jump. I wish I could sleep. I put down my paper or book and turn off all the lights, lie quietly in the dark. It may take hours, even years, for me to sleep again. There's nothing surprising or disappointing in that.

I know how all my dreams end anyway.

[1993]

"The Bullet or the Ballot"

By: Malcolm X

April 3, 1964

Reading Questions: What are Malcolm X's main points? How does Malcolm X's viewpoints support some Moslem beliefs and challenge another Muslim beliefs?

Mr. Moderator, Brother Lomax, brothers and sisters, friends and enemies: I just can't believe everyone in here is a friend, and I don't want to leave anybody out. The question tonight, as I understand it, is "The Negro Revolt, and Where Do We Go From Here?" or What Next?" In my little humble way of understanding it, it points toward either the ballot or the bullet.

Before we try and explain what is meant by the ballot or the bullet, I would like to clarify something concerning myself. I'm still a Muslim; my religion is still Islam. That's my personal belief. Just as Adam Clayton Powell is a Christian minister who heads the Abyssinian Baptist Church in New York, but at the same time takes part in the political struggles to try and bring about rights to the black people in this country; and Dr. Martin Luther King is a Christian minister down in Atlanta, Georgia, who heads another organization fighting for the civil rights of black people in this country; and Reverend Galamison, I guess you've heard of him, is another Christian minister in New York who has been deeply involved in the school boycotts to eliminate segregated education; well, I myself am a minister, not a Christian minister, but a Muslim minister; and I believe in action on all fronts by whatever means necessary.

Although I'm still a Muslim, I'm not here tonight to discuss my religion. I'm not here to try and change your religion. I'm not here to argue or discuss anything that we differ about, because it's time for us to submerge our differences and realize that it is best for us to first see that we have the same problem, a common problem, a problem that will make you catch hell whether you're a Baptist, or a Methodist, or a Muslim, or a nationalist. Whether you're educated or illiterate, whether you live on the boulevard or in the alley, you're going to catch hell just like I am. We're all in the same boat and we all are going to catch the same hell from the same man. He just happens to be a white man. All of us have suffered here, in this country, political oppression at the hands of the white man, economic exploitation at the hands of the white man, and social degradation at the hands of the white man.

Now in speaking like this, it doesn't mean that we're anti-white, but it does mean we're anti-exploitation, we're anti-degradation, we're anti-oppression. And if the white man doesn't want us to be anti-him, let him stop oppressing and exploiting and degrading us. Whether we are Christians or Muslims or nationalists or agnostics or atheists, we must first learn to forget our differences. If we have differences, let us differ in the closet; when we come out in front, let us not have anything to argue about until we get finished arguing with the man. If the late President Kennedy could get together with Khrushchev and exchange some wheat, we certainly have more in common with each other than Kennedy and Khrushchev had with each other.

If we don't do something real soon, I think you'll have to agree that we're going to be forced either to use the ballot or the bullet. It's one or the other in 1964. It isn't that time is running out -- time has run out!

1964 threatens to be the most explosive year America has ever witnessed. The most explosive year. Why? It's also a political year. It's the year when all of the white politicians will be back in the so-called Negro community jiving you and me for some votes. The year when all of the white political crooks will be right back in your and my community with their false promises, building up our hopes for a letdown, with their trickery and their treachery, with their false promises which they don't intend to keep. As they nourish these dissatisfactions, it can only lead to one thing, an explosion; and now we have the type of black man on the scene in America today -- I'm sorry, Brother Lomax -- who just doesn't intend to turn the other cheek any longer.

Don't let anybody tell you anything about the odds are against you. If they draft you, they send you to Korea and make you face 800 million Chinese. If you can be brave over there, you can be brave right here. These odds aren't as great as those odds. And if you fight here, you will at least know what you're fighting for.

I'm not a politician, not even a student of politics; in fact, I'm not a student of much of anything. I'm not a Democrat. I'm not a Republican, and I don't even consider myself an American. If you and I were Americans, there'd be no problem. Those Honkies that just got off the boat, they're already Americans; Polacks are already Americans; the Italian refugees are already Americans. Everything that came out of Europe, every blue-eyed thing, is already an American. And as long as you and I have been over here, we aren't Americans yet.

Well, I am one who doesn't believe in deluding myself. I'm not going to sit at your table and watch you eat, with nothing on my plate, and call myself a diner. Sitting at the table doesn't make you a diner, unless you eat some of what's on that plate. Being here in America doesn't make you an American. Being born here in America doesn't make you an American. Why, if birth made you American, you wouldn't need any legislation; you wouldn't need any amendments to the Constitution; you wouldn't be faced with civil-rights filibustering in Washington, D.C., right now. They don't have to pass civil-rights legislation to make a Polack an American.

No, I'm not an American. I'm one of the 22 million black people who are the victims of Americanism. One of the 22 million black people who are the victims of democracy, nothing but disguised hypocrisy. So, I'm not standing here speaking to you as an American, or a patriot, or a flag-saluter, or a flag-waver -- no, not I. I'm speaking as a victim of this American system. And I see America through the eyes of the victim. I don't see any American dream; I see an American nightmare.

These 22 million victims are waking up. Their eyes are coming open. They're beginning to see what they used to only look at. They're becoming politically mature. They are realizing that there are new political trends from coast to coast. As they see these new political trends, it's possible for them to see that every time there's an election the races are so close that they have to have a recount. They had to recount in Massachusetts to see who was going to be governor, it was so close. It was the same way in Rhode Island, in Minnesota, and in many other parts of the country. And the same with Kennedy and Nixon when they ran for president. It was so close they had to count all over again. Well, what does this mean? It means that when white people are evenly divided, and black people have a bloc of votes of their own, it is left up to them to determine who's going to sit in the White House and who's going to be in the dog house.

It. was the black man's vote that put the present administration in Washington, D.C. Your vote, your dumb vote, your ignorant vote, your wasted vote put in an administration in Washington, D.C., that has seen fit to pass every kind of legislation imaginable, saving you until last, then filibustering on top of that. And your and my leaders have the audacity to run around clapping their hands and talk about how much progress we're making. And what a good president we have. If he wasn't good in Texas, he sure can't be good in Washington, D.C. Because Texas is a lynch state. It is in the same breath as Mississippi, no different; only they lynch you in Texas with a Texas accent and lynch you in Mississippi with a Mississippi accent. And these Negro leaders have the audacity to go and have some coffee in the White House with a Texan, a Southern cracker -- that's all he is -- and then come out and tell you and me that he's going to be better for us because, since he's from the South, he knows how to deal with the Southerners. What kind of logic is that? Let Eastland be president, he's from the South too. He should be better able to deal with them than Johnson.

In this present administration they have in the House of Representatives 257 Democrats to only 177 Republicans. They control two-thirds of the House vote. Why can't they pass something that will help you and me? In the Senate, there are 67 senators who are of the Democratic Party. Only 33 of them are Republicans. Why, the Democrats have got the government sewed up, and you're the one who sewed it up for them. And what have they given you for it? Four years in office, and just now getting around to some civil-rights legislation. Just now, after everything else is gone, out of the way, they're going to sit down now and play with you all summer long -- the same old giant con game that they call filibuster. All those are in cahoots together. Don't you ever think they're not in cahoots together, for the man that is heading the civil-rights filibuster is a man from Georgia named Richard Russell. When Johnson became president, the first man he asked for when he got back to Washington, D.C., was "Dicky" -- that's how tight they are. That's his boy, that's his pal, that's his buddy. But they're playing that old con game. One of them makes believe he's for you, and he's got it fixed where the other one is so tight against you, he never has to keep his promise.

So it's time in 1964 to wake up. And when you see them coming up with that kind of conspiracy, let them know your eyes are open. And let them know you -- something else that's wide open too. It's got to be the ballot or the bullet. The ballot or the bullet. If you're afraid to use an expression like that, you should get on out of the country; you should get back in the cotton patch; you should get back in the alley. They get all the Negro vote, and after they get it, the Negro gets nothing in return. All they did when they got to Washington was give a few big Negroes big jobs. Those big Negroes didn't need big jobs, they already had jobs. That's camouflage, that's trickery, that's treachery, window-dressing. I'm not trying to knock out the Democrats for the Republicans. We'll get to them in a minute. But it is true; you put the Democrats first and the Democrats put you last.

Look at it the way it is. What alibis do they use, since they control Congress and the Senate? What alibi do they use when you and I ask, "Well, when are you going to keep your promise?" They blame the Dixiecrats. What is a Dixiecrat? A Democrat. A Dixiecrat is nothing but a Democrat in disguise. The titular head of the Democrats is also the head of the Dixiecrats, because the Dixiecrats are a part of the Democratic Party. The Democrats have never kicked the Dixiecrats out of the party. The Dixiecrats bolted themselves once, but the Democrats didn't put them out. Imagine, these lowdown Southern segregationists put the Northern Democrats down. But the Northern Democrats have never put the Dixiecrats down. No, look at that thing the way it is. They have got a con game going on, a political con game, and you and I are in the middle. It's time for you and me to wake up and start looking at it like it is, and trying to understand it like it is; and then we can deal with it like it is.

The Dixiecrats in Washington, D.C., control the key committees that run the government. The only reason the Dixiecrats control these committees is because they have seniority. The only reason they have seniority is because they come from states where Negroes can't vote. This is not even a government that's based on democracy. It. is not a government that is made up of representatives of the people. Half of the people in the South can't even vote. Eastland is not even supposed to be in Washington. Half of the senators and congressmen who occupy these key positions in Washington, D.C., are there illegally, are there unconstitutionally.

I was in Washington, D.C., a week ago Thursday, when they were debating whether or not they should let the bill come onto the floor. And in the back of the room where the Senate meets, there's a huge map of the United States, and on that map it shows the location of Negroes throughout the country. And it shows that the Southern section of the country, the states that are most heavily concentrated with Negroes, are the ones that have senators and congressmen standing up filibustering and doing all other kinds of trickery to keep the Negro from being able to vote. This is pitiful. But it's not pitiful for us any longer; it's actually pitiful for the white man, because soon now, as the Negro awakens a little more and sees the vise that he's in, sees the bag that he's in, sees the real game that he's in, then the Negro's going to develop a new tactic.

These senators and congressmen actually violate the constitutional amendments that guarantee the people of that particular state or county the right to vote. And the Constitution itself has within it the machinery to expel any representative from a state where the voting rights of the people are violated. You don't even need new legislation. Any person in Congress right now, who is there from a state or a district where the voting rights of the people are violated, that particular person should be expelled from Congress. And when you expel him, you've removed one of the obstacles in the path of any real meaningful legislation in this country. In fact, when you expel them, you don't need new legislation, because they will be replaced by black representatives from counties and districts where the black man is in the majority, not in the minority.

If the black man in these Southern states had his full voting rights, the key Dixiecrats in Washington, D. C., which means the key Democrats in Washington, D.C., would lose their seats. The Democratic Party itself would lose its power. It would cease to be powerful as a party. When you see the amount of power that would be lost by the Democratic Party if it were to lose the Dixiecrat wing, or branch, or element, you can see where it's against the interests of the Democrats to give voting rights to Negroes in states where the Democrats have been in complete power and authority ever since the Civil War. You just can't belong to that Party without analyzing it.

I say again, I'm not anti-Democrat, I'm not anti-Republican, I'm not anti-anything. I'm just questioning their sincerity, and some of the strategy that they've been using on our people by promising them promises that they don't intend to keep. When you keep the Democrats in power, you're keeping the Dixiecrats in power. I doubt that my good Brother Lomax will deny that. A vote for a Democrat is a vote for a Dixiecrat. That's why, in 1964, it's time now for you and me to become more politically mature and realize what the ballot is for; what we're supposed to get when we cast a ballot; and that if we don't cast a ballot, it's going to end up in a situation where we're going to have to cast a bullet. It's either a ballot or a bullet.

In the North, they do it a different way. They have a system that's known as gerrymandering, whatever that means. It means when Negroes become too heavily concentrated in a certain area, and begin to gain too much political power, the white man comes along and changes the district lines. You may say, "Why do you keep saying white man?" Because it's the white man who does it. I haven't ever seen any Negro changing any lines. They don't let him get near the line. It's the white man who does this. And usually, it's the white man who grins at you the most, and pats you on the back, and is supposed to be your friend. He may be friendly, but he's not your friend.

So, what I'm trying to impress upon you, in essence, is this: You and I in America are faced not with a segregationist conspiracy, we're faced with a government conspiracy. Everyone who's filibustering is a senator -- that's the government. Everyone who's finagling in Washington, D.C., is a congressman -- that's the government. You don't have anybody putting blocks in your path but people who are a part of the government. The same government that you go abroad to fight for and die for is the government that is in a conspiracy to deprive you of your voting rights, deprive you of your economic opportunities, deprive you of decent housing, deprive you of decent education. You don't need to go to the employer alone, it is the government itself, the government of America, that is responsible for the oppression and exploitation and degradation of black people in this country. And you should drop it in their lap. This government has failed the Negro. This so-called democracy has failed the Negro. And all these white liberals have definitely failed the Negro.

So, where do we go from here? First, we need some friends. We need some new allies. The entire civil-rights struggle needs a new interpretation, a broader interpretation. We need to look at this civil-rights thing from another angle -- from the inside as well as from the outside. To those of us whose philosophy is black nationalism, the only way you can get involved in the civil-rights struggle is give it a new interpretation. That old interpretation excluded us. It kept us out. So, we're giving a new interpretation to the civil-rights struggle, an interpretation that will enable us to come into it, take part in it. And these handkerchief-heads who have been dillydallying and pussy footing and compromising -- we don't intend to let them pussyfoot and dillydally and compromise any longer.

How can you thank a man for giving you what's already yours? How then can you thank him for giving you only part of what's already yours? You haven't even made progress, if what's being given to you, you should have had already. That's not progress. And I love my Brother Lomax, the way he pointed out we're right back where we were in 1954. We're not even as far up as we were in 1954. We're behind where we were in 1954. There's more segregation now than there was in 1954. There's more racial animosity, more racial hatred, more racial violence today in 1964, than there was in 1954. Where is the progress?

And now you're facing a situation where the young Negro's coming up. They don't want to hear that "turn the-other-cheek" stuff, no. In Jacksonville, those were teenagers, they were throwing Molotov cocktails. Negroes have never done that before. But it shows you there's a new deal coming in. There's new thinking coming in. There's new strategy coming in. It'll be Molotov cocktails this month, hand grenades next month, and something else next month. It'll be ballots, or it'll be bullets. It'll be liberty, or it will be death. The only difference about this kind of death -- it'll be reciprocal. You know what is meant by "reciprocal"? That's one of Brother Lomax's words. I stole it from him. I don't usually deal with those big words because I don't usually deal with big people. I deal with small people. I find you can get a whole lot of small people and whip hell out of a whole lot of big people. They haven't got anything to lose, and they've got every thing to gain. And they'll let you know in a minute: "It takes two to tango; when I go, you go."

The black nationalists, those whose philosophy is black nationalism, in bringing about this new interpretation of the entire meaning of civil rights, look upon it as meaning, as Brother Lomax has pointed out, equality of opportunity. Well, we're justified in seeking civil rights, if it means equality of opportunity, because all we're doing there is trying to collect for our investment. Our mothers and fathers invested sweat and blood. Three hundred and ten years we worked in this country without a dime in return -- I mean without a dime in return. You let the white man walk around here talking about how rich this country is, but you never stop to think how it got rich so quick. It got rich because you made it rich.

You take the people who are in this audience right now. They're poor. We're all poor as individuals. Our weekly salary individually amounts to hardly anything. But if you take the salary of everyone in here collectively, it'll fill up a whole lot of baskets. It's a lot of wealth. If you can collect the wages of just these people right here for a year, you'll be rich -- richer than rich. When you look at it like that, think how rich Uncle Sam had to become, not with this handful, but millions of black people. Your and my mother and father, who didn't work an eight-hour shift, but worked from "can't see" in the morning until "can't see" at night, and worked for nothing, making the white man rich, making Uncle Sam rich. This is our investment. This is our contribution, our blood.

Not only did we give of our free labor, we gave of our blood. Every time he had a call to arms, we were the first ones in uniform. We died on every battlefield the white man had. We have made a greater sacrifice than anybody who's standing up in America today. We have made a greater contribution and have collected less. Civil rights, for those of us whose philosophy is black nationalism, means: "Give it to us now. Don't wait for next year. Give it to us yesterday, and that's not fast enough."

I might stop right here to point out one thing. Whenever you're going after something that belongs to you, anyone who's depriving you of the right to have it is a criminal. Understand that. Whenever you are going after something that is yours, you are within your legal rights to lay claim to it. And anyone who puts forth any effort to deprive you of that which is yours, is breaking the law, is a criminal. And this was pointed out by the Supreme Court decision. It outlawed segregation.

Which means segregation is against the law. Which means a segregationist is breaking the law. A segregationist is a criminal. You can't label him as anything other than that. And when you demonstrate against segregation, the law is on your side. The Supreme Court is on your side.

Now, who is it that opposes you in carrying out the law? The police department itself. With police dogs and clubs. Whenever you demonstrate against segregation, whether it is segregated education, segregated housing, or anything else, the law is on your side, and anyone who stands in the way is not the law any longer. They are breaking the law; they are not representatives of the law. Any time you demonstrate against segregation and a man has the audacity to put a police dog on you, kill that dog, kill him, I'm telling you, kill that dog. I say it, if they put me in jail tomorrow, kill that dog. Then you'll put a stop to it. Now, if these white people in here don't want to see that kind of action, get down and tell the mayor to tell the police department to pull the dogs in. That's all you have to do. If you don't do it, someone else will.

If you don't take this kind of stand, your little children will grow up and look at you and think "shame." If you don't take an uncompromising stand, I don't mean go out and get violent; but at the same time you should never be nonviolent unless you run into some nonviolence. I'm nonviolent with those who are nonviolent with me. But when you drop that violence on me, then you've made me go insane, and I'm not responsible for what I do. And that's the way every Negro should get. Any time you know you're within the law, within your legal rights, within your moral rights, in accord with justice, then die for what you believe in. But don't die alone. Let your dying be reciprocal. This is what is meant by equality. What's good for the goose is good for the gander.

When we begin to get in this area, we need new friends, we need new allies. We need to expand the civil-rights struggle to a higher level -- to the level of human rights. Whenever you are in a civil-rights struggle, whether you know it or not, you are confining yourself to the jurisdiction of Uncle Sam. No one from the outside world can speak out in your behalf as long as your struggle is a civil-rights struggle. Civil rights comes within the domestic affairs of this country. All of our African brothers and our Asian brothers and our Latin-American brothers cannot open their mouths and interfere in the domestic affairs of the United States. And as long as it's civil rights, this comes under the jurisdiction of Uncle Sam.

But the United Nations has what's known as the charter of human rights; it has a committee that deals in human rights. You may wonder why all of the atrocities that have been committed in Africa and in Hungary and in Asia, and in Latin America are brought before the UN, and the Negro problem is never brought before the UN. This is part of the conspiracy. This old, tricky blue eyed liberal who is supposed to be your and my friend, supposed to be in our corner, supposed to be subsidizing our struggle, and supposed to be acting in the capacity of an adviser, never tells you anything about human rights. They keep you wrapped up in civil rights. And you spend so much time barking up the civil-rights tree, you don't even know there's a human-rights tree on the same floor.

When you expand the civil-rights struggle to the level of human rights, you can then take the case of the black man in this country before the nations in the UN. You can take it before the General Assembly. You can take Uncle Sam before a world court. But the only level you can do it on is the level of human rights. Civil rights keeps you under his restrictions, under his jurisdiction. Civil rights keeps you in his pocket. Civil rights means you're asking Uncle Sam to treat you right. Human rights are something you were born with. Human rights are your God-given rights. Human rights are the rights that are recognized by all nations of this earth. And any time any one violates your human rights, you can take them to the world court.

Uncle Sam's hands are dripping with blood, dripping with the blood of the black man in this country. He's the earth's number-one hypocrite. He has the audacity -- yes, he has -- imagine him posing as the leader of the free world. The free world! And you over here singing "We Shall Overcome." Expand the civil-rights struggle to the level of human rights. Take it into the United Nations, where our African brothers can throw their weight on our side, where our Asian brothers can throw their weight on our side, where our Latin-American brothers can throw their weight on our side, and where 800 million Chinamen are sitting there waiting to throw their weight on our side.

Let the world know how bloody his hands are. Let the world know the hypocrisy that's practiced over here. Let it be the ballot or the bullet. Let him know that it must be the ballot or the bullet.

When you take your case to Washington, D.C., you're taking it to the criminal who's responsible; it's like running from the wolf to the fox. They're all in cahoots together. They all work political chicanery and make you look like a chump before the eyes of the world. Here you are walking around in America, getting ready to be drafted and sent abroad, like a tin soldier, and when you get over there, people ask you what are you fighting for, and you have to stick your tongue in your cheek. No, take Uncle Sam to court, take him before the world.

By ballot I only mean freedom. Don't you know -- I disagree with Lomax on this issue -- that the ballot is more important than the dollar? Can I prove it? Yes. Look in the UN. There are poor nations in the UN; yet those poor nations can get together with their voting power and keep the rich nations from making a move. They have one nation -- one vote, everyone has an equal vote. And when those brothers from Asia, and Africa and the darker parts of this earth get together, their voting power is sufficient to hold Sam in check. Or Russia in check. Or some other section of the earth in check. So, the ballot is most important.

Right now, in this country, if you and I, 22 million African-Americans -- that's what we are -- Africans who are in America. You're nothing but Africans. Nothing but Africans. In fact, you'd get farther calling yourself African instead of Negro. Africans don't catch hell. You're the only one catching hell. They don't have to pass civil-rights bills for Africans. An African can go anywhere he wants right now. All you've got to do is tie your head up. That's right, go anywhere you want. Just stop being a Negro. Change your name to Hoogagagooba. That'll show you how silly the white man is. You're dealing with a silly man. A friend of mine who's very dark put a turban on his head and went into a restaurant in Atlanta before they called themselves desegregated. He went into a white restaurant, he sat down, they served him, and he said, "What would happen if a Negro came in here? And there he's sitting, black as night, but because he had his head wrapped up the waitress looked back at him and says, "Why, there wouldn't no nigger dare come in here."

So, you're dealing with a man whose bias and prejudice are making him lose his mind, his intelligence, every day. He's frightened. He looks around and sees what's taking place on this earth, and he sees that the pendulum of time is swinging in your direction. The dark people are waking up. They're losing their fear of the white man. No place where he's fighting right now is he winning. Everywhere he's fighting, he's fighting someone your and my complexion. And they're beating him. He can't win any more. He's won his last battle. He failed to win the Korean War. He couldn't win it. He had to sign a truce. That's a loss.

Any time Uncle Sam, with all his machinery for warfare, is held to a draw by some rice eaters, he's lost the battle. He had to sign a truce. America's not supposed to sign a truce. She's supposed to be bad. But she's not bad any more. She's bad as long as she can use her hydrogen bomb, but she can't use hers for fear Russia might use hers. Russia can't use hers, for fear that Sam might use his. So, both of them are weapon-less. They can't use the weapon because each's weapon nullifies the other's. So the only place where action can take place is on the ground. And the white man can't win another war fighting on the ground. Those days are over The black man knows it, the brown man knows it, the red man knows it, and the yellow man knows it. So they engage him in guerrilla warfare. That's not his style. You've got to have heart to be a guerrilla warrior, and he hasn't got any heart. I'm telling you now.

I just want to give you a little briefing on guerrilla warfare because, before you know it, before you know it. It takes heart to be a guerrilla warrior because you're on your own. In conventional warfare you have tanks and a whole lot of other people with you to back you up -- planes over your head and all that kind of stuff. But a guerrilla is on his own. All you have is a rifle, some sneakers and a bowl of rice, and that's all you need -- and a lot of heart. The Japanese on some of those islands in the Pacific, when the American soldiers landed, one Japanese sometimes could hold the whole army off. He'd just wait until the sun went down, and when the sun went down they were all equal. He would take his little blade and slip from bush to bush, and from American to American. The white soldiers couldn't cope with that. Whenever you see a white soldier that fought in the Pacific, he has the shakes, he has a nervous condition, because they scared him to death.

The same thing happened to the French up in French Indochina. People who just a few years previously were rice farmers got together and ran the heavily-mechanized French army out of Indochina. You don't need it -- modern warfare today won't work. This is the day of the guerrilla. They did the same thing in Algeria. Algerians, who were nothing but Bedouins, took a rine and sneaked off to the hills, and de Gaulle and all of his highfalutin' war machinery couldn't defeat those guerrillas. Nowhere on this earth does the white man win in a guerrilla warfare. It's not his speed. Just as guerrilla warfare is prevailing in Asia and in parts of Africa and in parts of Latin America, you've got to be mighty naive, or you've got to play the black man cheap, if you don't think some day he's going to wake up and find that it's got to be the ballot or the bullet.

I would like to say, in closing, a few things concerning the Muslim Mosque, Inc., which we established recently in New York City. It's true we're Muslims and our religion is Islam, but we don't mix our religion with our politics and our economics and our social and civil activities -- not any more We keep our religion in our mosque. After our religious services are over, then as Muslims we become involved in political action, economic action and social and civic action. We become involved with anybody, any where, any time and in any manner that's designed to eliminate the evils, the political, economic and social evils that are afflicting the people of our community.

The political philosophy of black nationalism means that the black man should control the politics and the politicians in his own community; no more. The black man in the black community has to be re-educated into the science of politics so he will know what politics is supposed to bring him in return. Don't be throwing out any ballots. A ballot is like a bullet. You don't throw your ballots until you see a target, and if that target is not within your reach, keep your ballot in your pocket.

The political philosophy of black nationalism is being taught in the Christian church. It's being taught in the NAACP. It's being taught in CORE meetings. It's being taught in SNCC Student Nonviolent Coordinating Committee meetings. It's being taught in Muslim meetings. It's being taught where nothing but atheists and agnostics come together. It's being taught everywhere. Black people are fed up with the dillydallying, pussyfooting, compromising approach that we've been using toward getting our freedom. We want freedom now, but we're not going to get it saying "We Shall Overcome." We've got to fight until we overcome.

The economic philosophy of black nationalism is pure and simple. It only means that we should control the economy of our community. Why should white people be running all the stores in our community? Why should white people be running the banks of our community? Why should the economy of our community be in the hands of the white man? Why? If a black man can't move his store into a white community, you tell me why a white man should move his store into a black community. The philosophy of black nationalism involves a re-education program in the black community in regards to economics. Our people have to be made to see that any time you take your dollar out of your community and spend it in a community where you don't live, the community where you live will get poorer and poorer, and the community where you spend your money will get richer and richer.

Then you wonder why where you live is always a ghetto or a slum area. And where you and I are concerned, not only do we lose it when we spend it out of the community, but the white man has got all our stores in the community tied up; so that though we spend it in the community, at sundown the man who runs the store takes it over across town somewhere. He's got us in a vise.

So the economic philosophy of black nationalism means in every church, in every civic organization, in every fraternal order, it's time now for our people to be come conscious of the importance of controlling the economy of our community. If we own the stores, if we operate the businesses, if we try and establish some industry in our own community, then we're developing to the position where we are creating employment for our own kind. Once you gain control of the economy of your own community, then you don't have to picket and boycott and beg some cracker downtown for a job in his business.

The social philosophy of black nationalism only means that we have to get together and remove the evils, the vices, alcoholism, drug addiction, and other evils that are destroying the moral fiber of our community. We our selves have to lift the level of our community, the standard of our community to a higher level, make our own society beautiful so that we will be satisfied in our own social circles and won't be running around here trying to knock our way into a social circle where we're not wanted. So I say, in spreading a gospel such as black nationalism, it is not designed to make the black man re-evaluate the white man -- you know him already -- but to make the black man re-evaluate himself. Don't change the white man's mind -- you can't change his mind, and that whole thing about appealing to the moral conscience of America -- America's conscience is bankrupt. She lost all conscience a long time ago. Uncle Sam has no conscience.

They don't know what morals are. They don't try and eliminate an evil because it's evil, or because it's illegal, or because it's immoral; they eliminate it only when it threatens their existence. So you're wasting your time appealing to the moral conscience of a bankrupt man like Uncle Sam. If he had a conscience, he'd straighten this thing out with no more pressure being put upon him. So it is not necessary to change the white man's mind. We have to change our own mind. You can't change his mind about us. We've got to change our own minds about each other. We have to see each other with new eyes. We have to see each other as brothers and sisters. We have to come together with warmth so we can develop unity and harmony that's necessary to get this problem solved ourselves. How can we do this? How can we avoid jealousy? How can we avoid the suspicion and the divisions that exist in the community? I'll tell you how.

I have watched how Billy Graham comes into a city, spreading what he calls the gospel of Christ, which is only white nationalism. That's what he is. Billy Graham is a white nationalist; I'm a black nationalist. But since it's the natural tendency for leaders to be jealous and look upon a powerful figure like Graham with suspicion and envy, how is it possible for him to come into a city and get all the cooperation of the church leaders? Don't think because they're church leaders that they don't have weaknesses that make them envious and jealous -- no, everybody's got it. It's not an accident that when they want to choose a cardinal, as Pope I over there in Rome, they get in a closet so you can't hear them cussing and fighting and carrying on.

Billy Graham comes in preaching the gospel of Christ. He evangelizes the gospel. He stirs everybody up, but he never tries to start a church. If he came in trying to start a church, all the churches would be against him. So, he just comes in talking about Christ and tells everybody who gets Christ to go to any church where Christ is; and in this way the church cooperates with him. So we're going to take a page from his book.

Our gospel is black nationalism. We're not trying to threaten the existence of any organization, but we're spreading the gospel of black nationalism. Anywhere there's a church that is also preaching and practicing the gospel of black nationalism, join that church. If the NAACP is preaching and practicing the gospel of black nationalism, join the NAACP. If CORE is spreading and practicing the gospel of black nationalism, join CORE. Join any organization that has a gospel that's for the uplift of the black man. And when you get into it and see them pussyfooting or compromising, pull out of it because that's not black nationalism. We'll find another one.

And in this manner, the organizations will increase in number and in quantity and in quality, and by August, it is then our intention to have a black nationalist convention which will consist of delegates from all over the country who are interested in the political, economic and social philosophy of black nationalism. After these delegates convene, we will hold a seminar; we will hold discussions; we will listen to everyone. We want to hear new ideas and new solutions and new answers. And at that time, if we see fit then to form a black nationalist party, we'll form a black nationalist party. If it's necessary to form a black nationalist army, we'll form a black nationalist army. It'll be the ballot or the bullet. It'll be liberty or it'll be death.

It's time for you and me to stop sitting in this country, letting some cracker senators, Northern crackers and Southern crackers, sit there in Washington, D.C., and come to a conclusion in their mind that you and I are supposed to have civil rights. There's no white man going to tell me anything about my rights. Brothers and sisters, always remember, if it doesn't take senators and congressmen and presidential proclamations to give freedom to the white man, it is not necessary for legislation or proclamation or Supreme Court decisions to give freedom to the black man. You let that white man know, if this is a country of freedom, let it be a country of freedom; and if it's not a country of freedom, change it.

We will work with anybody, anywhere, at any time, who is genuinely interested in tackling the problem head-on, nonviolently as long as the enemy is nonviolent, but violent when the enemy gets violent. We'll work with you on the voter-registration drive, we'll work with you on rent strikes, we'll work with you on school boycotts; I don't believe in any kind of integration; I'm not even worried about it, because I know you're not going to get it anyway; you're not going to get it because you're afraid to die; you've got to be ready to die if you try and force yourself on the white man, because he'll get just as violent as those crackers in Mississippi, right here in Cleveland. But we will still work with you on the school boycotts because we're against a segregated school system. A segregated school system produces children who, when they graduate, graduate with crippled minds. But this does not mean that a school is segregated because it's all black. A segregated school means a school that is controlled by people who have no real interest in it whatsoever.

Let me explain what I mean. A segregated district or community is a community in which people live, but outsiders control the politics and the economy of that community. They never refer to the white section as a segregated community. It's the all-Negro section that's a segregated community. Why? The white man controls his own school, his own bank, his own economy, his own politics, his own everything, his own community; but he also controls yours. When you're under someone else's control, you're segregated. They'll always give you the lowest or the worst that there is to offer, but it doesn't mean you're segregated just because you have your own. You've got to control your own. Just like the white man has control of his, you need to control yours.

You know the best way to get rid of segregation? The white man is more afraid of separation than he is of integration. Segregation means that he puts you away from him, but not far enough for you to be out of his jurisdiction; separation means you're gone. And the white man will integrate faster than he'll let you separate. So we will work with you against the segregated school system because it's criminal, because it is absolutely destructive, in every way imaginable, to the minds of the children who have to be exposed to that type of crippling education.

Last but not least, I must say this concerning the great controversy over rifles and shotguns. The only thing that I've ever said is that in areas where the government has proven itself either unwilling or unable to defend the lives and the property of Negroes, it's time for Negroes to defend themselves. Article number two of the constitutional amendments provides you and me the right to own a rifle or a shotgun. It is constitutionally legal to own a shotgun or a rifle. This doesn't mean you're going to get a rifle and form battalions and go out looking for white folks, although you'd be within your rights -- I mean, you'd be justified; but that would be illegal and we don't do anything illegal. If the white man doesn't want the black man buying rifles and shotguns, then let the government do its job.

That's all. And don't let the white man come to you and ask you what you think about what Malcolm says -- why, you old Uncle Tom. He would never ask you if he thought you were going to say, "Amen!" No, he is making a Tom out of you." So, this doesn't mean forming rifle clubs and going out looking for people, but it is time, in 1964, if you are a man, to let that man know.

If he's not going to do his job in running the government and providing you and me with the protection that our taxes are supposed to be for, since he spends all those billions for his defense budget, he certainly can't begrudge you and me spending $12 or $15 for a single-shot, or double-action. I hope you understand. Don't go out shooting people, but any time -- brothers and sisters, and especially the men in this audience; some of you wearing Congressional Medals of Honor, with shoulders this wide, chests this big, muscles that big -- any time you and I sit around and read where they bomb a church and murder in cold blood, not some grownups, but four little girls while they were praying to the same God the white man taught them to pray to, and you and I see the government go down and can't find who did it.

Why, this man -- he can find Eichmann hiding down in Argentina somewhere. Let two or three American soldiers, who are minding somebody else's business way over in South Vietnam, get killed, and he'll send battleships, sticking his nose in their business. He wanted to send troops down to Cuba and make them have what he calls free elections -- this old cracker who doesn't have free elections in his own country.

No, if you never see me another time in your life, if I die in the morning, I'll die saying one thing: the ballot or the bullet, the ballot or the bullet.

If a Negro in 1964 has to sit around and wait for some cracker senator to filibuster when it comes to the rights of black people, why, you and I should hang our heads in shame. You talk about a march on Washington in 1963, you haven't seen anything. There's some more going down in '64.

And this time they're not going like they went last year. They're not going singing "We Shall Overcome." They're not going with white friends. They're not going with placards already painted for them. They're not going with round-trip tickets. They're going with one way tickets. And if they don't want that non-nonviolent army going down there, tell them to bring the filibuster to a halt.

The black nationalists aren't going to wait. Lyndon B. Johnson is the head of the Democratic Party. If he's for civil rights, let him go into the Senate next week and declare himself. Let him go in there right now and declare himself. Let him go in there and denounce the Southern branch of his party. Let him go in there right now and take a moral stand -- right now, not later. Tell him, don't wait until election time. If he waits too long, brothers and sisters, he will be responsible for letting a condition develop in this country which will create a climate that will bring seeds up out of the ground with vegetation on the end of them looking like something these people never dreamed of. In 1964, it's the ballot or the bullet.

Thank you.

Phillis Wheatley
[1753?–1784]

PHILLIS WHEATLEY *was brought as a small child to Boston on a slave ship. A Fulani child, she had come from Senegal in West Africa. A tailor, John Wheatley, purchased her in 1761 as a companion for his wife, Susannah. Boston had none of the Southern laws against teaching a slave to read so Phillis was able to learn easily in this religious and very literate household. She mastered English in sixteen months and was able to read the Bible with ease at an age that would have been impressive for a native English speaker. Her eagerness to learn led to her mastery of mythology, classical languages, and English verse. By age thirteen she was writing compositions such as "To the University of Cambridge in New England." This essay still has relevance because Wheatley wrote about the circumstances that enable one person to receive a good education while another does not. Not only did she study at home, but she also studied with the pastor of the Old North Church, the Reverend Dr. Richard Sewall, for whom she wrote an elegy at his death. She also wrote an elegy for the evangelist George Whitefield titled "On the Death of the Rev. Mr. George Whitefield." This elegy was her first publication (1770).*

She quickly became well known as a prodigy and began writing letters to famous Christian writers and to members of the Transatlantic abolitionist network. At about the same time she became ill and was sent to England with Wheatley's son Nathaniel for her health. There she met the Countess of Huntingdon, Sebina Hastings, a woman with whom she had exchanged letters. Hastings became Wheatley's patron, a form of support that brought Wheatley's book, Poems on Various Subjects, Religious and Moral *(1773) to the public eye. Wheatley quickly became not only famous but an example of proof that an African could be both learned and talented in letters. In 1772 the Somerset Decision in England could have freed her, but John Wheatley persuaded her to come home to be with his dying wife on the promise of manumission. She did come back to Boston and was rewarded with her freedom. She married John Peters in 1778 and worked on a second book. The book was never published though many of the poems have been recovered from other publications such as magazines and newspapers. Her later life was plagued by illness and the death of her two children. Her work stayed in front of the public eye thanks to abolitionists and African-American women's literary societies. She has received much critical interest in recent years, and the poems for her second book have become objects of archival treasure hunts.*

On Being Brought from Africa to America

PHILLIS WHEATLEY

'Twas mercy brought me from my *Pagan*[1] land,
Taught my benighted soul to understand
That there's a God, that there's a *Saviour* too:
Once I redemption neither sought nor knew.
Some view our sable race with scornful eye,   5
"Their colour is a diabolic die."
Remember, *Christians*, *Negros*, black as *Cain*,
May be refin'd, and join th'angelic train.

[1773]

---

[1]The peoples of Senegal were animists.

From *Poems on Various Subjects, Religious and Moral* (1773).

Kwame Anthony Appiah
[1954–   ]

The distinguished career of philosopher **KWAME ANTHONY APPIAH** *spans multiple continents; son of a Ghanaian politician and diplomat, and an English art historian, Appiah was the first person of African descent to receive a doctoral degree from Cambridge University in England. He has taught in Ghana, England, and the United States, where he is now a citizen. Appiah's work includes co-editing* Africana: The Encyclopedia of African and African American Experience *(1999) with the distinguished educator and scholar Henry Louis Gates, Jr., and co-founding the Web site* Africana: Gateway to the Black World. *He co-authored books with Amy Gutmann including* Color Conscious: The Political Morality of Race *(1996) and with Saskia Sassen,* Globalization and Its Discontents: Essays on the New Mobility of People and Money *(1999). He is best known, however, for his controversial book* In My Father's House: Africa in the Philosophy of Culture *(1992). In this book, Appiah rejects both biological and cultural definitions of "race," and argues that certain strains of cultural nationalism and Pan-Africanism are similarly suspect, as they are founded in myths about essential racial identity. His work throughout his career has focused on the intersections of ethics, politics, and identity.*

from *In My Father's House: Africa In The Philosophy of Culture*

KWAME ANTHONY APPIAH

Au delà du refus de toute domination extérieure, c'est la
volonté de renouer en profondeur avec l'héritage culturel de
l'Afrique, trop longtemps méconnu et refusé. Loin d'être un
effort superficiel ou folklorique pour faire revivre quelques
traditions ou pratiques ancestrales, il s'agit de construire une
nouvelle société dont l'identité n'est pas conférée du dehors.[1]

CARDINAL PAUL ZOUNGRANA

Topologies of Nativism

MARTIN FARQUHAR TUPPER, AN Englishman who lived through most of the nineteenth century, was an extremely prolific writer; in his day the verses in his *Proverbial Maxims* were read by millions, and his two novels and many other writings gathered him a respectable public. Nowadays, Tupper is known only to those with a historical interest in popular writers of the nineteenth century or an antiquarian interest in bad verse. But in 1850 Tupper was at the height of his popularity and his powers, and in that year he published these soon-to-be-famous words in a new journal called the *Anglo-Saxon*.

Stretch forth! stretch forth! from the south to the north,
From the east to the west,—stretch forth! stretch forth!
Strengthen thy stakes and lengthen thy cords,—
The world is a tent for the world's true lords!
Break forth and spread over every place
The world is a world for the Saxon race!

[1]"Beyond the refusal of all exterior domination is the urge to reconnect in a deep way with Africa's cultural heritage, which has been for too long misunderstood and rejected. Far from being a superficial or folkloric attempt to bring back to life some of the traditions or practices of our ancestors, it is a matter of constructing a new African society, whose identity is not conferred from outside." Cited by Valentin Mudimbe in "African Gnosis. Philosophy and the order of Knowledge: An Introduction," 164.

Reprinted from *In My Father's House: Africa in the Philosophy of Culture,* by permission of Oxford University Press. Copyright © 1992 by Anthony Appiah.

The *Anglo-Saxon* lasted only a year, but its tone is emblematic of an important development in the way educated Englishmen and women thought of themselves and of what it was that made them English—a development that was itself part of a wider movement of ideas in Europe and North America. As heirs to the culture of the modern world, a culture so crucially shaped by the ideas that Tupper's poem represents, almost all twentieth-century readers, not merely in Europe and America but throughout the world, are able to take for granted a set of assumptions about what Tupper means by "race." Those assumptions, which amounted to a new theory of race, color our modern understanding of literature—indeed of most symbolic culture—in fundamental ways, and this despite the fact that many of these assumptions have been officially discarded.

Race, nation, literature: these terms are bound together in the recent intellectual history of the West, and we shall need, as we shall see, to bear this in mind when we turn to Crummell's and Du Bois's postcolonial literary heirs.[2] For while the ideas of racialism are familiar and no one needs to be reminded of the connection between racialism and the sort of imperialism that Tupper celebrated, it is perhaps a less familiar thought that many of those works that are central to the recent history of our understanding of what *literature* is are also thematically preoccupied with racial issues. But the reason for this is not far to seek: it lies in the dual connection made in eighteenth- and nineteenth-century Euro-American thought between, on the one hand, race and nationality, and, on the other, nationality and literature. In short, the nation is the key middle term in understanding the relations between the concept of *race* and the idea of literature.

The first of these linkages, between nation and race, will surely be the less puzzling, even to an American reader raised in a self-consciously multiracial nation. Since the seventeenth century, Americans have believed that part of what is distinctive about New World culture and politics is the variety of the national (and later the "racial") origins of the peoples who have settled here. America was a new nation, conceived of by the Puritans as the product of the free choice of its immigrants. The Puritan community was established in self-conscious contrast to the European kingdoms and principalities from which the first immigrants came, states where which ruler you were the subject of was a matter of birth. These first immigrants thought of their new community as the product not of descent but of choice; of the bonds, in a familiar phrase, of brotherly love. As John Winthrop put it in 1630 "the ligaments of this body [the Puritan commu-

---

[2]Alexander Crummel (1819–1898), African-American scholar and proponent of Pan-Africanism, discussed in an earlier chapter of Appiah's book; W. E. B. Du Bois (1868–1963), African-American scholar and author of *The Souls of Black Folk* (1903). [Ed. note.]

nity] which knit [it] together are love."[3] Precisely because Americans from the beginning contrasted their situation as having consented to live together in the New World, with that in the Old World, where people were the hereditary subjects of monarchies, they have always known that European nations conceived of themselves in terms of descent. From this perspective, all that happened was that descent came in the mid-nineteenth century to be understood in terms of *race*.

Yet the increasing identification of race and nation in European—and more particularly in *English*—thought was a complex process. The Anglo-Saxonism of the nineteenth century in Britain—Crummell's Anglo-Saxonism—has its roots deep in the soil of historical argument about the English constitution; in the fascinating process through which a rising commercial class transformed the monarchy in Britain from its feudal roots into the "constitutional monarchy" that was established at the Restoration of 1660. In the arguments that surround this development, a mythology developed in the seventeenth century of a free Anglo-Saxon people, living under parliamentary government in the period before the Norman Conquest of 1066. Increasingly, Anglo-Saxon institutions were seen both to account for the Englishman's "natural love of freedom" and to underlie the "immemorial rights" of free men against the crown.

This mythology was counterposed against the mainstream historiography of the Middle Ages, which traced the *History of the Kings of Britain*—as Geoffrey of Monmouth's seminal work of 1136 was called—to Brutus, grandson of Aeneas of Troy.[4] It was Geoffrey who established the story of King Arthur, son of Uther-pendragon, as forever part of British mythology; his work played a significant part in providing a framework within which the different cultural streams—Roman, Saxon, Danish, and Norman—that had come together over the first millennium in Britain could be gathered into a single unifying history.

When Richard Verstegen published his influential *Restitution of Decayed Intelligence* in 1605, he claimed that England's Anglo-Saxon past was the past of a Germanic people, who shared their language and institutions with the Germanic tribes whose great courage and fierce independence Tacitus had described many centuries earlier.[5] Verstegen argued that these tribes were also

---

[3]This is cited in Sollors's *Beyond Ethnicity* (57), which gives a lucid discussion of the role of notions of descent in the understanding of ethnicity in America; see my discussion of Sollors in "Are We Ethnic? The Theory and Practice of American Pluralism." My discussion here is much indebted to Sollors's work.

[4]See Hugh B. MacDougall's *Racial Myth in English History: Trojans, Teutons, and Anglo-Saxons.* The discussion of these paragraphs is based on MacDougall's account.

[5]Cornelius Tacitus (c. 55–117 C.E.), Roman historian. [Ed. note.]

the ancestors of the Danes and the Normans, whose invasions of Britain had thus not essentially disturbed the unity of the English as a Germanic people. The effect of this argument, of course, was to provide for the seventeenth century what the *History of the Kings of Britain* had provided in the Middle Ages: a framework within which the peoples of England could be conceived as united.

By the eve of the American Revolution, Anglo-Saxon historiography and the study of Anglo-Saxon law, language, and institutions were established scholarly pursuits, and the notion of a free Anglo-Saxon past, whose reestablishment would be an escape from the monarchy's potential to develop into a tyranny, was one that appealed naturally to such figures as Thomas Jefferson. Anglo-Saxonism spread easily to a United States whose dominant culture imagined itself—even after the Revolution—as British. And when Jefferson, himself no mean Anglo-Saxon scholar, designed a curriculum for the University of Virginia, he included the study of the Anglo-Saxon language, because, as he said, reading the "histories and laws left us in that . . . dialect," students would "imbibe with the language their free principles of government."

Jefferson himself also "suspected," as he argued in his *Notes on the State of Virginia*, that the Anglo-Saxon people were superior to blacks "in the endowments both of body and of mind," though he never directly challenged the biblical orthodoxy that Africans were, like all human beings, descended from Adam and Eve. And this language, with its focus on *endowments*, that is, on heredity, and in its linking of the physical bodily inheritance with the endowments of the mind, is one of the earliest statements of what was then a radical view: the view that the cultural inferiority of the nonwhite races flowed from an inherited racial essence.

But Jefferson is, in many ways, not yet the complete racialist. For one thing, his view is not totally generalized, so that he does not have the idea that *every* person belongs to a race with its own distinctive essence and its own place in the order of moral and intellectual endowments. While his attitude toward blacks was less than enthusiastic, his beliefs about the "endowments" of native Americans, who were plainly not of Anglo-Saxon descent, were largely positive, and he actively favored interbreeding to produce a new strain of Americans of "mixed blood." But, in the half century following the *Notes on the State of Virginia*, the generalization of race thinking—to produce the racialism of Crummell and Du Bois—was completed.[6]

---

[6]See Reginald Horsman's *Race and Manifest Destiny: The Origins of American Racial Anglo-Saxonism.* My discussion of Jefferson is based on Horsman's account, from which these citations come; see 19, 101, 108.

In the different circumstances of the New World, where racial slavery had become a central fact of life, Jefferson anticipated an intellectual process that began in Britain only later. In England, Anglo-Saxonist mythology had so far been used largely in arguments within the United Kingdom, arguments that centered on the shift of power from the feudal aristocracy to the rising bourgeoisie. In the period from the end of the Napoleonic Wars to the midcentury, the celebration of the Anglo-Saxon people and their institutions was turned outward to justify the domination of the nonwhite world. And it is the lineaments of this fully racialized nation—what I earlier called the linkage between nation and race—that we recognize so easily in Tupper's verse.

But the deep-rooted character of the second linkage—between nation and literature—will probably be less naturally intelligible. And our starting point for understanding the role of the idea of a national literature in the development of the concept of a national culture must be in the work of the man who developed its first real theoretical articulation (a man I have already mentioned—almost inevitably—in connection with Crummell)—namely, Johann Gottfried Herder.

In his *On the New German Literature: Fragments* of 1767, Herder—who is in some ways the first important philosopher of modern nationalism—proposed the notion that language is not just "a tool of the arts and sciences" but "a part of them." "Whoever writes about the literature of a country," Herder continued, "must not neglect its language." Herder's notion of the *Sprachgeist*—literally, the "spirit" of the language—embodies the thought that language is more than the medium through which speakers communicate. As Hans Kohn, one of the great historians of nationalism, has written, for Herder a

> nationality lived above all in its civilization; its main instrument was its language, not an artificial instrument, but a gift of God, the guardian of the national community and the matrix of its civilization. Thus language, national language, became a sacred instrument; each man could be himself only by thingking and creating in his own language. With the respect for all other nationalities went a respect for their languages.[7]

Herder had, of course, to make a sharp distinction between nations and states because in eighteenth-century Europe there was not even an approximate correlation between linguistic and political boundaries. (It is important to remember that the correlation remains in most parts of the world quite rough-and-ready.) The modern European nationalism that produced, for

---

[7]See Hans Kohn, *The Idea of Nationalism*, 431–32, which includes the reference to Herder's *On the New German Literature: Fragments.*

example, the German and Italian states, involved an attempt to create states to correspond to nationalities: nationalities conceived of as sharing a civilization and, more particularly, a language and literature. Exactly because political geography did not correspond to Herder's nationalities, he was obliged to draw a distinction between the nation as a natural entity and the state as the product of culture, as a human artifice.

The opposition between nature and culture is one of the oldest in Western intellectual history (indeed, Claude Lévi-Strauss, has argued that it is one of the central oppositions of human thought). But this opposition has been understood in radically different ways in different periods. For Herder and his contemporaries, as Hans Kohn makes clear, human nature was still largely a matter of God's intentions for human beings; the nation was natural, as Crummell wrote about a century after Herder's *Fragments* (in a passage I have already cited), because "races, like families, are the organisms and ordinances of God."[8]

But with the increasing influence of the natural sciences in the period since Herder's day, what is natural in human beings—"human nature"—has come increasingly to be thought of in terms of the sciences of biology and anthropology. Inevitably, then, the nation comes more and more to be identified as a biological unit, defined by the shared essence that flows from a common descent; even when, as in the case of Alexander Crummell, the reality of races was also itself seen, theologically—as the Hebrews had seen it—as a product of the divine will.

Superimposing the Herderian identification of the core of the nation with its national literature on the racial conception of the nation, we arrive at the racial understanding of literature that flourishes from the mid-nineteenth century in the work of the first modern literary historians. Hippolyte Taine's monumental *History of English Literature*—perhaps the first modern literary history of English, published in France in the 1860s—begins with the words: "History has been transformed, within a hundred years in Germany, within sixty in France, and that by the study of their literatures."[9] But he is soon telling us that:

> a race, like the Old Aryans, scattered from the Ganges as far as the Hebrides, settled in every clime, and every stage of civilization, transformed by thirty centuries of revolutions, nevertheless manifests in its languages, religions, literatures, philosophies, the community of blood and of intellect which to this day binds its offshoots together.[10]

---

[8]Alexander Crummell, "The Race Problem in America," in Brotz, *Negro Social and Political Thought,* 184.

[9]Hippolyte A. Taine, *History of English Literature,* 1.

[10]Ibid., 17.

What is revealed, in short, by the study of literature that has transformed the discipline of history is the "moral state" of the race whose literature it is. It is because of this conception that Taine finds it proper to start his study of English literature with a chapter on the Saxons, so that Taine's *History* begins not in England at all but in Holland:

> As you coast the North Sea from Scheldt to Jutland, you will mark in the first place that the characteristic feature is the want of slope: marsh, waster, shoal; the rivers hardly drag themselves along, swollen and sluggish, with long, black-looking waves.[11]

The "Saxons, Angles, Jutes, Frisians . . . [and] Danes"[12] who occupied this region of Holland at the beginning of the first millennium are, according to Taine, the ancestors of the English, but since they, themselves, are of German descent, Taine also refers, in describing this "race" a few pages later, to some of their traits reported in Tacitus.

It is the conception of the binding core of the English nation as the Anglo-Saxon *race* that accounts for Taine's decision to identify the origins of English literature not in its antecedents in the Greek and Roman classics that provided the models and themes of so much of the best-known works of English "poesy"; not in the Italian models that influenced the drama of Marlowe and Shakespeare; but in *Beowulf*, a poem in the Anglo-Saxon tongue, a poem that was unknown to Spenser and Shakespeare, the first poets to write in a version of the English language that we can still almost understand.[13]

Yet this decision was quite representative. When the teaching of English literature was institutionalized in the English universities in the nineteenth century, students were required to learn Anglo-Saxon in order to study *Beowulf*. Anglo-Saxonism thus played a major role in the establishment of the canon of literary works that are to be studied in both British and American colleges, and the teachers who came from these colleges to the high schools brought the Anglo-Saxon canon with them.

It hardly needs pointing out that explicit Anglo-Saxonism is not exactly in favor; it has succumbed, we may happily say, first to the political and then to the intellectual onslaughts of antiracism. So there is something of a historical irony in the fact that among the most prominent reflections of racially under-

---

[11]Ibid., 37.

[12]Ibid., 39.

[13]Christopher Marlowe (1564–1593), English playwright; Edmund Spenser (1552–1599), English poet.

stood ethnicity in literary studies in recent years is in the development of African-American literary criticism. For anyone who has followed the argument so far, it will not be surprising that the persistent stream of African-American nationalist argument—a tradition whose origins can be traced back to well before the rise of racial Anglo-Saxonism—has been accompanied by appeals to an African cultural heritage expressed in black folk music, poetry, and song. Such intellectual pioneers as Du Bois from the latter nineteenth century on attempted to articulate a racial tradition of black letters, in part as a natural expression of the Herderian view of the nation as identified above all else with its expression in "poesy." Many African-American theorists would have agreed with Carlyle—there is another irony in this happy consensus between "niggers" and the author of the "Occasional Discourse on the Nigger Question"—when he wrote in *The Edinburgh Review* in 1831 (in a discussion of a history of German poetry):

> The history of a nation's poetry is the essence of its history, political, scientific, religious. With all these the complete Historian of Poetry will be familiar: the national physiognomy, in its finest traits, and through its successive stages of growth, will be clear to him; he will discern the grand spiritual tendency of every period.

But there is another reason why the identification of a history of black literature has been central not merely to African-American literary criticism but to the culture of African-Americans: namely, that for almost the whole period that there have been people of African descent in the New World, Europeans and Americans of European descent have consistently denied that black people were capable of contributing to "the arts and letters." Starting before the fixing of *race* as a biological concept, influential figures expressed their doubts about the "capacity of the Negro" to produce literature. Even in the Enlightenment, which emphasized the universality of reason, Voltaire in France, Hume in Scotland, and Kant in Germany, like Jefferson in the New World, denied literary capacity to people of African descent.[14] As Hume—surely a philosopher of more than negligible influence—wrote in a famous footnote to his essay *Of National Characters* (1748): "I am apt to suspect the Negroes to be naturally inferior to the Whites. There scarcely ever was a civilized nation of that complexion, nor even any individual, eminent either in action or speculation."[15] And, as we have seen, once race was conceptualized

---

[14]Voltaire, pen name of François Marie Arouet (1694–1778), David Hume (1711–1776), and Immanuel Kant (1724–1804), French, English, and German philosophers of the Enlightenment, respectively. [Ed. note.]

[15]David Hume, *Of National Characters* (1748), 521–22 n. [M].

in biological terms, such low opinions of black people would lead easily to the implication that these incapacities were part of an inescapable racial essence.

In response to this long line of antiblack invective, black writers in the United States since the very first African-American poet (Phillis Wheatley, who lived in Boston in the latter part of the eighteenth century) have sought to establish the "capacity of the Negro" by writing and publishing first poetry and then, later—as literature came to be conceived as encompassing the novel, the essay, and the autobiography—in each of these forms.[16] More than this, the major proportion of the published writing of African-Americans, even when not directed to countering racist mythology, has been concerned thematically with issues of race, a fact that is hardly surprising in a country where black people were subjected to racial slavery until the mid-nineteenth century and then treated legally as second-class citizens in many places until the 1960s.

The recognition, especially in recent years, of the role of Anglo-Saxonism, in particular, and racism, more generally, in the construction of the canon of literature studied in American university departments of English has led many scholars to argue for the inclusion of texts by African-Americans in that canon, in part because their initial exclusion was an expression of racism. It has led others to argue for the recognition of an African-American tradition of writing, with its own major texts, which can be studied as a canon of their own.

What has not been so clear—despite the close affiliations of anglophone African and African-American criticisms—is the role of the conjunction of nation and literature in anglophone African criticism; it is to that issue, which I believe we should understand in the context I have just described, that I want to turn now.

Not long ago, I heard the Congolese writer Sony Labou Tansi discuss his ambivalent relation to the French language. Raised first by his Zairian kin in the (Belgian) Congo and then sent to school in (French) Congo-Brazzaville, he arrived at his formal schooling unfamiliar with its (French) language of instruction. He reported, with a strange mildness, the way in which his colonial teachers daubed him with human feces as a punishment for his early grammatical solecisms; then, a moment later, he went on to talk about his own remarkable work as a novelist and playwright in French. Labou Tansi has fashioned out of an experience with such unpromising beginnings a use for a language he ought surely to hate—a language literally shit-stained in his childhood—a use in the project of postcolonial literary nationalism.

---

[16]See Henry Louis Gates's preface to *Black Literature and Literary Theory*.

In Africa and around the world, so much of our writing and, more espe-cially, of our writing about writing touches on these issues of the nation and its language, on the conjunction captured almost at the start of modern theo-ries of the nation in the Herderian conception of the *Sprachgeist*. For intellec-tuals everywhere are now caught up—whether as volunteers, draftees, or resisters—in a struggle for the articulation of their respective nations, and everywhere, it seems, language and literature are central to that articulation.

The power of the idea of the nation in the nonindustrialized world is more than a consequence of the cultural hegemony of the Europeans and Americans whose ancestors invented both the idea and most of the world's juridical nationalities. As Ben Anderson has argued—in his elegant *Imagined Communities*—though the national idea was introduced to much of the world by way of contacts with European imperialism, the appeal of the idea to the "natives" soon outran the control and the interests of the metropole. African and Asian intellectuals do not believe in national self-determination simply because it was forced upon them, because it was imposed as a tool of their continued neocolonial domination; rather, the idea of the nation provided— first for the local elite, then for the newly proletarianized denizens of the colo-nial city, and finally even for a peasantry attempting to come to terms with its increasing incorporation into the world system—a way to articulate a resis-tance both to the material domination of the world empires and to the more nebulous threat to precolonial modes of thought represented by the Western project of cultural ascendancy.

I began with the tradition that leads through Tupper to the present day not merely because, as we shall see, it informs recent African criticism, but also because I want to insist on the extent to which the issues of language and nation that are so central to the situation I want to discuss in this essay—that of sub-Saharan African writers and critics—are also the problems of European and American criticism. This is not—as it is often presented as being—a voyage into the exotic, a flirtation with a distant Other. Voltaire or one of his *philosophe* comrades in a European culture before the heyday of the world empires once said that when we travel, what we discover is always our-selves. It seems to me that this thought has, so to speak, become true. In the world after those world empires, a world where center and periphery are mutually constitutive, political life may be conceived of (however mislead-ingly) in national terms, but what Voltaire might have called the life of the mind cannot. If I seek to locate my discussion of the African situation with a few elements of context, then, it is in part so that others can recognize how much of that situation is familiar territory.

That the territory *is* so familiar is a consequence of the way in which intel-lectuals from what I will call, with reservations, the Third World, are a historical product of an encounter with what I will continue, with similar reservations, to call the West. As we have seen, most African writers have received a Western-style education; their ambiguous relations to the world of their foremothers and forefathers and to the world of the industrialized countries are part of their distinctive cultural (dis)location, a condition that Abiola Irele has eloquently described in "In Praise of Alienation."

> We are wedged uncomfortably between the values of our traditional culture and those of the West. The process of change which we are going through has created a dualism of forms of life which we experience at the moment less as a mode of challenging complexity than as one of confused disparateness.

Of course, there are influences—some of them (as we shall see) important—that run from the precolonial intellectual culture to those who have received colonial or postcolonial educations in the Western manner. Nevertheless, in sub-Saharan Africa, most literate people are literate in the colonial languages; most writing with a substantial readership (with the important exception of Swahili) is in those languages, and the only writing with a genuinely subcontinental audience and address is in English or in French. For many of their most important cultural purposes, African intellectuals, south of the Sahara, are what I have called "europhone."

There *are* intellectual workers—priests, shamans, griots, for example—in Africa and Asia (and some in South America and Australasia, too) who still operate in worlds of thought that are remote from the influences of Western literate discourse. But we surely live in the last days of that phase of human life in culture; and whether or not we choose to call these people "intellectuals"—and this strikes me as a decision whose outcome is less important than recognizing that it has to be made—they are surely *not* the intellectuals who are producing the bulk of what we call Third World literature, nor are they articulating what we call literary theory or criticism. Literature, by and large, in sub-Saharan Africa means europhone literature (except in the Swahili culture area, where Swahili and the colonial languages are active together). And what matters in its being europhone is more than its inscription in the languages of the colonizers.

For language here is, of course, a synecdoche. When the colonialists attempted to tame the threatening cultural alterity of the African (whether through what the French called *assimilation* or through the agency of missionary "conversion"), the instrument of pedagogy was their most formidable weapon. So that the problem is not only, or not so much, the English or the French or the Portuguese languages as the cultural imposition that they each represent. Colonial education, in short, produced a generation immersed in the literature of the colonizers, a literature that often reflected and transmitted the imperialist vision.

This is, surely, no new thing: literary pedagogy played a similar role in Roman education in the provinces of that empire, an empire that still provides perhaps our most powerful paradigm of imperialism. John Guillory has recently focused our attention on a standard—dare I say, magisterial—treatment, by R. R. Bolgar in *The Classical Heritage and Its Beneficiaries*, of the process in which "the legions withdraw and are replaced by schools."

> As the protective might of the legions weakened, so the imperial government came to rely to an ever greater extent on its intangible assets. . . . Steel was in short supply . . . so the provinces were to be grappled to the soul of Rome by hoops of a different make.[17]

The role of the colonial (and, alas, the postcolonial) school in the reproduction of Western culture is crucial to African criticism because of the intimate connection between the idea of criticism and the growth of literary pedagogy, for (as John Guillory reminds us in the same place) the role of literature, indeed, the formation of the concept, the institution of "literature," is indissoluble from pedagogy. Roland Barthes expressed the point in a characteristic apothegm: " 'L'enseignement de la littérature' est pour moi presque tautologique. La littérature, c'est ce qui s'enseigne, un point c'est tout. C'est un objet d'enseignement."[18] Abstracted from its context, this formulation no doubt requires some qualifying glosses. But one cannot too strongly stress the importance of the fact that what we discuss under the rubric of modern African writing is largely what is *taught* in high schools all around the continent. Nor should we ignore the crucial psychological importance of the possibility of such an African writing. The weapon of pedagogy changes hands simply because we turn from reading Buchan and Conrad and Graham Greene to reading Abrahams, Achebe, Armah[19]—to begin an alphabet of writers in the Heinemann African Writer's series, which constitutes in the most

---

[17]Cited in John Guillory, "Canonical and Non-Canonical: A Critique of the Current Debate." This essay will surely come to be seen as a definitive analysis.

[18]" 'The teaching of literature' is for me almost tautological. Literature is what is taught, that is all. It's an object of teaching." Roland Barthes, "Reflections sur un manuel," 170.

[19]John Buchan (1875–1940), English novelist and author of *A Lodge in the Wilderness;* Joseph Conrad (1857–1924), English novelist and author of *Heart of Darkness;* Graham Greene (1904–1991), English novelist and author of *The Heart of the Matter;* all three novels focus on colonial Africa. These three novelists are contrasted with African authors Peter Abrahams (1919–), author of *Mine Boy,* Chinua Achebe (1930–), author of *Things Fall Apart,* and Ayi Kwei Armah (1939–), author of *The Beautyful Ones are Not Yet Born.* [Ed. note.]

concrete sense the pedagogical canon of anglophone African writing. The decolonized subject people write themselves, now, as the subject of a literature of their own. The simple gesture of writing for and about oneself—there are fascinating parallels here with the history of African-American writing—has a profound political significance.

Writing for and about ourselves, then, helps constitute the modern community of the nation, but we do it largely in languages imposed by "the might of the legions." Now that the objects of European imperialism have at last become the subjects of a discourse addressed both to each other and to the West, European languages and European disciplines have been "turned," like double agents, from the projects of the metropole to the intellectual work of post colonial cultural life.

But though officially in the service of new masters, these tools remain, like all double agents, perpetually under suspicion. Even when the colonizer's language is creolized, even when the imperialist's vision is playfully subverted in the lyrics of popular songs, there remains the suspicion that a hostile *Sprachgeist* is at work. Both the complaints against defilement by alien traditions in an alien tongue and the defenses of them as a practical necessity (a controversy that recalls similar debates in situations as otherwise different as, say, the early-twentieth-century Norwegian debate over "New Norwegian" and the nineteenth-century German Jewish debates over Yiddish) seem often to reduce to a dispute between a sentimental Herderian conception of Africa's languages and traditions as expressive of the collective essence of a pristine traditional community, on the one hand, and, on the other, a positivistic conception of European languages and disciplines as mere tools; tools that can be cleansed of the accompanying imperialist—and, more specifically, racist—modes of thought.

The former view is often at the heart of what we can call "nativism": the claim that true African independence requires a literature of one's own. Echoing the debate in nineteenth-century Russia between "Westerners" and "Slavophiles," the debate in Africa presents itself as an opposition between "universalism" and "particularism," the latter defining itself, above all else, by its opposition to the former. But there are only two real players in this game: us, inside; them, outside. That is all there is to it.

Operating with this topology of inside and outside—indigene and alien, Western and traditional—the apostles of nativism are able in contemporary Africa to mobilize the undoubted power of a nationalist rhetoric, one in which the literature of one's own is that of one's own nation. But nativists may appeal to identities that are both wider and narrower than the nation: to "tribes" and towns, below the nation-state; to Africa, above. And, I believe, we shall have the best chance of redirecting nativism's power if we challenge not the rhetoric of the tribe, the nation, or the continent but the topology that it presupposes, the opposition it asserts.

Consider, then, that now-classic manifesto of African cultural nationalism, *Toward the Decolonization of African Literature*. This much-discussed book is the work of three Nigerian authors—Chinweizu, Onwuchekwa Jemie, and Ihechukwu Madubuike—all of them encumbered with extensive Western university educations. Dr. Chinweizu, a widely published poet and quondam editor of the Nigerian literary magazine *Okike*, was an undergraduate at MIT and holds a doctorate from SUNY Buffalo; he has emerged (from a career that included time on the faculty at MIT and at San Jose State) as one of the leading figures in contemporary Nigerian journalism, writing for a long period a highly influential column in *The Guardian* of Lagos. Dr. Jemie holds a doctorate from Columbia University in English and comparative literature, is also a distinguished poet, and has published an introduction to the poetry of Langston Hughes. And Dr. Ihechukwu Madubuike—who has been Nigeria's minister of education—studied at Laval in Canada, the Sorbonne, and SUNY Buffalo. All of these critics have taught in black studies programs in the United States—in their preface they thank the Department of Afro-American Studies at the University of Minnesota and the Black Studies Department at Ohio State University for "supportive clerical help." If their rhetoric strikes responsive chords in the American ear, we shall not find it too surprising.

Not that their language fails to incorporate Nigerian elements. The term *bolekaja*—which means, "Come down, let's fight"—is used in western Nigeria to refer to the "mammy-wagons" that are the main means of popular transportation; it reflects "the outrageous behaviour of their touts." In their preface, Chinweizu, Jemie, and Madubuike call themselves "*bolekaja* critics, outraged touts for the passenger lorries of African literature."

> There comes a time, we believe, in the affairs of men and of nations, when it becomes necessary for them to engage in bolekaja criticism for them to drag the stiflers of their life down to earth for a corrective tussle. A little wrestle in the sands never killed a sturdy youth.[20]

And it is clear that it is not really the "sturdy youth" of African criticism that they take to be at risk; for the work of the succeeding chapters is to wrestle the critical ethnocentrism of their Eurocentric opponents to the ground in the name of an Afrocentric particularism. If this is to be a struggle to the death,

---

[20]Chinweizu, Onwuchekwa Jemie, and Ihechukwu Madubuike, *Toward the Decolonization of African Literature*, xiv, text and footnote.

Chinweizu and his compatriots expect to be the survivors. They assert, for example, that

> most of the objections to thematic and ideological matters in the African novel sound like admonitions from imperialist motherhens to their wayward or outright rebellious captive chickens. They cluck: "Be Universal! Be Universal!"[21]

And they condemn

> the modernist retreat of our poets into privatist universalism [which] makes it quite easy for them to shed whatever African nationalist consciousness they have before they cross the threshold into the sanctum of "poetry in the clouds." And that suits the English literary establishment just fine, since they would much prefer it if an African nationalist consciousness, inevitably anti-British, was not promoted or cultivated, through literature, in the young African elite.[22]

Thus, when the British critic Adrian Roscoe urges African poets to view themselves as "inheritors of a universal tradition of art and letters and not just as the recipients of an indigenous legacy," he reaps the nationalists' scorn.[23] For their central insistence is that "African literature *is* an autonomous entity separate and apart from all other literature. It has its own traditions, models and norms."[24]

Now we should recognize from the start that such polemics can be a salutary corrective to a great deal of nonsense that has been written about African literature, by critics for whom literary merit is gauged by whether a work can be inserted into a Great White Tradition of masterpieces. It is hard not to be irritated by high-handed pronouncements from critics for whom detailed description of locale amounts to mere travelogue, unless, say, the locale is "Wessex" and the author is Thomas Hardy; for whom the evocation of local custom amounts to mere ethnography, unless, say, they are the customs of a northern English mining town and the author is D. H. Lawrence; and for whom the recounting of historical event amounts to mere journalism, unless the event is the Spanish civil war and the author is Hemingway.[25]

---

[21]Ibid., 89.

[22]Ibid., 151.

[23]Ibid., 147.

[24]Ibid., 4.

[25]Thomas Hardy (1840–1928) and D. H. Lawrence (1885–1930), English novelists; Ernest Hemingway (1899–1961), American novelist. [Ed. note.]

What Chinweizu and his colleagues are objecting to, in other words, is the posture that conceals its privileging of one national (or racial) tradition against others in false talk of the Human Condition. It is not surprising, then, that Chinweizu and his colleagues also endorse T. S. Eliot's view that "although it is only too easy for a writer to be local without being universal, I doubt whether a poet or novelist can be universal without being local too."[26] And here, of course, it is plain enough that "universal" is hardly a term of derogation.

Indeed it is characteristic of those who pose as antiuniversalists to use the term *universalism* as if it meant *pseudouniversalism,* and the fact is that their complaint is not with universalism at all. What they truly object to—and who would not?—is Eurocentric hegemony *posing* as universalism. Thus, while the debate is couched in terms of the competing claims of particularism and universalism, the actual ideology of universalism is never interrogated, and, indeed, is even tacitly accepted. Ironically, as we shall see later, the attack on something called "universalism" leads to the occlusion of genuine local difference.

The appeal of this nativist rhetoric is most easily understood in the context of the subcontinent's politico-linguistic geography, a geography I rehearsed at the start of the book. The essential fact to recall here is the association of a europhone elite and a noneurophone populace, for it is this combination that makes for the appeal of nativism. That the European languages—and, in particular, the dialects of them in which elite writing goes on—are far from being the confident possession of the populace does not, of course, distinguish Third World literature—the writings that are taught—from the bulk of contemporary European or American taught writings. But the fact that contemporary African literature operates in a sphere of language that is so readily identifiable as the product of schooling—and schooling that is fully available only to an elite—invites the nativist assimilation of formal literature to the alien. This association is reinforced by the recognition that there is, in Africa as in the West, a body of distinctive cultural production—over the whole range of popular culture—that *does* have a more immediate access to the citizen with less formal education.

So, for example, there are certainly, as I have already once said, strong living practices of oral culture—religious, mythological, poetic, and narrative—in most of the thousand and more languages of sub-Saharan Africa, and there is no doubt as to the importance of the few languages that were already (as we

---

[26]Eliot is cited on p. 106. When Chinweizu et al. assert, typically, that "there was in pre-colonial Africa an abundance of oral narratives which are in no way inferior to European novels" (27), they presuppose the universalist view that there is some (universal) value-metric by which the relative excellence of the two can be gauged.

say) reduced to writing before the colonial era. But we must not fall for the sentimental notion that the "people" have held onto an indigenous national tradition, that only the educated bourgeoisie are "children of two worlds." At the level of popular culture, too, the currency is not a holdover from an unbroken stream of tradition; indeed, it is, like most popular culture in the age of mass production, hardly national at all. Popular culture in Africa encompasses the (Americans) Michael Jackson and Jim Reeves; when it picks up cultural production whose sources are geographically African, what it picks up is not usually in any plausible sense traditional. Highlife music is both recognizably West African and distinctly not precolonial; and the sounds of Fela Kuti would have astonished the musicians of the last generation of court musicians in Yorubaland. As they have developed new forms of music, drawing on instrumental repertoires and musical ideas with a dazzling eclecticism, Africa's musicians have also done astonishing things with a language that used to be English. But it is *as* English that that language is accessible to millions around the continent (and around the world).

If we are to move beyond nativist hand waving, the right place to start is by defamiliarizing the concepts with which we think about—and teach—literature. Too often, attempts at cultural analysis are short-circuited by a failure to recall the histories of the analytical terms—*culture, literature, nation*—through which we have come to speak about the postcolonial world. So it is as well to remind ourselves of the original twinning of literature and nationalism, with which I began this essay, and with the ways in which each is essentialized through narratives. We are familiar, from Ernest Renan, with the selective remembering and forgetting of the past that undergirds group identity. And recent historiography has stressed again and again the ways in which the "national heritage" is constructed through the invention of traditions; the careful filtering of the rough torrent of historical event into the fine stream of an official narrative; the creation of a homogeneous legacy of values and experience.[27]

In the specific context of the history of "literature" and its study, recent debates have also left us attuned to the ways in which the factitious "excavation" of the literary canon can serve to solidify a particular cultural identity. The offical constitution of a national history bequeaths us the nation, and the discipline of literary history, as Michel de Certeau has aptly remarked, "transforms the text into an institution"—and so bequeaths us what we call literature.[28]

---

[27]Renan's influential essay "Qu'est-ce qu'une nation" is the locus classicus of attempts to define nationality through a "common memory." For recent work on the invention of traditions see Eric Hobsbawm and Terence Ranger, eds., *The Invention of Tradition.*

[28]Michel de Certeau, *Heterologies: Discourse on the Other,* 32.

The late Raymond Williams once noted that as the term *literature* begins to acquire its modern semantic freight, we find "a development of the concept of 'tradition' within national terms, resulting in the more effective definition of 'a national literature.' "[29] As I argued at the start of this essay, "literature" and "nation" could hardly fail to belong together: from the very start they were made for each other. Once the concept of literature was taken up by African intellectuals, the African debate about literary nationalism was inevitable.

So that what we see in *Toward the Decolonization of African Literature* is, in effect, the establishment of a "reverse discourse": the terms of resistance are already given us, and our contestation is entrapped within the Western cultural conjuncture we affect to dispute. The pose of repudiation actually presupposes the cultural institutions of the West and the ideological matrix in which they, in turn, are imbricated. Railing against the cultural hegemony of the West, the nativists are of its party without knowing it.[30] Indeed, the very arguments, the rhetoric of defiance, that our nationalists muster are, in a sense, canonical, time-tested. For they enact a conflict that is *interior* to the same nationalist ideology that provided the category of "literature" its conditions of emergence: defiance is determined less by "indigenous" notions of resistance than by the dictates of the West's own Herderian legacy—its highly elaborated ideologies of national autonomy, of language and literature as their cultural substrate. Nativist nostalgia, in short, is largely fueled by that Western sentimentalism so familiar after Rousseau[31]; few things, then, are less native than nativism in its current forms.

In this debate among African intellectuals we see recapitulated the classic gestures of nation formation in the domain of culture. And surely this is exactly as we should expect. In postcolonial discourse the project of nation formation—what used to be, in the eighteenth century, the attempt to define (and thus to invent) the "national character"—always lies close to the surface. But, as any Americanist would remind us, the emergence of American litera-

---

[29]"The sources of each of these tendencies can be discerned from the Renaissance, but it was in the eighteenth and nineteenth centuries that they came through most powerfully, until they became, in the twentieth century, in effect received assumptions." Raymond Williams, *Marxism and Literature,* 47. See also Louis Montrose, "Of Gentlemen and Shepherds: The Politics of Elizabethan Pastoral Form," and Michel Beaujour, "Genus Universum."

[30]Ernesto Laclau and Chantal Mouffe write: "Only if it is accepted that the subject positions cannot be led back to a positive and unitary founding principle—only then can pluralism be considered radical. Pluralism is *radical* only to the extent that each term of this plurality of identities finds within itself the principle of its own validity, without this having to be sought in a transcendent or underlying positive ground for the hierarchy of meaning of them all and the source and guarantee of their legitimacy." *Hegemony and Socialist Strategy,* 167.

[31]Jean-Jacques Rousseau (1712–1778), French philosopher. [Ed. note.]

ture in the nineteenth century was circumscribed by just such concerns, coupled with a strong sense of being at the periphery vis-à-vis the European center. So it is with a sense of recognition that one turns from the rhetoric of postcolonial criticism today to read, say, William Carlos Williams's anxious observation:

> Americans have never recognized themselves. How can they? It is impossible until someone invent the original terms. As long as we are content to be called by somebody's else terms, we are incapable of being anything but our own dupes.[32]

In their ideological inscription, the cultural nationalists remain in a position of counteridentification (to borrow Michel Pêcheux's convenient schematism), which is to continue to participate in an institutional configuration— to be subjected to cultural identities—one officially decries.[33]

Once we lay aside the "universalism" that Chinweizu and others rightly attack as a disguised particularism, we can understand how an Afrocentric particularism—Chinweizu's cultural nationalism—is itself covertly universalist. Nativism organizes its vaunted particularities into a "culture" that is, in fact, an artifact of Western modernity. While Western criteria of evaluation are challenged, the way in which the contest is framed is not. The "Eurocentric" bias of criticism is scrutinized, but not the way in which its defining subject is constructed. For to acknowledge *that* would be to acknowledge that outside is not outside at all, so that the topology of nativism would be irretrievably threatened.

Ideologies succeed to the extent that they are invisible, in the moment that their fretwork of assumptions passes beneath consciousness; genuine victories are won without a shot being fired. Inasmuch as the most ardent of Africa's cultural nationalists participates in naturalizing—universalizing— the value-laden categories of "literature" and "culture," the triumph of universalism has, in the face of a silent nolo contendere, already taken place. The Western emperor has ordered the natives to exchange their robes for trousers: their act of defiance is to insist on tailoring them from homespun material. Given their arguments, plainly, the cultural nationalists do not go far enough; they are blind to the fact that their nativist demands inhabit a Western architecture.

---

[32]William Carlos Williams, *In the American Grain*, 226.

[33]For Pêcheux the more radical move is toward what he terms dis-identification, in which we are no longer invested in the specific institutional determinations of the West. Michel Pêcheux, *Language, Semantics and Ideology*, 156–59.

It is as well to insist on a point that is neglected almost as often as it has been made, namely that nativism and nationalism (in all their many senses) are different creatures. Certainly, they fit together uneasily for many reasons. A return to traditions, after all, would never be a return to the contemporary nation-state. Nor could it mean, in Africa (where Pan-Africanism is a favorite form of nationalism) a return to an earlier continental unity, since—to insist on the obvious—the continent was not united in the past. [. . . V]arious projects of African solidarity have their uses on the continent and in her diaspora: but these forms of "nationalism" look to the future not to the past.

I think that once we see the larger context more clearly, we will be less prone to the anxieties of nativism, less likely to be seduced by the rhetoric of ancestral purity. More than a quarter of a century ago, Frantz Fanon exposed the artificiality of nativist intellectuals, whose ersatz populism only estranges them from the *Volk* they venerate. The intellectual

> . . . sets a high value on the customs, traditions, and the appearances of his people, but his inevitable, painful experience only seems to be a banal search for exoticism. The sari becomes sacred, and shoes that come from Paris or Italy are left off in favor of pampooties, while suddenly the language of the ruling power is felt to burn your lips.[34]

Inevitably, though, the "culture that the intellectual leans toward is often no more than a stock of particularisms. He wishes to attach himself to the people, but instead he only catches hold of their outer garments."[35] Fanon does not dismiss the products of the modern cultural worker in the colonial or postcolonial era, but he urges that the native poet who has taken his people as subject "cannot go forward resolutely unless he first realizes the extent of his estrangement from them."[36] Intellectuals betray this estrangement by a fetishistic attitude toward the customs, folklore, and vernacular traditions of their people, an atti-

---

[34]Frantz Fanon, *The Wretched of the Earth*, 221.

[35]Ibid., 223–24.

[36]Ibid., 226. For Ngugi, the cause of cultural nationalism has lead him to write in Gikuyu, eschewing the languages of Europe. In fact, he insists of his europhone compeers that "despite any claims to the contrary, what they have produced is not African literature," and he consigns the work of Achebe, Soyinka, Sembene, and others to a mere hybrid aberrancy that "can only be termed Afro-European literature" (Ngugi wa Thiong'o, "The Language of African Literature," p. 125). So it is interesting to note that, despite his *linguistic* nativism, he does not eschew innovations rooted in Western expressive media. Recently he explained some of the effects he achieved in his latest Gikuyu novel, *Matigari ma Njirugi*, by the happy fact of his being "influenced by film technique. . . . I write as if each scene is captured in a frame, so the whole novel is a series of camera shots." "Interview with Ngugi wa Thiong'o by Hansel Nolumbe Eyoh," 166.

tude that, Fanon argues, must, in the end, set them against the people in their time of struggle.

One focus of this estrangement that has not, perhaps, been sufficiently appreciated is the very conception of an African identity. Although most discourse about African literature has moved beyond the monolithic notions of negritude or the "African personality," the constructed nature of the modern African identity (like all identities) is not widely enough understood. Terence Ranger has written of how the British colonialist's "own respect for 'tradition' disposed them to look with favour upon what they took to be traditional in Africa."[37] British colonial officers, traveling in the footsteps of Lord Lugard (and with the support of that curious creature, the government anthropologist) collected, organized, and enforced these "traditions," and such works as Rattray's *Ashanti Law and Constitution* had the effect of monumentalizing the flexible operations of precolonial systems of social control as what came to be called "customary law." Ironically, for many contemporary African intellectuals, these invented traditions have now acquired the status of national mythology, and the invented past of Africa has come to play a role in the political dynamics of the modern state.

> The invented traditions imported from Europe not only provided whites with models of command but also offered many Africans models of "modern" behavior. The invented traditions of African societies—whether invented by the Europeans or by Africans themselves in response—distorted the past but became in themselves realities through which a good deal of colonial encounter was expressed.[38]

So it is, Ranger observes, that "those like Ngugi who repudiate bourgeois elite culture face the ironic danger of embracing another set of colonial inventions instead."[39] The English, who knew all about nations, could extend a similar comprehension to its stand-in, the "tribe," and that could mean inventing

---

[37]Terence Ranger, "Invention of Tradition in Colonial Africa," in Hobsbawm and Ranger, *The Invention of Tradition*, 212.

[38]Ibid.

[39]Ibid., 262. Al-Amin M. Mazrui has argued, to the point, that "empirical observations have tended to suggest a shift towards increasing ethnic consciousness, despite the reverse trend towards decreasing ethnic behavior. Losing sight of such observations necessarily culminates in the distortion of the nature of tribal identity and in the mystification of cultural revival as an aid to tribal identity. In fact, this tendency to mystify tribal identity is precisely the factor which has made imperialist countries realise that there is no conflict of interest in their sponsoring all sorts of parochial tribal cultural festivals in the guise of reviving African cultural heritage, while attempting to infuse our societies with a 'new' cultural ethos that will be conducive to further consolidation of neocolonial capitalism in Africa." Al-Amin M. Mazrui, "Ideology or Pedagogy: The Linguistic Indigenisation of African Literature," 67.

tribes where none quite existed before. The point extends beyond the anglophone domain. In Zaire we find that a sweeping linguistic division (between Lingala and Swahili) is a product of recent history, an outcome of worker stratification imposed by the Belgian administration.[40] Indeed, [...], the very invention of Africa (as something more than a geographical entity) must be understood, ultimately, as an outgrowth of European racialism; the notion of Pan-Africanism was founded on the notion of the African, which was, in turn, founded not on any genuine cultural commonality but, as we have seen, on the very European concept of the Negro. "The Negro," Fanon writes, is "never so much a Negro as since he has been dominated by whites."[41] But the reality is that the very category of the Negro is at root a European product: for the "whites" invented the Negroes in order to dominate them. Simply put, the course of cultural nationalism in Africa has been to make real the imaginary identities to which Europe has subjected us.

[1992]

---

[40]Johannes Fabian, *Language and Colonial Power*, 42–43. The dominance of Swahili in many areas is, itself, a colonial product (see p. 6).

[41]Fanon, The *Wretched of the Earth*, 212.

Maya Angelou
[1928–   ]

Born Marguerite Johnson in St. Louis, Missouri, **MAYA ANGELOU** *was reared in rural Arkansas, which she portrays in her autobiography* I Know Why the Caged Bird Sings *(1970). After being violently attacked as a child, she refused to speak for several years, but she eventually found a voice that would influence millions during her lifetime. She grew up with a respected uncle and was a part of a larger Southern community that gave her both a voice and the ambition to change the lives of oppressed children and adults around the world. She married a South African freedom fighter and moved to Cairo, Egypt, where she edited the only English news source, the* Arab Observer. *She also began a career as an actor and dancer at this stage in her life. Next she moved to Ghana where she taught at the University of Ghana and edited the* African Review. *Upon her return to the United States Angelou was persuaded by Dr. Martin Luther King, Jr. to become the Northern leader of the Southern Christian Leadership Conference during the unrest of the sixties. She lent her powerful voice to the American civil rights movement and opened many doors for African Americans through her powerful presence and careful diplomacy. President Carter appointed her to the National Commission on the Observance of International Women's Year, and President Ford appointed her to the Bicentennial Commission so that she used her voice to speak for women around the world. During the seventies she was recipient of the* Ladies Home Journal Woman of the Year *Award. In 1981 she was nominated for the Pulitzer Prize and the National Book award. She received the Golden Eagle award for her PBS series* Afro-Americans in the Arts *and an Emmy for her performance in the acclaimed TV series* Roots. *She wrote the screenplay* Georgia *and was the first black woman to see her play filmed. She also produced, directed, and starred in* Cabaret for Freedom, *a political review.*

Angelou's career has included writing poetry, drama, and prose; acting, producing, and directing drama for both television and the theater; and civil rights activism at home and abroad. At the same time, she has thrilled audiences around the world with her brilliant readings and lectures and has moved many to follow her lead toward a positive advocacy for civil rights for all. She speaks French, Spanish, Italian, and West African Fanti. In 1993 she read at President Clinton's inauguration. She is currently Reynolds Professor of English at Wake Forest University in North Carolina and continues to travel widely, generously giving of her time and energy for political causes, poetry readings, and human rights.

Africa

MAYA ANGELOU

Thus she had lain
sugar cane sweet
deserts her hair
golden her feet
mountains her breasts   5
two Niles her tears
Thus she has lain
Black through the years.

Over the white seas
rime white and cold   10
brigands ungentled
icicle bold
took her young daughters
sold her strong sons
churched her with Jesus   15
bled her with guns.
Thus she has lain.

Now she is rising
remember her pain
remember the losses   20
her screams loud and vain
remember her riches
her history slain
now she is striding   25
although she had lain.

[1975]

Reprinted from *Oh, Pray My Wings Are Gonna Fit Me Well*, by permission of Random House, Inc. Copyright © 1975 by Maya Angelou.

W. E. B. Du Bois
[1868–1963]

"The problem of the twentieth century is the problem of the color line," wrote African-American author W. E. B. DU BOIS *in the foreword to his masterpiece,* The Souls of Black Folk *(1903), and arguably with that statement, he established the field that has since developed into critical race theory. Du Bois was the first African American to receive a doctorate from Harvard University, and his first published book was his dissertation,* The Suppression of the African Slave-Trade to the United States of America, 1638–1870 *(1896). He wrote in numerous genres, publishing volumes of criticism, essays, fiction, poetry, biography, and history throughout his life. In 1905, Du Bois founded the Niagara Movement, the first all-black protest movement in U.S. history, and in 1910, he participated in the founding of, and became the director of publicity and research for, the National Association for the Advancement of Colored People (NAACP). A long-standing conflict with black leader Booker T. Washington was brought into public debate in a chapter of* The Souls of Black Folk, *in which Du Bois took Washington to task for advocating policies of conciliation toward whites, and the gradual improvement of the lives of African Americans through vocational training. Du Bois insisted, above all, that liberal education was necessary for blacks to achieve true equality in American culture. Barring such an achievement, African Americans would be condemned to a life of what he termed "double-consciousness," always excluded from the mainstream of American life. Du Bois worked throughout his life to eliminate racial barriers, but, disillusioned with the failures of the United States to make genuine progress in that regard, Du Bois joined the Communist party and emigrated to Ghana in 1961 where he died in 1963, a Ghanaian citizen. Throughout his writings, however, Du Bois sought for African Americans not a remove from, but a greater participation in, the civic life and the culture of the United States.*

The Souls of Black Folk: Chapter I
Of Our Spiritual Strivings

W.E.B. DU BOIS

O water, voice of my heart, crying in the sand,
All night long crying with a mournful cry,
As I lie and listen, and cannot understand
The voice of my heart in my side or the voice of the sea,
O water, crying for rest, is it I, is it I?
All night long the water is crying to me.

Unresting water, there shall never be rest
Till the last moon droop and the last tide fail,
And the fire of the end begin to burn in the west;
And the heart shall be weary and wonder and cry
like the sea,
All life long crying without avail,
As the water all night long is crying to me.

Arthur Symons.[1]

BETWEEN ME AND THE other world there is ever an unasked question: unasked by some through feelings of delicacy; by others through the difficulty of rightly framing it. All, nevertheless, flutter round it. They approach me in a half-hesitant sort of way, eye me curiously or compassionately, and then, instead of saying directly, *How does it feel to be a problem?* they say, I know an

---

[1]Arthur Symons (1865–1945), Welsh writer and translator.

First published in 1903.

excellent colored man in my town; or, I fought at Mechanicsville; or, Do not these Southern outrages make your blood boil? At these I smile, or am interested, or reduce the boiling to a simmer, as the occasion may require. *To the real question, How does it feel to be a problem? I answer seldom a word.*

And yet, being a problem is a strange experience—peculiar even for one who has never been anything else, save perhaps in babyhood and in Europe. It is in the early days of rollicking boyhood that the revelation first bursts upon one, all in a day, as it were. I remember well when the shadow swept across me. I was a little thing, away up in the hills of New England, where the dark Housatonic winds between Hoosac and Taghkanic to the sea.[2] In a wee wooden schoolhouse, something put it into the boys' and girls' heads to buy gorgeous visiting-cards—ten cents a package—and exchange. The exchange was merry, till one girl, a tall newcomer, refused my card,—refused it peremptorily, with a glance. Then it dawned upon me with a certain suddenness that I was different from the others; or like, mayhap, in heart and life and longing, but *shut out from their world by a vast veil.* I had thereafter no desire to tear down that veil, to creep through; I held all beyond it in common contempt, and lived above it in a region of blue sky and great wandering shadows. That sky was bluest when I could beat my mates at examination time, or beat them at a foot-race, or even beat their stringy heads. Alas, with the years all this fine contempt began to fade; for the worlds I longed for, and all their dazzling opportunities, were theirs, not mine. But they should not keep these prizes, I said; some, all, I would wrest from them. Just how I would do it I could never decide: by reading law, by healing the sick, by telling the wonderful tales that swam in my head,—some way. With other black boys the strife was not so fiercely sunny: their youth shrunk into tasteless sycophancy, or into silent hatred of the pale world about them and mocking distrust of everything white; or wasted itself in a bitter cry, Why did God make me an outcast and a stranger in mine own house? The shades of the prison-house closed round about us all: walls strait and stubborn to the whitest, but relentlessly narrow, tall, and unscalable to sons of night who must plod darkly on in resignation, or beat unavailing palms against the stone, or steadily, half hopelessly, watch the streak of blue above.

After the Egyptian and Indian, the Greek and Roman, the Teuton and Mongolian, *the Negro is a sort of seventh son, born with a veil, and gifted with second sight in this American world—a world which yields him no true self-consciousness, but only lets him see himself through the revelation of the other world.* It is a peculiar sensation, this *double-consciousness*, this sense of always

---

[2]The Housatonic is a river in the Berkshires that passes between the towns of Hoosac in western Massachusetts and Taghkanic in eastern New York, before continuing south to Long Island Sound.

looking at one's self through the eyes of others, of measuring one's soul by the tape of a world that looks on in amused contempt and pity. *One ever feels his twoness,—an American, a Negro*; two souls, two thoughts, two unreconciled strivings; two warring ideals in one dark body, whose dogged strength alone keeps it from being torn asunder.

The history of the American Negro is the history of this strife,—this longing to attain self-conscious manhood, to merge his double self into a better and truer self. In this merging he wishes neither of the older selves to be lost. He would not Africanize America, for America has too much to teach the world and Africa. He would not bleach his Negro soul in a flood of white Americanism, for he knows that Negro blood has a message for the world. *He simply wishes to make it possible for a man to be both a Negro and an American, without being cursed and spit upon by his fellows, without having the doors of Opportunity closed roughly in his face.*

This, then, is the end of his striving: to be a co-worker in the kingdom of culture, to escape both death and isolation, to husband and use his best powers and his latent genius. These powers of body and mind have in the past been strangely wasted, dispersed, or forgotten. The shadow of a mighty Negro past flits through the tale of Ethiopia the Shadowy and of Egypt the Sphinx. Throughout history, the powers of single black men flash here and there like falling stars, and die sometimes before the world has rightly gauged their brightness. Here in America, in the few days since Emancipation, the black man's turning hither and thither in hesitant and doubtful striving has often made his very strength to lose effectiveness, to seem like absence of power, like weakness. And yet it is not weakness,—it is the contradiction of double aims. The double-aimed struggle of the black artisan—on the one hand to escape white contempt for a nation of mere hewers of wood and drawers of water, and on the other hand to plough and nail and dig for a poverty-stricken horde—could only result in making him a poor craftsman, for he had but half a heart in either cause. By the poverty and ignorance of his people, the Negro minister or doctor was tempted toward quackery and demagogy; and by the criticism of the other world, toward ideals that made him ashamed of his lowly tasks. The would-be black *savant* was confronted by the paradox that the knowledge his people needed was a twice-told tale to his white neighbors, while the knowledge which would teach the white world was Greek to his own flesh and blood. The innate love of harmony and beauty that set the ruder souls of his people a-dancing and a-singing raised but confusion and doubt in the soul of the black artist; for the beauty revealed to him was the soul-beauty of a race which his larger audience despised, and he could not articulate the message of another people. This waste of double aims, this seeking to satisfy two unreconciled ideals, has wrought sad havoc with the courage and faith and deeds of ten thousand thousand people,—has sent them often wooing false gods and invoking false means of salvation, and at times has even seemed about to make them ashamed of themselves.

Away back in the days of bondage they thought to see in one divine event the end of all doubt and disappointment; few men ever worshipped Freedom with half such unquestioning faith as did the American Negro for two centuries. To him, so far as he thought and dreamed, slavery was indeed the sum of all villainies, the cause of all sorrow, the root of all prejudice; Emancipation was the key to a promised land of sweeter beauty than ever stretched before the eyes of wearied Israelites. In song and exhortation swelled one refrain—Liberty; in his tears and curses, the God he implored had Freedom in his right hand. At last it came,—suddenly, fearfully, like a dream. With one wild carnival of blood and passion came the message in his own plaintive cadences:—

> "Shout, O children!
> Shout, you're free!
> For God has bought your liberty!"[3]

Years have passed away since then,—ten, twenty, forty; forty years of national life, forty years of renewal and development, and yet the swarthy spectre sits in its accustomed seat at the Nation's feast. In vain do we cry to this our vastest social problem:—

> "Take any shape but that, and my firm nerves
> Shall never tremble!"[4]

The Nation has not yet found peace from its sins; the freedman has not yet found in freedom his promised land. Whatever of good may have come in these years of change, the shadow of a deep disappointment rests upon the Negro people,—a disappointment all the more bitter because the unattained ideal was unbounded save by the simple ignorance of a lowly people.

The first decade was merely a prolongation of the vain search for freedom, the boon that seemed ever barely to elude their grasp,—like a tantalizing will-o'-the-wisp, maddening and misleading the headless host. The holocaust of war, the terrors of the Ku-Klux Klan, the lies of carpetbaggers, the disorganization of industry, and the contradictory advice of friends and foes, left the bewildered serf with no new watchword beyond the old cry for freedom. As the time flew, however, he began to grasp a new idea. The ideal of lib-

---

[3]From a nineteenth century Negro spiritual.

[4]Shakespeare, *Macbeth*, Act 3, scene 4, lines 101–102.

erty demanded for its attainment powerful means, and these the Fifteenth Amendment gave him. The ballot, which before he had looked upon as a visible sign of freedom, he now regarded as the chief means of gaining and perfecting the liberty with which war had partially endowed him. And why not? Had not votes made war and emancipated millions? Had not votes enfranchised the freedmen? Was anything impossible to a power that had done all this? A million black men started with renewed zeal to vote themselves into the kingdom. So the decade flew away, the revolution of 1876 came, and left the half-free serf weary, wondering, but still inspired. Slowly but steadily, in the following years, a new vision began gradually to replace the dream of political power,—a powerful movement, the rise of another ideal to guide the unguided, another pillar of fire by night after a clouded day. It was the *ideal of "book-learning"*; the curiosity, born of compulsory ignorance, to know and test the power of the cabalistic letters of the white man, the longing to know. Here at last seemed to have been discovered the mountain path to Canaan; longer than the highway of Emancipation and law, steep and rugged, but straight, leading to heights high enough to overlook life.

Up the new path the advance guard toiled, slowly, heavily, doggedly; only those who have watched and guided the faltering feet, the misty minds, the dull understandings of the dark pupils of these schools know how faithfully, how piteously, this people strove to learn. It was weary work. The cold statistician wrote down the inches of progress here and there, noted also where here and there a foot had slipped or some one had fallen. To the tired climbers, the horizon was ever dark, the mists were often cold, the Canaan was always dim and far away. If, however, the vistas disclosed as yet no goal, no resting-place, little but flattery and criticism, the journey at least gave leisure for reflection and self-examination; it changed the child of Emancipation to the youth with dawning self-consciousness, self-realization, self-respect. In those sombre forests of his striving his own soul rose before him, and he saw himself,— darkly as through a veil; and yet he saw in himself some faint revelation of his power, of his mission. He began to have a dim feeling that, to attain his place in the world, he must be himself, and not another. For the first time he sought to analyze the burden he bore upon his back, that dead-weight of social degradation partially masked behind a half-named Negro problem. He felt his poverty; without a cent, without a home, without land, tools, or savings, he had entered into competition with rich, landed, skilled neighbors. To be a poor man is hard, but to be a poor race in a land of dollars is the very bottom of hardships. He felt the weight of his ignorance,—not simply of letters, but of life, of business, of the humanities; the accumulated sloth and shirking and awkwardness of decades and centuries shackled his hands and feet. Nor was his burden all poverty and ignorance. The red stain of bastardy, which two centuries of systematic legal defilement of Negro women had stamped upon his race, meant not only the loss of ancient African chastity, but also the hereditary weight of a mass of corruption from white adulterers, threatening almost the obliteration of the Negro home.

A people thus handicapped ought not to be asked to race with the world, but rather allowed to give all its time and thought to its own social problems. But alas! while sociologists gleefully count his bastards and his prostitutes, the very soul of the toiling, sweating black man is darkened by the shadow of a vast despair. Men call the shadow prejudice, and learnedly explain it as the natural defence of culture against barbarism, learning against ignorance, purity against crime, the "higher" against the "lower" races. To which the Negro cries Amen! and swears that to so much of this strange prejudice as is founded on just homage to civilization, culture, righteousness, and progress, he humbly bows and meekly does obeisance. But before that nameless prejudice that leaps beyond all this he stands helpless, dismayed, and well-nigh speechless; before that personal disrespect and mockery, the ridicule and systematic humiliation, the distortion of fact and wanton license of fancy, the cynical ignoring of the better and the boisterous welcoming of the worse, the all-pervading desire to inculcate disdain for everything black, from Toussaint[5] to the devil,—before this there rises a sickening despair that would disarm and discourage any nation save that black host to whom "discouragement" is an unwritten word.

But the facing of so vast a prejudice could not but bring the inevitable self-questioning, self-disparagement, and lowering of ideals which ever accompany repression and breed in an atmosphere of contempt and hate. Whisperings and portents came borne upon the four winds. Lo! we are diseased and dying, cried the dark hosts; we cannot write, our voting is vain; what need of education, since we must always cook and serve? And the nation echoed and enforced this self-criticism, saying: Be content to be servants, and nothing more; what need of higher culture for half-men? Away with the black man's ballot, by force or fraud,—and behold the suicide of a race! Nevertheless, out of the evil came something of good,—the more careful adjustment of education to real life, the clearer perception of the Negroes' social responsibilities, and the sobering realization of the meaning of progress.

So dawned the time of *Sturm und Drang*[6]: storm and stress to-day rocks our little boat on the mad waters of the world-sea; there is within and with-

---

[5]The reference here is likely to Toussaint Louverture (1743–1803), who liberated Haiti from the French in 1800; he was captured and imprisoned by French forces in 1802. The reference is, however-er, most important for its wordplay, juxtaposing Toussaint ("all-saint") with the devil.

[6]"Storm and stress" (German), a phrase taken from the name of a school of late eighteenth century German literature.

out the sound of conflict, the burning of body and rending of soul; inspiration strives with doubt, and faith with vain questionings. The bright ideals of the past,—physical freedom, political power, the training of brains and the training of hands,—all these in turn have waxed and waned, until even the last grows dim and overcast. Are they all wrong,—all false? No, not that, but each alone was over-simple and incomplete,—the dreams of a credulous race-childhood, or the fond imaginings of the other world which does not know and does not want to know our power. To be really true, all these ideals must be melted and welded into one. The training of the schools we need to-day more than ever,—the training of deft hands, quick eyes and ears, and above all the broader, deeper, higher culture of gifted minds and pure hearts. The power of the ballot we need in sheer self-defence, else what shall save us from a second slavery? Freedom, too, the long-sought, we still seek,—the freedom of life and limb, the freedom to work and think, the freedom to love and aspire. Work, culture, liberty,—all these we need, not singly but together, not successively but together, each growing and aiding each, and all striving toward that vaster ideal that swims before the Negro people, the ideal of human brotherhood, gained through the unifying ideal of Race; the ideal of fostering and developing the traits and talents of the Negro, not in opposition to or contempt for other races, but rather in large conformity to the greater ideals of the American Republic, in order that some day on American soil two world-races may give each to each those characteristics both so sadly lack. We the darker ones come even now not altogether empty-handed: there are to-day no truer exponents of the pure human spirit of the Declaration of Independence than the American Negroes; there is no true American music but the wild sweet melodies of the Negro slave; the American fairy tales and folklore are Indian and African; and, all in all, we black men seem the sole oasis of simple faith and reverence in a dusty desert of dollars and smartness. Will America be poorer if she replace her brutal dyspeptic blundering with light-hearted but determined Negro humility? or her coarse and cruel wit with loving jovial good-humor? or her vulgar music with the soul of the Sorrow Songs?

Merely a concrete test of the underlying principles of the great republic is the Negro Problem, and the spiritual striving of the freedmen's sons is the travail of souls whose burden is almost beyond the measure of their strength, but who bear it in the name of an historic race, in the name of this the land of their fathers' fathers, and in the name of human opportunity.

[1903]

Amiri Baraka
[1934–   ]

AMIRI BARAKA was born LeRoi Jones in Newark, New Jersey. After attending Howard University, he served in the United States Air Force. In the 1950s, Baraka began his poetic career in association with the literary avant-garde of the period. He lived in Greenwich Village during the late fifties, associating with Beat poets such as Allen Ginsberg and Frank O'Hara. He was also influenced by Charles Olson, the leader of an experimental group of poets and artists working at Black Mountain College. At this time, he believed that poetry should seek its own form, and rejected traditional forms such as the sonnet or the sestina. His play, Dutchman, won an Obie award in 1964, which brought him national recognition.

After the assassination of Malcolm X in 1965, Jones became a Black Nationalist, moving to Harlem and ending his association with white culture. His book Black Magic, published in 1967, emblematized his break and subsequent powerful identification with blackness, and black people as "a race, a culture, a Nation." He established the Black Repertory Theater Arts School in Harlem. After nearly ten years of this association, Baraka reversed his position and declared himself a Third-World Marxist, rejecting the ideas of black separatism and violence against whites and white institutions. Rather, he came to believe in the destruction of the capitalist state and the institution of a socialist community; he defended art as "a weapon of revolution." His work during this period, after 1974, included Hard Facts, Poetry for the Advanced, and What Was the Relationship of the Lone Ranger and the Means of Production? Profoundly revisionist of dominant cultural forms, Baraka has sought throughout his career to write in such a way that readers can find the means, through language, to envision an alternative to social arrangements as they are—an artistic practice the author has called revolutionary.

Ka 'Ba

AMIRI BARAKA

A closed window looks down
on a dirty courtyard, and black people
call across or scream across or walk across
defying physics in the stream of their will
Our world is full of sound   5
Our world is more lovely than anyone's
tho we suffer, and kill each other
and sometimes fail to walk the air

We are beautiful people
with african imaginations   10
full of masks and dances and swelling chants
with african eyes, and noses, and arms,
though we sprawl in grey chains in a place
full of winters, when what we want is sun.
We have been captured,   15
brothers. And we labor
to make our getaway, into
the ancient image, into a new

correspondence with ourselves
and our black family. We need magic   20
now we need the spells, to raise up
return, destroy, and create. What will be

the sacred words?

[1969]

Reprinted from *Black Magic Poetry*, by permission of Sterling Lord Literistic. Copyright
© 1969 by Amiri Baraka.

America

CLAUDE McKAY

Although she feeds me bread of bitterness,
And sinks into my throat her tiger's tooth,
Stealing my breath of life, I will confess
I love this cultured hell that tests my youth!
Her vigor flows like tides into my blood,   5
Giving me strength erect against her hate.
Her bigness sweeps my being like a flood.
Yet as a rebel fronts a king in state,
I stand within her walls with not a shred
Of terror, malice, not a word of jeer.   10
Darkly I gaze into the days ahead,
And see her might and granite wonders there,
Beneath the touch of Time's unerring hand,
Like priceless treasures sinking in the sand.

[1922]

First published in 1922, in the October edition of *The Literary Digest* and in McKay's collection, *Harlem Shadows*.

Langston Hughes
[1902–1967]

A major figure of the Harlem Renaissance, **LANGSTON HUGHES** *was born in Joplin, Missouri. His father left for Mexico in 1903, and after traveling for a time with his mother, Hughes moved to Lawrence, Kansas to live with his grandmother. He graduated from high school in Cleveland—again living with his mother—and then spent fifteen months with his father in Mexico and a year at Columbia University before he shipped on a merchant vessel abroad traveling to Africa. He worked for a year in Paris and Venice before returning to the United States.*

Hughes became interested in literature while still young, and published some of his most important poems before his trip abroad. In fact, by the time he was "discovered," working as a busboy, by poet Vachel Lindsay in 1925, he had already established himself as one of the central poets of the Harlem Renaissance. In 1921 The Crisis, *an important journal of African-American letters edited by W. E. B. Du Bois, was published. "The Negro Speaks of Rivers," and "The Weary Blues" appeared two years later in the* Amsterdam News *(a journal published in New York).*

Hughes worked in many genres, including drama, prose fiction, and journalism. He also edited literary anthologies, and offered support and encouragement for emerging writers such as Alice Walker and Gwendolyn Brooks. His first book of poetry, The Weary Blues, *was published in 1926, and his first novel,* Not Without Laughter, *appeared in 1930. He also collaborated for many years writing children's books with novelist Arna Bontemps. Besides the widely anthologized poems mentioned here, Hughes was also widely known for his sketches in the* Chicago Defender *featuring Harlem sage Jesse B. Semple. With Semple, Hughes created a persona through which he could humorously but pointedly address issues of race relations and the condition of African Americans.*

As a member of the Harlem Renaissance and a noted black man of letters, Hughes created controversy with his rejection of the bourgeois aspirations of upper-middle class African Americans, whose value systems he saw as a slavish imitation of white society. He worked toward a literature that was uniquely African American, rather than one that derived its structures and standards from the literatures of Europe. In poems such as "The Weary Blues" he sought to reproduce the rhythms of the blues and to focus on the realities of African-American life. His was a dominant voice in African-American literature, and he shed light on the concerns of black America far beyond the dissolution of the Harlem Renaissance.

—David L. G. Arnold, *University of Wisconsin, Stevens Point*

Dream Variations

LANGSTON HUGHES

To fling my arms wide
In some place of the sun,
To whirl and to dance
Till the white day is done.
Then rest at cool evening   5
Beneath a tall tree
While night comes on gently,
    Dark like me–
That is my dream!

To fling my arms wide   10
In the face of the sun,
Dance! Whirl! Whirl!
Till the quick day is done.
Rest at pale evening . . .
A tall, slim tree . . .   15
Night coming tenderly
    Black like me.

[1924]

Reprinted from *The Collected Poems of Langston Hughes,* by permission of Alfred A. Knopf, a division of Random House, Inc. Copyright © 1994 by The Estate of Langston Hughes.

Dream Boogie

LANGSTON HUGHES

Good morning, daddy!
Ain't you heard
The boogie-woogie rumble
Of a dream deferred?

Listen closely: 5
You'll hear their feet
Beating out and beating out a—

You think
It's a happy beat?

Listen to it closely: 10
Ain't you heard
something underneath
like a–

What did I say?

Sure,   15
I'm happy!
Take it away!

Hey, pop!
Re-bop!
Mop!   20

Y-e-a-h!

[1951]

Reprinted from *The Collected Poems of Langston Hughes,* by permission of Alfred A. Knopf, a division of Random House, Inc. Copyright © 1994 by The Estate of Langston Hughes.

Harlem [2]

LANGSTON HUGHES

What happens to a dream deferred?

Does it dry up
like a raisin in the sun?
Or fester like a sore—
And then run?   5
Does it stink like rotten meat?
Or crust and sugar over—
like a syrupy sweet?

Maybe it just sags
like a heavy load.   10

Or does it explode?

[1951]

Reprinted from *The Collected Poems of Langston Hughes,* by permission of Alfred A. Knopf, a division of Random House, Inc. Copyright © 1994 by The Estate of Langston Hughes.

Theme for English B

LANGSTON HUGHES

The instructor said,

   Go home and write
   a page tonight.
   And let that page come out of you—
   Then, it will be true.   5

I wonder if it's that simple?
I am twenty-two, colored, born in Winston-Salem.
I went to school there, then Durham,[1] then here
to this college on the hill above Harlem.[2]
I am the only colored student in my class.   10
The steps from the hill lead down into Harlem,
through a park, then I cross St. Nicholas,
Eighth Avenue, Seventh, and I come to the Y,[3]
the Harlem Branch Y, where I take the elevator
up to my room, sit down, and write this page: 15

It's not easy to know what is true for you or me
at twenty-two, my age. But I guess I'm what
I feel and see and hear, Harlem, I hear you:
hear you, hear me—we two—you, me, talk on this page.
(I hear New York, too.) Me—who?   20

---

[1] Winston-Salem and Durham are both cities in North Carolina.

[2] A famous African-American community in New York City. The college in question is the City College of New York.

[3] "The Y" is a nickname for the YMCA—the Young Men's Christian Association, which historically provides inexpensive accommodations.

Reprinted from *The Collected Poems of Langston Hughes,* by permission of Alfred A. Knopf, a division of Random House, Inc. Copyright © 1994 by The Estate of Langston Hughes.

Well, I like to eat, sleep, drink, and be in love.
I like to work, read, learn, and understand life.
I like a pipe for a Christmas present,
or records—Bessie, bop, or Bach.[4]
I guess being colored doesn't make me *not* like   25
the same things other folks like who are other races.
So will my page be colored that I write?
Being me, it will not be white.
But it will be
a part of you, instructor.   30
You are white—
yet a part of me, as I am a part of you.
That's American.
Sometimes perhaps you don't want to be a part of me.
Nor do I often want to be a part of you.   35
But we are, that's true!
As I learn from you,
I guess you learn from me—
although you're older—and white—
and somewhat more free.   40

This is my page for English B.

                                                              [1951]

---

[4]The speaker refers here to blues singer Bessie Smith (1894–1937), along with "bop" style jazz music, and German composer Johann Sebastian Bach (1685–1750).

I, Too

LANGSTON HUGHES

I, too, sing America.

I am the darker brother.
They send me to eat in the kitchen
When company comes,
But I laugh, 5
And eat well,
And grow strong.

Tomorrow,
I'll be at the table
When company comes. 10
Nobody'll dare
Say to me,
"Eat in the kitchen,"
Then.

Besides, 15
They'll see how beautiful I am
And be ashamed—

I, too, am America.

[1925]

Reprinted from *The Collected Poems of Langston Hughes,* by permission of Alfred A. Knopf, a division of Random House, Inc. Copyright © 1994 by The Estate of Langston Hughes.

Big Meeting

LANGSTON HUGHES

THE EARLY STARS HAD begun to twinkle in the August night as Bud and I neared the woods. A great many Negroes, old and young, were plodding down the dirt road on foot on their way to the Big Meeting. Long before we came near the lantern-lighted tent, we could hear early arrivals singing, clapping their hands lustily, and throwing out each word distinct like a drum-beat. Songs like "When the Saints Go Marching Home" and "That Old-Time Religion" filled the air.

In the road that ran past the woods, a number of automobiles and buggies belonging to white people had stopped near the tent so that their occupants might listen to the singing. The whites stared curiously through the hickory trees at the rocking figures in the tent. The canvas, except behind the pulpit, was rolled up on account of the heat, and the meeting could easily be seen from the road, so there beneath a tree Bud and I stopped, too. In our teens, we were young and wild and didn't believe much in revivals, so we stayed outside in the road where we could smoke and laugh like the white folks. But both Bud's mother and mine were under the tent singing, actively a part of the services. Had they known we were near, they would certainly have come out and dragged us in.

From frequent attendance since childhood at these Big Meetings held each summer in the South, we knew the services were divided into three parts. The testimonials and the song-service came first. This began as soon as two or three people were gathered together, continuing until the minister himself arrived. Then the sermon followed, with its accompanying songs and shouts from the audience. Then the climax came with the calling of the lost souls to the mourners' bench, and the prayers for sinners and backsliders. This was where Bud and I would leave. We were having too good a time being sinners, and we didn't want to be saved—not yet, anyway.

When we arrived, old Aunt Ibey Davis was just starting a familiar song:

> "Where shall I be when that first trumpet sound?
> Lawdy, where shall I be when it sound so loud?"

Reprinted from *Something in Common,* by permission of Farrar, Straus and Giroux, LLC. Copyright © 1963 by Langston Hughes.

The rapidly increasing number of worshipers took up the tune in full volume, sending a great flood of melody billowing beneath the canvas roof. With heads back, feet and hands patting time, they repeated the chorus again and again. And each party of new arrivals swung into rhythm as they walked up the aisle by the light of the dim oil lanterns hanging from the tent poles.

Standing there at the edge of the road beneath a big tree, Bud and I watched the people as they came—keeping our eyes open for the girls. Scores of Negroes from the town and nearby villages and farms came, drawn by the music and the preaching. Some were old and gray-headed; some in the prime of life; some mere boys and girls; and many little barefooted children. It was the twelfth night of the Big Meeting. They came from miles around to bathe their souls in a sea of song, to shout and cry and moan before the flow of Reverend Braswell's eloquence, and to pray for all the sinners in the county who had not yet seen the light. Although it was a colored folks' meeting, whites liked to come and sit outside in the road in their cars and listen. Sometimes there would be as many as ten or twelve parties of whites parked there in the dark, smoking and listening, and enjoying themselves, like Bud and I, in a not very serious way.

Even while old Aunt Ibey Davis was singing, a big red Buick drove up and parked right behind Bud and me beneath the tree. It was full of white people, and we recognized the driver as Mr. Parkes, the man who owned the drugstore in town where colored people couldn't buy a glass of soda at the fountain.

> *"It will sound so loud it will wake up the dead!*
> *Lawdy, where shall I be when it sound?"*

"You'll hear some good singing out here," Mr. Parkes said to a woman in the car with him.

"I always did love to hear darkies singing," she answered from the back seat.

Bud nudged me in the ribs at the word "darkie."

"I hear 'em," I said, sitting down on one of the gnarled roots of the tree and pulling out a cigarette.

The song ended as an old black woman inside the tent got up to speak. "I rise to testify dis evenin' fo' Jesus!" she said. "Ma Saviour an' ma Redeemer an' de chamber wherein I resusticates ma soul. Pray fo' me, brothers and sisters. Let yo' mercies bless me in all I do an' yo' prayers go with me on each travelin' voyage through dis land."

"Amen! Hallelujah!" cried my mother.

Just in front of us, near the side of the tent, a woman's clear soprano voice began to sing:

> *"I am a Po' pilgrim of sorrow*
> *Out in this wide world alone . . ."*

Soon others joined with her and the whole tent was singing:

> *"Sometimes I am tossed and driven,*
> *Sometimes I don't know where to go . . ."*

"Real pretty, ain't it?" said the white woman in the car behind us.

> *"But I've heard of a city called heaven*
> *And I've started to make it my home."*

When the woman finished her song, she rose and told how her husband left her with six children, her mother died in a poorhouse, and the world had always been against her—but still she was going on!

"My, she's had a hard time," giggled the woman in the car.

"Sure has," laughed Mr. Parkes, "to hear her tell it."

And the way they talked made gooseflesh come out on my skin.

"Trials and tribulations surround me—but I'm goin' on," the woman in the tent cried. Shouts and exclamations of approval broke out all over the congregation.

"Praise God!"

"Bless His Holy Name!"

"That's right, sister!"

"Devils beset me—but I'm goin' on!" said the woman. "I ain't got no friends—but I'm goin' on!"

"Jesus yo' friend, sister! Jesus yo' friend!" came the answer.

"God bless Jesus! I'm goin' on!"

"Dat's right!" cried Sister Mabry, Bud's mother, bouncing in her seat and flinging her arms outward. "Take all this world, but gimme Jesus!"

"Look at Mama," Bud said half amused, sitting there beside me smoking. "She's getting happy."

"Whoo-ooo-o-o! Great Gawd A'mighty!" yelled old man Walls near the pulpit. "I can't hold it dis evenin'! Dis mawnin', dis evenin', dis mawnin', Lawd!"

"Pray for me—cause I'm goin' on!" said the woman. In the midst of the demonstration she had created, she sat down exhausted, her armpits wet with sweat and her face covered with tears.

"Did you hear her, Jehover?" someone asked.

"Yes! He heard her! Halleloo!" came the answer.

"Dis mawnin', dis evenin', dis mawnin', Lawd!"
Brother Nace Eubanks began to line a song:

> *"Must Jesus bear his cross alone*
> *An' all de world go free?"*

Slowly they sang it line by line. Then the old man rose and told of a vision that had come to him long ago on that day when he had been changed from a sinner to a just man.

"I was layin' in ma bed," he said, "at de midnight hour twenty-two years past at Seven hundred fourteen Pine Street in dis here city when a snow-white sheep come in ma room an' stood behind de washbowl. Dis here sheep, hit spoke to me wid tongues o' fiah an' hit said, 'Nace, git up! Git up, an' come wid me!' Yes, suh! He had a light round 'bout his head like a moon, an' wings like a dove, an' he walked on hoofs o' gold an' dis sheep hit said, 'I once were lost, but now I'm saved, an' you kin be like me!" Yes, suh! An' ever since dat night, brothers an' sisters, I's been a chile o' de Lamb! Pray fo' me!"

"Help him, Jesus!" Sister Mabry shouted.

"Amen!" chanted Deacon Laws. "Amen! Amen!"

> *"Glory! Hallelujah!*
> *Let de halleluian roll*
>
> *I'll sing ma Saviour's praises far an' wide!"*

It was my mother's favorite song, and she sang it like a paean of triumph, rising from her seat.

"Look at Ma," I said to Bud, knowing that she was about to start her nightly shouting.

"Yah," Bud said. "I hope she don't see me while she's standing up there, or she'll come out here and make us go up to the mourners' bench."

"We'll leave before that," I said.

> *"I've opened up to heaven*
> *All de windows of ma soul,*
>
> *An' I'm livin' on de halleluian side!"*

Rocking proudly to and fro as the second chorus boomed and swelled beneath the canvas, Mama began to clap her hands, her lips silent now in this sea of song she had started, her head thrown back in joy—for my mother was a great shouter. Stepping gracefully to the beat of the music, she moved out toward the center aisle into a cleared space. Then she began to spring on her toes with little short rhythmical hops. All the way up the long aisle to the pulpit gently she leaped to the clap-clap of hands, the pat of feet, and the steady booming song of her fellow worshipers. Then Mama began to revolve in a dignified circle, slowly, as a great happiness swept her gleaming black features, and her lips curved into a smile.

> *"I've opened up to heaven*
> *All de windows of my soul . . ."*

Mama was dancing before the Lord with her eyes closed, her mouth smiling, and her head held high.

> *"I'm livin on de halleluian side!"*

As she danced, she threw her hands upward away from her breasts, as though casting off all the cares of the world.

Just then the white woman in Mr. Parkes's car behind us laughed. "My Lord, John, it's better than a show!"

Something about the way she laughed made my blood boil. That was *my mother* dancing and shouting. Maybe it was better than a show, but nobody had any business laughing at her, least of all white people.

I looked at Bud, but he didn't say anything. Maybe he was thinking how often we, too, made fun of the shouters, laughing at our parents as though they were crazy—but deep down inside us we understood why they came to Big Meeting. Working all day all their lives for white folks, they *had* to believe there was a "halleluian side."

I looked at Mama standing there singing, and I thought about how many years she had prayed and shouted and praised the Lord at church meetings and revivals, then came home for a few hours' sleep before getting up at dawn to go cook and scrub and clean for others. And I didn't want any white folks, especially whites who wouldn't let a Negro drink a glass of soda in their drugstore or give one a job, sitting in a car laughing at Mama.

"Gimme a cigarette, Bud. If these dopes behind us say any more, I'm gonna get up and tell 'em something they won't like."

"To hell with 'em," Bud answered.

I leaned back against the gnarled roots of the tree by the road and inhaled deeply. The white people were silent again in their car, listening to the singing. In the dark I couldn't see their faces to tell if they were still amused or not. But that was mostly what they wanted out of Negroes—work and fun—without paying for it, I thought, work and fun.

To a great hand-clapping body-rocking foot-patting rhythm, Mama was repeating the chorus over and over. Sisters leaped and shouted and perspiring brothers walked the aisles, bowing left and right, beating time, shaking hands, laughing aloud for joy, and singing steadily when, at the back of the tent, the Reverend Duke Braswell arrived.

A tall, powerful jet-black man, he moved with long steps through the center of the tent, his iron-gray hair uncovered, his green-black coat jim-swinging to his knees, his fierce eyes looking straight toward the altar. Under his arm he carried a Bible.

Once on the platform, he stood silently wiping his brow with a large white handkerchief while the singing swirled around him. Then he sang, too, his voice roaring like a cyclone, his white teeth shining. Finally he held up his palms for silence and the song gradually lowered to a hum, hum, hum, hands and feet patting, bodies still moving. At last, above the broken cries of the shouters and the undertones of song, the minister was able to make himself heard.

"Brother Garner, offer up a prayer."

Reverend Braswell sank on his knees and every back bowed. Brother Garner, with his head in his hands, lifted his voice against a background of moans:

"Oh, Lawd, we comes befo' you dis evenin' wid fear an' tremblin'—unworthy as we is to enter yo' house an' speak yo' name. We comes befo' you, Lawd, 'cause we knows you is mighty an' powerful in all de lands, an' great above de stars, an' bright above de moon. Oh, Lawd, you is bigger den de world. You holds de sun in yo' right hand an' de mornin' star in you' left, an' we po' sinners ain't nothin', not even so much as a grain o' sand beneath yo' feet. Yet we calls on you dis evenin' to hear us, Lawd, to send down yo' sweet Son Jesus to walk wid us in our sorrows to comfort us on our weary road 'cause sometimes we don't know which-a-way to turn! We pray you dis evenin', Lawd, to look down at our wanderin' chilluns what's gone from home. Look down in St. Louis, Lawd, an' look in Memphis, an' look down in Chicago if they's usin' Thy name in vain dis evenin', if they's gamblin' tonight, Lawd, if they's doin' any ways wrong—reach down an' pull 'em up, Lawd, an' say, 'Come wid me, cause I am de Vine an' de Husbandman an' de gate dat leads to Glory!' "

Remembering sons in faraway cities, "Help him, Jesus!" mothers cried.

"Whilst you's lookin' down on us dis evenin', keep a mighty eye on de sick an' de 'flicked. Ease Sister Hightower, Lawd, layin' in her bed at de pint o' death. An' bless Bro' Carpenter what's come out to meetin' here dis evenin' in spite o' his broken arm from fallin' off de roof. An' Lawd, aid de pastor dis evenin' to fill dis tent wid yo' Spirit, an' to make de sinners tremble an' back-sliders shout, an' dem dat is without de church to come to de moaners' bench an' find rest in Jesus! We ask Thee all dese favors dis evenin'. Also to guide us an' bless us wid Thy bread an' give us Thy wine to drink fo' Christ de Holy Saviour's sake, our Shelter an' our Rock. Amen!"

"There's not a friend like de lowly Jesus . . ."

Some sister began, high and clear after the passion of the prayer,

"No, not one! . . . No, not one!"

Then the preacher took his text from the open Bible. "Ye now therefore have sorrow: but I will see you again, and your hearts shall rejoice, and your joy no man taketh from you."

He slammed shut the Holy Book and walked to the edge of the platform. "That's what Jesus said befo' he went to the cross, children—'I will see you again, and yo' hearts shall rejoice!' "

"Yes sir!" said the brothers and sisters. "'Deed he did!"

Then the minister began to tell the familiar story of the death of Christ. Standing in the dim light of the smoking oil lanterns, he sketched the life of the man who had had power over multitudes.

"Power," the minister said. "Power! Without money and without titles, without position, he had power! And that power went out to the poor and afflicted. For Jesus said, 'The first shall be last, and the last shall be first.' "

"He sho did!" cried Bud's mother.

"Hallelujah!" Mama agreed loudly. "Glory be to God!"

"Then the big people of the land heard about Jesus," the preacher went on, "the chief priests and the scribes, the politicians, the bootleggers, and the bankers—and they begun to conspire against Jesus because *He had power!* This Jesus with His twelve disciples preachin' in Galilee. Then came that eve of the Passover, when he set down with His friends to eat and drink of the vine and the settin' sun fell behind the hills of Jerusalem. And Jesus knew that ere the cock crew, Judas would betray Him, and Peter would say, 'I know Him not,' and all alone by Hisself He would go to His death. Yes, sir, He knew! So He got up from the table and went into the garden to pray. In this hour of trouble, Jesus went to pray!"

Away at the back of the tent some old sister began to sing:

> *"Oh, watch with me one hour*
> *While I go yonder and pray . . ."*

And the crowd took up the song, swelled it, made its melody fill the hot tent while the minister stopped talking to wipe his face with his white handkerchief.

Then, to the humming undertone of the song, he continued, "They called it Gethsemane—that garden where Jesus fell down on His face in the grass and cried to the Father, 'Let this bitter hour pass from me! Oh, God, let this hour pass.' Because He was still a young man who did not want to die, He rose up and went back into the house—but His friends was all asleep. While Jesus prayed, His friends done gone to sleep! But, 'Sleep on,' he said, 'for the hour is at hand.' Jesus said, 'Sleep on.' "

"Sleep on, sleep on," chanted the crowd, repeating the words of the minister.

"He was not angry with them. But as Jesus looked out of the house, He saw that garden alive with men carryin' lanterns and swords and staves, and the mob was everywhere. So He went to the door. Then Judas come out from among the crowd, the traitor Judas, and kissed Him on the cheek—oh, bitter friendship! And the soldiers with handcuffs fell upon the Lord and took Him prisoner.

"The disciples was awake by now, oh yes! But they fled away because they was afraid. And the mob carried Jesus off.

"Peter followed Him from afar, followed Jesus in chains till they come to the palace of the high priest. There Peter went in, timid and afraid, to see the trial. He set in the back of the hall. Peter listened to the lies they told about Christ—and didn't dispute 'em. He watched the high priest spit in Christ's face—and made no move. He saw 'em smite Him with the palms of they hands—and Peter uttered not a word for his poor mistreated Jesus."

"Not a word! . . . Not a word! . . . Not a word!"

"And when the servants of the high priest asked Peter, 'Does you know this man?' he said, 'I do not!'

"And when they asked him a second time, he said, 'No!'

"And yet a third time, 'Do you know Jesus?'

"And Peter answered with an oath, 'I told you, no!'

"Then the cock crew."

"De cock crew!" cried Aunt Ibey Davis. "De cock crew! Oh, ma Lawd! De cock crew!"

"The next day the chief priests taken counsel against Jesus to put Him to death. They brought Him before Pilate, and Pilate said, 'What evil hath he done?'

"But the people cried, 'Crucify Him!' because they didn't care. So Pilate called for water and washed his hands.

"The soldiers made sport of Jesus where He stood in the Council Hall. They stripped Him naked, and put a crown of thorns on His head, a red robe about His body, and a reed from the river in His hands.

"They said, 'Ha! Ha! So you're the King! Ha! Ha!' And they bowed down in mockery before Him, makin' fun of Jesus.

"Some of the guards threw wine in His face. Some of the guards was drunk and called Him out o' His name—and nobody said, 'Stop! That's Jesus!' "

The Reverend Duke Braswell's face darkened with horror as he pictured the death of Christ. "Oh yes! Peter denied Him because he was afraid. Judas betrayed Him for thirty pieces of silver. Pilate said, 'I wash my hands—take Him and kill Him.'

"And His friends fled away! . . . Have mercy on Jesus! . . . His friends done fled away!"

"His friends!"

"His friends done fled away!"

The preacher chanted, half moaning his sentences, not speaking them. His breath came in quick, short gasps, with an indrawn "umn!" between each rapid phrase. Perspiration poured down his face as he strode across the platform, wrapped in this drama that he saw in the very air before his eyes. Peering over the heads of his audience out into the darkness, he began the ascent to Golgotha, describing the taunting crowd at Christ's heels and the heavy cross on His shoulders.

"Then a black man named Simon, blacker than me, come and took the cross and bore it for Him. Umn!

"Then Jesus were standin' alone on a high hill, in the broilin' sun, while they put the crosses in the ground. No water to cool His throat! No tree to shade His achin' head! Nobody to say a friendly word to Jesus! Umn!

"Alone, in that crowd on the hill of Golgotha, with two thieves bound and dyin', and the murmur of the mob all around. Umn!

"They laid they hands on Him, and they tore the clothes from His body— and then, and then"—loud as a thunderclap, the minister's voice broke through the little tent—"they raised Him to the cross!"

A great wail went up from the crowd. Bud and I sat entranced in spite of ourselves, forgetting to smoke. Aunt Ibey Davis wept. Sister Mabry moaned. In their car behind us the white people were silent as the minister went on:

> *"They brought four long iron nails*
> *And put one in the palm of His left hand.*

> *The hammer said . . . Bam!*
> *They put one in the palm of His right hand.*
> *The hammer said . . . Bam!*
> *They put one through His left foot . . . Bam!*
> *And one through His right foot . . . Bam!"*

"Don't drive it!" a woman screamed. "Don't drive them nails! For Christ's sake! Oh! Don't drive 'em!"

> *"And they left my Jesus on the cross!*
> *Nails in His hands! Nails in His feet!*
> *Sword in His side! Thorns circlin' His head!*
> *Mob cussin' and hootin' my Jesus! Umn!*
> *The spit of the mob in His face! Umn!*
> *His body hangin' on the cross! Umn!*
> *Gimme piece of His garment for a souvenir! Umn!*
> *Castin' lots for His garments! Umn!*
> *Blood from His wounded side! Umn!*
> *Streamin' down His naked legs! Umn!*
> *Droppin' in the dust—umn—*
> *That's what they did to my Jesus!*
> *They stoned Him first, they stoned Him!*
> *Called Him everything but a child of God.*
> *Then they lynched Him on the cross."*

In song I heard my mother's voice cry:

> *"Were you there when they crucified my Lord?*
> *Were you there when they nailed Him to the tree?"*

The Reverend Duke Braswell stretched wide his arms against the white canvas of the tent. In the yellow light his body made a cross-like shadow on the canvas.

> *"Oh, it makes me to tremble, tremble!*
> *Were you there when they crucified my Lord?"*

"Let's go," said the white woman in the car behind us. "This is too much for me!" They started the motor and drove noisily away in a swirl of dust.

"Don't go," I cried from where I was sitting at the root of the tree. "Don't go," I shouted, jumping up. "They're about to call for sinners to come to the mourners' bench. Don't go!" But their car was already out of earshot.

I didn't realize I was crying until I tasted my tears in my mouth.

[1935]

Robert Hayden
[1913–1980]

ROBERT HAYDEN *was born in Detroit. He was raised primarily in a foster home, a result of his parents having separated shortly after his birth. The marriage of his foster parents was contentious, and he suffered abuses in that home. He compensated for these and other unhappy conditions by voracious reading. He attended Detroit City College (later Wayne State University) in the early 1930s. He left there in 1936 to work in the Federal Writers' Project, where he researched black history and folk culture. Many other African-American writers at the time did the same, including Ralph Ellison, Richard Wright, and Margaret Walker. The two years he spent on the project gave him material he would employ in his poetry and dramatic work.*

The first volume of Hayden's poetry, Heart-Shape in the Dust *was published in 1940, after which he enrolled at the University of Michigan, where he studied with W. H. Auden. Hayden remained at the University of Michigan for several years before moving to Fisk University in 1946, where he taught for twenty-three years. His second volume of poetry, though never published, drew heavily on the research he did during the Federal Writers' Project years, investigating the force of the African-American presence in American history. Many of these poems appeared in the* Selected Poems *of 1966. Other collections included* The Lion and the Archer, Figures of Time *(1955);* A Ballad of Remembrance *(1962);* Words in the Mourning Time *(1970);* Night-Blooming Cereus *(1972);* Angle of Ascent *(1975);* American Journal *(1978 and 1982); and* Collected Poems *(1985). Hayden was also selected to be the Consultant in Poetry to the Library of Congress, from 1976 to 1978.*

Critical readings of Hayden's body of work reveal a great deal about the temper of the times. For instance, during the sixties, some partisans of the Black Arts Movement saw him as "insufficiently black," in the words of Pontheolla Williams. Other critics saw his work as driven by racial grievance, and thus not universal. Such debates are most useful in reconstructing the emergence of an adequate critical language for considering the writing of those whose work emerges from oppressive social circumstances. Reading Hayden now, attentive readers will appreciate his care with language, his view of African-American culture and history, and the emotional textures of his poems.

Homage to the Empress of the Blues[1]

ROBERT HAYDEN

Because there was a man somewhere in a candystripe silk shirt,
gracile and dangerous as a jaguar and because a woman moaned
for him in sixty-watt gloom and mourned him Faithless Love
Twotiming Love Oh Love Oh Careless Aggravating Love,

      She came out on the stage in yards of pearls, emerging like   *5*
      a favorite scenic view, flashed her golden smile and sang.

Because grey laths began somewhere to show from underneath
torn hurdygurdy[2] lithographs of dollfaced heaven;
and because there were those who feared alarming fists of snow
on the door and those who feared the riot-squad of statistics,   *10*

      She came out on the stage in ostrich feathers, beaded satin,
      and shone that smile on us and sang.

                              [1962]

---

[1]Bessie Smith (1895–1937), classic blues singer who recorded in the 1920s with jazz greats Fletcher
Henderson, Coleman Hawkins, and Louis Armstrong, among others.

[2]A hurdy-gurdy is a stringed instrument in which the strings are rubbed by a rosined wheel instead
of a bow; associated with street music.

Reprinted from *Collected Poems of Robert Hayden*, edited by Frederick Glaysher. Copyright
© 1966 by Robert Hayden. Reprinted by permission of Liveright Publishing Corporation.

Song Lyrics for HUMNT 1110: The Arts and Cultural Diversity

Reading Questions: What does each of these songs tell us about the African-American experience?

"Brown Sugar" Song Lyrics by The Rolling Stones

Gold coast slave ship bound for cotton fields
Sold in a market down in New Orleans
Scarred old slaver knows he's doing alright
Hear him whip the women just around midnight

Brown sugar how come you taste so good?
Brown sugar just like a young girl should

Drums beating, cold English blood runs hot
Lady of the house wonderin' where it's gonna stop
House boy knows that he's doing alright
You shoulda heard him just around midnight

Brown sugar how come you taste so good, now?
Brown sugar just like a young girl should, now

Ah, get along, brown sugar how come you taste so good, baby?
Ah, got me feelin' now, brown sugar just like a black girl should

I bet your mama was a tent show queen
And all here boyfriends were sweet sixteen
I'm no schoolboy but I know what I like
You shoulda heard me just around midnight

Brown sugar how come you taste so good, baby?
Ah, brown sugar just like a young girl should, yeah

I said yeah, yeah, yeah, woo
How come you...how come you taste so good?
Yeah, yeah, yeah, woo
Just like a...just like a black girl should
Yeah, yeah, yeah, woo

<u>Swing Low, Sweet Chariot</u>
Swing low, sweet chariot,
Coming for to carry me home,
Swing low, sweet chariot,
Coming for to carry me home.
I looked over Jordan, and what did I see?
Coming for to carry me home,
A band of angels coming after me,
Coming for to carry me home.
(Refrain)
If you get there before I do,
Coming for to carry me home,
Tell all my friends I'm coming, too.
Coming for to carry me home.
(Refrain)
I'm sometimes up and sometimes down,
Coming for to carry me home,
But still my soul feels heavenly bound,
Coming for to carry me home.
(Refrain)
The brightest day that I can say,
Coming for to carry me home,
When Jesus washed my sins away,
Coming for to carry me home.
(Refrain)

Follow the Drinking Gourd

When the sun goes back
and the first quail calls
Follow the drinking gourd
The old man is a-waitin' for
to carry you to freedom
Follow the drinking gourd

Chorus

Follow the drinking gourd,
follow the drinking gourd
For the old man is a-waitin'
to carry you to freedom
Follow the drinking gourd
The river bed makes a mighty fine road,
Dead trees to show you the way
And it's left foot, peg foot, traveling on
Follow the drinking gourd
The river ends between two hills
Follow the drinking gourd
There's another river on the other side
Follow the drinking gourd

<u>Stand by Me</u> by Ben E. King

When the night has come
And the land is dark
And the moon is the only light we'll see
No I won't be afraid, no I won't be afraid
Just as long as you stand, stand by me

And darlin', darlin', stand by me, oh now now stand by me
Stand by me, stand by me

If the sky that we look upon
Should tumble and fall
And the mountains should crumble to the sea
I won't cry, I won't cry, no I won't shed a tear
Just as long as you stand, stand by me

And darlin', darlin', stand by me, oh stand by me
Stand by me, stand by me, stand by me-e, yeah

Whenever you're in trouble won't you stand by me, oh now now stand by me
Oh stand by me, stand by me, stand by me

Darlin', darlin', stand by me-e, stand by me
Oh stand by me, stand by me, stand by me

Song Lyrics: <u>What's Going On</u> by Marvin Gaye

Mother, mother
There's too many of you crying
Brother, brother, brother
There's far too many of you dying
You know we've got to find a way
To bring some lovin' here today - Ya

Father, father
We don't need to escalate
You see, war is not the answer
For only love can conquer hate
You know we've got to find a way
To bring some lovin' here today

Picket lines and picket signs
Don't punish me with brutality
Talk to me, so you can see
Oh, what's going on
What's going on
Ya, what's going on
Ah, what's going on

In the mean time
Right on, baby
Right on
Right on

Father, father, everybody thinks we're wrong
Oh, but who are they to judge us
Simply because our hair is long
Oh, you know we've got to find a way
To bring some understanding here today
Oh

Picket lines and picket signs
Don't punish me with brutality
Talk to me
So you can see
What's going on
Ya, what's going on
Tell me what's going on
I'll tell you what's going on - Uh
Right on baby. Right on baby

Lyrics to "The Message" by Grandmaster Flash & the Furious Five
Broken glass everywhere
People pissing on the stairs, you know they just don't care
I can't take the smell, I can't take the noise
Got no money to move out, I guess I got no choice
Rats in the front room, roaches in the back
Junkie's in the alley with a baseball bat
I tried to get away, but I couldn't get far
Cause the man with the tow-truck repossessed my car

Chorus:
Don't push me, cause I'm close to the edge
I'm trying not to loose my head
It's like a jungle sometimes, it makes me wonder
How I keep from going under

Standing on the front stoop, hangin' out the window
Watching all the cars go by, roaring as the breezes blow
Crazy lady, livin' in a bag
Eating out of garbage piles, used to be a fag-hag
Search and test a tango, skips the life and then go
To search a prince to see the last of senses
Down at the peepshow, watching all the creeps
So she can tell the stories to the girls back home
She went to the city and got so so so ditty
She had to get a pimp, she couldn't make it on her
Own

Chorus:
It's like a jungle sometimes, it makes me wonder
How I keep from goin' under

My brother's doing fast on my mother's t.v.
Says she watches to much, is just not healthy
All my children in the daytime, dallas at night
Can't even see the game or the sugar ray fight
Bill collectors they ring my phone
And scare my wife when I'm not home
Got a bum education, double-digit inflation
Can't take the train to the job, there's a strike
At the station
Me on king kong standin' on my back
Can't stop to turn around, broke my sacroiliac
Midrange, migraine, cancered membrane
Sometimes I think I'm going insane, I swear I might
Hijack a plane!

Chorus:

My son said daddy I don't wanna go to school
Cause the teacher's a jerk, he must think I'm a fool
And all the kids smoke reefer, I think it'd be cheaper
If I just got a job, learned to be a street sweeper
I dance to the beat, shuffle my feet
Wear a shirt and tie and run with the creeps
Cause it's all about money, ain't a damn thing funny

You got to have a con in this land of milk and honey
They push that girl in front of a train
Took her to a doctor, sowed the arm on again
Stabbed that man, right in his heart
Gave him a transplant before a brand new start
I can't walk through the park, cause it's crazy
After the dark
Keep my hand on the gun, cause they got me on the run
I feel like an outlaw, broke my last fast jaw
Hear them say you want some more, livin' on a seesaw

Chorus:

A child was born, with no state of mind
Blind to the ways of mankind
God is smiling on you but he's frowning too
Cause only God knows what you go through
You grow in the ghetto, living second rate
And your eyes will sing a song of deep hate
The places you play and where you stay
Looks like one great big alley way
You'll admire all the number book takers
Thugs, pimps, pushers and the big money makers
Driving big cars, spending twenties and tens
And you wanna grow up to be just like them
Smugglers, scrambles, burglars, gamblers
Pickpockets, peddlers and even pan-handlers
You say I'm cool, I'm no fool
But then you wind up dropping out of high school
Now you're unemployed, all null 'n' void
Walking around like you're pretty boy floyd
Turned stickup kid, look what you done did
Got send up for a eight year bid
Now your man is took and you're a may tag
Spend the next two years as an undercover fag
Being used and abused, and served like hell
Till one day you was find hung dead in a cell
It was plain to see that your life was lost
You was cold and your body swung back and forth
But now your eyes sing the sad sad song
Of how you lived so fast and died so young

Public Enemy's: "Fight the Power" Song Lyrics

1989 the number another summer (get down)
Sound of the funky drummer
Music hittin' your heart cause I know you got soul
(Brothers and sisters, hey)
Listen if you're missin' y'all
Swingin' while I'm singin'
Givin' whatcha gettin'
Knowin' what I know
While the Black bands sweatin'
And the rhythm rhymes rollin'
Got to give us what we want
Gotta give us what we need
Our freedom of speech is freedom or death
We got to fight the powers that be
Lemme hear you say
Fight the power

Chorus

As the rhythm designed to bounce
What counts is that the rhymes
Designed to fill your mind
Now that you've realized the prides arrived
We got to pump the stuff to make us tough
from the heart
It's a start, a work of art
To revolutionize make a change nothin's strange
People, people we are the same
No we're not the same
Cause we don't know the game
What we need is awareness, we can't get careless
You say what is this?
My beloved lets get down to business
Mental self defensive fitness
(Yo) bum rush the show
You gotta go for what you know
Make everybody see, in order to fight the powers that be
Lemme hear you say...
Fight the Power

Chorus

Elvis was a hero to most
But he never meant ---- to me you see
Straight up racist that sucker was
Simple and plain
Mother---- him and John Wayne
Cause I'm Black and I'm proud
I'm ready and hyped plus I'm amped
Most of my heroes don't appear on no stamps
Sample a look back you look and find
Nothing but rednecks for 400 years if you check
Don't worry be happy
Was a number one jam

Damn if I say it you can slap me right here
(Get it) lets get this party started right
Right on, c'mon
What we got to say
Power to the people no delay
To make everybody see
In order to fight the powers that be

(Fight the Power)

N.W.A.'s "Fuck the Police"
Right about now NWA court is in full effect.
Judge Dre presiding in the case of NWA versus the police department.
Prosecuting attourneys are MC Ren Ice Cube and Eazy muthafuckin E.
Order order order. Ice Cube take the muthafuckin stand.
Do you swear to tell the truth the whole truth
and nothin but the truth so help your black ass?
<YOU'RE right! goddamn
Why don't you tell everybody what the fuck you gotta say?

Fuck tha police
Comin straight from the underground
Young nigga got it bad cuz I'm brown
And not the other color so police think
They have the authority to kill a minority

Fuck that shit, cuz I ain't tha one
For a punk muthafucka with a badge and a gun
To be beatin on, and throwin in jail
We could go toe to toe in the middle of a cell

Fuckin with me cuz I'm a teenager
With a little bit of gold and a pager
Searchin my car, lookin for the product
Thinkin every nigga is sellin narcotics

You'd rather see me in the pen
Then me and Lorenzo rollin in the Benzo
Beat tha police outta shape
And when I'm finished, bring the yellow tape
To tape off the scene of the slaughter
Still can't swallow bread and water

I don't know if they fags or what
Search a nigga down and grabbin his nuts
And on the other hand, without a gun they can't get none
But don't let it be a black and a white one
Cuz they slam ya down to the street top
Black police showin out for the white cop

Ice Cube will swarm
On any muthafucka in a blue uniform
Just cuz I'm from the CPT, punk police are afraid of me
A young nigga on a warpath
And when I'm finished, it's gonna be a bloodbath
Of cops, dyin in LA
Yo Dre, I got somethin to say

Fuck the police (4X)

Toni Morrison
[1931–   ]

TONI MORRISON'S *relationship to American literature has a multiplicity unlike that of any other writer in U.S. history: She has primarily made her mark as a writer of novels, but she has also been a literary editor—working for nearly twenty years at Random House—and a literary scholar, educator at Princeton University, and the author highly influential volume of literary criticism,* Playing in the Dark: Whiteness and the Literary Imagination *(1992). Morrison received the Nobel Prize in literature in 1993—only the eighth woman and the first African American to do so—on the strength of a literary career that includes the novels* The Bluest Eye *(1970),* Sula *(1974),* Song of Solomon *(1977),* Tar Baby *(1981),* Beloved *(1987), and* Jazz *(1992). Since that time, she has published two more novels,* Paradise *(1998) and* Love *(2003), and a series of children's books co-authored with her son, Slade, as well as editing two important volumes of cultural criticism,* Race-ing Justice, En-Gendering Power: Essays on Anita Hill, Clarence Thomas, and the Construction of Social Reality *(1992), and* Birth of a Nation'Hood: Gaze, Script, and Spectacle in the O.J. Simpson Case *(1997).*

Throughout her career as a novelist, Morrison focuses her work on the history of the black experience in America; as a literary editor, she helps foster the writing careers of a number of important African American authors, including Toni Cade Bambara; as a critic, she unflinchingly explores the role that the Africanist presence in the United States played in shaping the white cultural imagination. As Time Magazine *said of her work, Morrison produced "seismic effects" on the American literary scene, not only through her own fiction, but also through her influence on other authors of color, and her contributions to a race-conscious criticism of U.S. literature.*

Black Matters

TONI MORRISON

I am moved by fancies that are curled
Around these images, and cling:
The notion of some infinitely gentle
Infinitely suffering thing.

—T. S. ELIOT FROM "PRELUDES, IV"

THESE CHAPTERS PUT FORTH an argument for extending the study of American literature into what I hope will be a wider landscape. I want to draw a map, so to speak, of a critical geography and use that map to open as much space for discovery, intellectual adventure, and close exploration as did the original charting of the New World—without the mandate for conquest. I intend to outline an attractive, fruitful, and provocative critical project, unencumbered by dreams of subversion or rallying gestures at fortress walls.

I would like it to be clear at the outset that I do not bring to these matters solely or even principally the tools of a literary critic. As a reader (before becoming a writer) I read as I had been taught to do. But books revealed themselves rather differently to me as a writer. In that capacity I have to place enormous trust in my ability to imagine others and my willingness to project consciously into the danger zones such others may represent for me. I am drawn to the ways all writers do this: the way Homer renders a heart-eating cyclops so that our hearts are wrenched with pity; the way Dostoevsky compels intimacy with Svidrigailov and Prince Myshkin. I am in awe of the authority of Faulkner's Benjy, James's Maisie, Flaubert's Emma, Melville's Pip, Mary Shelley's Frankenstein—each of us can extend the list.[1]

I am interested in what prompts and makes possible this process of entering what one is estranged from—and in what disables the foray, for purposes of fiction, into corners of the consciousness held off and away from the reach

---

[1]The references are to Homer (c. 800 B.C.E.), *The Odyssey*; Fyodor Dostoyevsky *Crime and Punishment* (1821–1881), and *The Idiot*; William Faulkner (1897–1962), *The Sound and the Fury*; Henry James (1843–1916), *What Maisie Knew*; Gustave Flaubert (1821–1880), *Madame Bovary*; Herman Melville (1819–1891), *Moby Dick*; and Mary Shelley (1797–1851), *Frankenstein*. [Ed. note.]

Reprinted from *Playing in the Dark*, by permission of Vintage Books, a division of Random House, Inc. Copyright © 1992 by Toni Morrison.

of the writer's imagination. My work requires me to think about how free I can be as an African-American woman writer in my genderized, sexualized, wholly racialized world. To think about (and wrestle with) the full implications of my situation leads me to consider what happens when other writers work in a highly and historically racialized society. For them, as for me, imagining is not merely looking or looking at; nor is it taking oneself intact into the other. It is, for the purposes of the work, *becoming.*

My project rises from delight, not disappointment. It rises from what I know about the ways writers transform aspects of their social grounding into aspects of language, and the ways they tell other stories, fight secret wars, limn out all sorts of debates blanketed in their text. And rises from my certainty that writers always know, at some level, that they do this.

For some time now I have been thinking about the validity or vulnerability of a certain set of assumptions conventionally accepted among literary historians and critics and circulated as "knowledge." This knowledge holds that traditional, canonical American literature is free of, uninformed, and unshaped by the four-hundred-year-old presence of, first, Africans and then African-Americans in the United States. It assumes that this presence—which shaped the body politic, the Constitution, and the entire history of the culture—has had no significant place or consequence in the origin and development of that culture's literature. Moreover, such knowledge assumes that the characteristics of our national literature emanate from a particular "Americanness" that is separate from and unaccountable to this presence. There seems to be a more or less tacit agreement among literary scholars that, because American literature has been clearly the preserve of white male views, genius, and power, those views, genius, and power are without relationship to and removed from the overwhelming presence of black people in the United States. This agreement is made about a population that preceded every American writer of renown and was, I have come to believe, one of the most furtively radical impinging forces on the country's literature. The contemplation of this black presence is central to any understanding of our national literature and should not be permitted to hover at the margins of the literary imagination.

These speculations have led me to wonder whether the major and championed characteristics of our national literature—individualism, masculinity, social engagement versus historical isolation; acute and ambiguous moral problematics; the thematics of innocence coupled with an obsession with figurations of death and hell—are not in fact responses to a dark, abiding, signing Africanist presence. It has occurred to me that the very manner by which American literature distinguishes itself as a coherent entity exists because of this unsettled and unsettling population. Just as the formation of the nation necessitated coded language and purposeful restriction to deal with the racial disingenuousness and moral frailty at its heart, so too did the literature, whose founding characteristics extend into the twentieth century, reproduce the necessity for codes and restriction. Through significant and underscored omissions, startling contradictions, heavily nuanced conflicts, through the way writers peopled their work with the signs and bodies of this presence—one can see that a real or fabricated Africanist presence was crucial to their sense of Americanness. And it shows.

My curiosity about the origins and literary uses of this carefully observed, and carefully invented, Africanist presence has become an informal study of what I call American Africanism. It is an investigation into the ways in which a non-white, Africanlike (or Africanist) presence or persona was constructed in the United States, and the imaginative uses this fabricated presence served. I am using the term "Africanism" not to suggest the larger body of knowledge on Africa that the philosopher Valentine Mudimbe means by the term "Africanism,"[2] nor to suggest the varieties and complexities of African people and their descendants who have inhabited this country. Rather I use it as a term for the denotative and connotative blackness that African peoples have come to signify, as well as the entire range of views, assumptions, readings, and misreadings that accompany Eurocentric learning about these people. As a trope, little restraint has been attached to its uses. As a disabling virus within literary discourse, Africanism has become, in the Eurocentric tradition that American education favors, both a way of talking about and a way of policing matters of class, sexual license, and repression, formations and exercises of power, and meditations on ethics and accountability. Through the simple expedient of demonizing and reifying the range of color on a palette, American Africanism makes it possible to say and not say, to inscribe and erase, to escape and engage, to act out and act on, to historicize and render timeless. It provides a way of contemplating chaos and civilization, desire and fear, and a mechanism for testing the problems and blessings of freedom.

The United States, of course, is not unique in the construction of Africanism. South America, England, France, Germany, Spain—the cultures of all these countries have participated in and contributed to some aspect of an "invented Africa." None has been able to persuade itself for long that criteria and knowledge could emerge outside the categories of domination. Among Europeans and the Europeanized, this shared process of exclusion—of assigning designation and value—has led to the popular and academic notion that

[2]See Valentine Mudimbe, *The Idea of Africa* (Bloomington: Indiana University Press, 1994). [Ed note.]

racism is a "natural," if irritating, phenomenon. The literature of almost all these countries, however, is now subject to sustained critiques of its racialized discourse. The United States is a curious exception, even though it stands out as being the oldest democracy in which a black population accompanied (if one can use that word) and in many cases preceded the white settlers. Here in that nexus, with its particular formulations, and in the absence of real knowledge or open-minded inquiry about Africans and African-Americans, under the pressures of ideological and imperialistic rationales for subjugation, an American brand of Africanism emerged: strongly urged, thoroughly serviceable, companionably ego-reinforcing, and pervasive. For excellent reasons of state—because European sources of cultural hegemony were dispersed but not yet valorized in the new country—the process of organizing American coherence through a distancing Africanism became the operative mode of a new cultural hegemony.

These remarks should not be interpreted as simply an effort to move the gaze of African-American studies to a different site. I do not want to alter one hierarchy in order to institute another. It is true that I do not want to encourage those totalizing approaches to African-American scholarship which have no drive other than the exchange of dominations—dominant Eurocentric scholarship *replaced* by dominant Afrocentric scholarship. More interesting is what makes intellectual domination possible; how knowledge is transformed from invasion and conquest to revelation and choice; what ignites and informs the literary imagination, and what forces help establish the parameters of criticism.

Above all I am interested in how agendas in criticism have disguised themselves and, in so doing, impoverished the literature it studies. Criticism as a form of knowledge is capable of robbing literature not only of its own implicit and explicit ideology but of its ideas as well; it can dismiss the difficult, arduous work writers do to make an art that becomes and remains part of and significant within a human landscape. It is important to see how inextricable Africanism is or ought to be from the deliberations of literary criticism and the wanton, elaborate strategies undertaken to erase its presence from view.

What Africanism became for, and how it functioned in, the literary imagination is of paramount interest because it may be possible to discover, through a close look at literary "blackness," the nature—even the cause—of literary "whiteness." What is it *for*? What parts do the invention and development of whiteness play in the construction of what is loosely described as "American"? If such an inquiry ever comes to maturity, it may provide access to a deeper reading of American literature—a reading not completely available now, not least, I suspect, because of the studied indifference of most literary criticism to these matters.

One likely reason for the paucity of critical material on this large and compelling subject is that, in matters of race, silence and evasion have historically ruled literary discourse. Evasion has fostered another, substitute language in which the issues are encoded, foreclosing open debate. The situation is aggravated by the tremor that breaks into discourse on race. It is further complicated by the fact that the habit of ignoring race is understood to be a graceful, even generous, liberal gesture. To notice is to recognize an already discredited difference. To enforce its invisibility through silence is to allow the black body a shadowless participation in the dominant cultural body. According to this logic, every well-bred instinct argues *against noticing* and forecloses adult discourse. It is just this concept of literary and scholarly moeurs[3] (which functions smoothly in literary criticism, but neither makes nor receives credible claims in other disciplines) that has terminated the shelf life of some once extremely well-regarded American authors and blocked access to remarkable insights in their works.

These moeurs are delicate things, however, which must be given some thought before they are abandoned. Not observing such niceties can lead to startling displays of scholarly lapses in objectivity. In 1936 an American scholar investigating the use of Negro so-called dialect in the works of Edgar Allan Poe (a short article clearly proud of its racial equanimity) opens this way: "Despite the fact that he grew up largely in the south and spent some of his most fruitful years in Richmond and Baltimore, Poe has little to say about the darky."[4]

Although I know this sentence represents the polite parlance of the day, that "darky" was understood to be a term more acceptable than "nigger," the grimace I made upon reading it was followed by an alarmed distrust of the scholar's abilities. If it seems unfair to reach back to the thirties for samples of the kind of lapse that can occur when certain manners of polite repression are waived, let me assure you equally egregious representations of the phenomenon are still common.

Another reason for this quite ornamental vacuum in literary discourse on the presence and influence of Africanist peoples in American criticism is the pattern of thinking about racialism in terms of its consequences on the victim—of always defining it assymetrically from the perspective of its impact on the object of racist policy and attitudes. A good deal of time and intelligence has been invested in the exposure of racism and the horrific results on its objects. There are constant, if erratic, liberalizing efforts to legislate these

---

[3]Customs or behavior typical of a social group; mores. [Ed. note.]

[4]Killis Campbell, "Poe's Treatment of the Negro and of the Negro Dialect," *Studies in English*, 16 (1936), p. 106.

matters. There are also powerful and persuasive attempts to analyze the origin and fabrication of racism itself, contesting the assumption that it is an inevitable, permanent, and eternal part of all social landscapes. I do not wish to disparage these inquiries. It is precisely because of them that any progress at all has been accomplished in matters of racial discourse. But that well-established study should be joined with another, equally important one: the impact of racism on those who perpetuate it. It seems both poignant and striking how avoided and unanalyzed is the effect of racist inflection on the subject. What I propose here is to examine the impact of notions of racial hierarchy, racial exclusion, and racial vulnerability and availability on non-blacks who held, resisted, explored, or altered those notions. The scholarship that looks into the mind, imagination, and behavior of slaves is valuable. But equally valuable is a serious intellectual effort to see what racial ideology does to the mind, imagination, and behavior of masters.

Historians have approached these areas, as have social scientists, anthropologists, psychiatrists, and some students of comparative literature. Literary scholars have begun to pose these questions of various national literatures. Urgently needed is the same kind of attention paid to the literature of the western country that has one of the most resilient Africanist populations in the world—a population that has always had a curiously intimate and unhingingly separate existence within the dominant one. When matters of race are located and called attention to in American literature, critical response has tended to be on the order of a humanistic nostrum—or a dismissal mandated by the label "political." Excising the political from the life of the mind is a sacrifice that has proven costly. I think of this erasure as a kind of trembling hypochondria always curing itself with unnecessary surgery. A criticism that needs to insist that literature is not only "universal" but also "race-free" risks lobotomizing that literature, and diminishes both the art and the artist.

I am vulnerable to the inference here that my inquiry has vested interests; that because I am an African-American and a writer I stand to benefit in ways not limited to intellectual fulfillment from this line of questioning. I will have to risk the accusation because the point is too important: for both black and white American writers, in a wholly racialized society, there is no escape from racially inflected language, and the work writers do to unhobble the imagination from the demands of that language is complicated, interesting, and definitive.

Like thousands of avid but nonacademic readers, some powerful literary critics in the United States have never read, and are proud to say so, *any* African-American text. It seems to have done them no harm, presented them with no discernible limitations in the scope of their work or influence. I suspect, with much evidence to support the suspicion, that they will continue to flourish without any knowledge whatsoever of African-American literature. What is fascinating, however, is to observe how their lavish exploration of literature manages *not* to see meaning in the thunderous, theatrical presence of black surrogacy—an informing, stabilizing, and disturbing element—in the literature they do study. It is interesting, not surprising, that the arbiters of critical power in American literature seem to take pleasure in, indeed relish, their ignorance of African-American texts. What is surprising is that their refusal to read black texts—a refusal that makes no disturbance in their intellectual life—repeats itself when they reread the traditional, established works of literature worthy of their attention.

It is possible, for example, to read Henry James scholarship exhaustively and never arrive at a nodding mention, much less a satisfactory treatment, of the black woman who lubricates the turn of the plot and becomes the agency of moral choice and meaning in *What Maisie Knew*. Never are we invited to a reading of "The Beast in the Jungle"[5] in which that figuration is followed to what seems to me its logical conclusion. It is hard to think of any aspect of Gertrude Stein's *Three Lives* that has not been covered, except the exploratory and explanatory uses to which she puts the black woman who holds center stage in that work. The urgency and anxiety in Willa Cather's rendering of black characters are liable to be missed entirely; no mention is made of the problem that race causes in the technique and the credibility of her last novel, *Sapphira and the Slave Girl*. These critics see no excitement or meaning in the tropes of darkness, sexuality, and desire in Ernest Hemingway or in his cast of black men. They see no connection between God's grace and Africanist "othering" in Flannery O'Connor. With few exceptions, Faulkner criticism collapses the major themes of that writer into discursive "mythologies" and treats the later works—whose focus is race and class—as minor, superficial, marked by decline.

An instructive parallel to this willed scholarly indifference is the centuries-long, hysterical blindness to feminist discourse and the way in which women and women's issues were read (or unread). Blatant sexist readings are on the decline, and where they still exist they have little effect because of the successful appropriation by women of their own discourse.

National literatures, like writers, get along the best way they can, and with what they can. Yet they do seem to end up describing and inscribing what is really on the national mind. For the most part, the literature of the United States has taken as its concern the architecture of a *new white man*. If I am disenchanted by the indifference of literary criticism toward examining the range of that concern, I do have a lasting resort: the writers themselves.

---

[5]Short story by Henry James. [Ed. note.]

Writers are among the most sensitive, the most intellectually anarchic, most representative, most probing of artists. The ability of writers to imagine what is not the self, to familiarize the strange and mystify the familiar, is the test of their power. The languages they use and the social and historical context in which these languages signify are indirect and direct revelations of that power and its limitations. So it is to them, the creators of American literature, that I look for clarification about the invention and effect of Africanism in the United States.

My early assumptions as a reader were that black people signified little or nothing in the imagination of white American writers. Other than as the objects of an occasional bout of jungle fever, other than to provide local color or to lend some touch of verisimilitude or to supply a needed moral gesture, humor, or bit of pathos, blacks made no appearance at all. This was a reflection, I thought, of the marginal impact that blacks had on the lives of the characters in the work as well as the creative imagination of the author. To imagine or write otherwise, to situate black people throughout the pages and scenes of a book like some government quota, would be ludicrous and dishonest.

But then I stopped reading as a reader and began to read as a writer. Living in a racially articulated and predicated world, I could not be alone in reacting to this aspect of the American cultural and historical condition. I began to see how the literature I revered, the literature I loathed, behaved in its encounter with racial ideology. American literature could not help being shaped by that encounter. Yes, I wanted to identify those moments when American literature was complicit in the fabrication of racism, but equally important, I wanted to see when literature exploded and undermined it. Still, those were minor concerns. Much more important was to contemplate how Africanist personae, narrative, and idiom moved and enriched the text in self-conscious ways, to consider what the engagement meant for the work of the writer's imagination.

How does literary utterance arrange itself when it tries to imagine an Africanist other? What are the signs, the codes, the literary strategies designed to accommodate this encounter? What does the inclusion of Africans or African-Americans do to and for the work? As a reader my assumption had always been that nothing "happens": Africans and their descendants were not, in any sense that matters, *there;* and when they were there, they were decorative—displays of the agile writer's technical expertise. I assumed that since the author was not black, the appearance of Africanist characters or narrative or idiom in a work could never be *about* anything other than the "normal," unracialized, illusory white world that provided the fictional backdrop. Certainly no American text of the sort I am discussing was ever written *for* black people—

no more than *Uncle Tom's Cabin* was written for Uncle Tom to read or be persuaded by. As a writer reading, I came to realize the obvious: the subject of the dream is the dreamer. The fabrication of an Africanist persona is reflexive; an extraordinary meditation on the self; a powerful exploration of the fears and desires that reside in the writerly conscious. It is an astonishing revelation of longing, of terror, of perplexity, of shame, of magnanimity. It requires hard work *not* to see this.

It is as if I had been looking at a fishbowl—the glide and flick of the golden scales, the green tip, the bolt of white careening back from the gills; the castles at the bottom, surrounded by pebbles and tiny, intricate fronds of green; the barely disturbed water, the flecks of waste and food, the tranquil bubbles traveling to the surface—and suddenly I saw the bowl, the structure that transparently (and invisibly) permits the ordered life it contains to exist in the larger world. In other words, I began to rely on my knowledge of how books get written, how language arrives; my sense of how and why writers abandon or take on certain aspects of their project. I began to rely on my understanding of what the linguistic struggle requires of writers and what they make of the surprise that is the inevitable concomitant of the act of creation. What became transparent were the self-evident ways that Americans choose to talk about themselves through and within a sometimes allegorical, sometimes metaphorical, but always choked representation of an Africanist presence.

I have made much here of a kind of willful critical blindness—a blindness that, if it had not existed, could have made these insights part of our routine literary heritage. Habit, manners, and political agenda have contributed to this refusal of critical insight. A case in point is Willa Cather's *Sapphira and the Slave Girl*, a text that has been virtually jettisoned from the body of American literature by critical consensus.

References to this novel in much Cather scholarship are apologetic, dismissive, even cutting in their brief documentation of its flaws—of which there are a sufficient number. What remains less acknowledged is the source of its flaws and the conceptual problems that the book both poses and represents. Simply to assert the failure of Cather's gifts, the exhaustion of her perception, the narrowing of her canvas, evades the obligation to look carefully at what might have caused the book to fail—if "failure" is an intelligent term to apply to any fiction. (It is as if the realms of fiction and reality were divided by a line that, when maintained, offers the possibility of winning but, when crossed, signals the inevitability of losing.)

I suspect that the "problem" of *Sapphira and the Slave Girl* is not that it has a weaker vision or is the work of a weaker mind. The problem is trying to come to terms critically and artistically with the novel's concerns: the power and license of a white slave mistress over her female slaves. How can that *content* be subsumed by some other meaning? How can the story of a white mistress be severed from a consideration of race and the violence entailed in the story's premise?

If *Sapphira and the Slave Girl* neither pleases nor engages us, it may be enlightening to discover why. It is as if this last book—this troublesome, quietly dismissed novel, very important to Cather—is not only about a fugitive but is itself a fugitive from its author's literary estate. It is also a book that describes and inscribes its narrative's own fugitive flight from itself.

Our first hint of this flight appears in the title, *Sapphira and the Slave Girl.* The girl referred to is named Nancy. To have called the book "Sapphira and Nancy" would have lured Cather into dangerous deep water. Such a title would have clarified and drawn attention immediately to what the novel obscures even as it makes a valiant effort at honest engagement: the sycophancy of white identity. The story, briefly, is this.

Sapphira Colbert, an invalid confined to her chair and dependent on slaves for the most intimate services, has persuaded herself that her husband is having or aching to have a liaison with Nancy, the pubescent daughter of her most devoted female slave. It is clear from the beginning that Mistress Colbert is in error: Nancy is pure to the point of vapidity; Master Colbert is a man of modest habits, ambition, and imagination.

Sapphira's suspicions, fed by her feverish imagination and by her leisure to have them, grow and luxuriate unbearably. She forms a plan. She will invite a malleable lecherous nephew, Martin, to visit and let his nature run its course: Nancy will be seduced. The purpose of arranging the rape of her young servant is to reclaim, for purposes not made clear, the full attentions of her husband.

Interference with these plans comes from Sapphira's daughter, Rachel, estranged from her mother primarily for her abolitionist views but also, we are led to believe, because Sapphira does not tolerate opposition. It is Rachel who manages to effect Nancy's escape to the north and freedom, with the timid help of her father, Mr. Colbert. A reconciliation of all of the white characters takes place when the daughter loses one of her children to diphtheria and is blessed with the recuperation of the other. The reconciliation of the two key black characters is rendered in a postscript in which many years later Nancy returns to see her aged mother and recount her post-flight adult narrative to the author, a child witnessing the return and the happiness that is the novel's denouement. The novel was published in 1940, but has the shape and feel of a tale written or experienced much earlier.

This précis in no way does justice to the novel's complexities and its problems of execution. Both arise, I believe, not because Cather was failing in narrative power, but because of her struggle to address an almost completely buried subject: the interdependent working of power, race, and sexuality in a white woman's battle for coherence.

In some ways this novel is a classic fugitive slave narrative: a thrilling escape to freedom. But we learn almost nothing of the trials of the fugitive's journey because the emphasis is on Nancy's fugitive state within the household *before her escape*. And the real fugitive, the text asserts, is the slave mistress. Furthermore, the plot escapes the author's control and, as its own fugitive status becomes clear, is destined to point to the hopelessness of excising racial considerations from formulations of white identity.

Escape is the central focus of Nancy's existence on the Colbert farm. From the moment of her first appearance, she is forced to hide her emotions, her thoughts, and eventually her body from pursuers. Unable to please Sapphira, plagued by the jealousy of the darker-skinned slaves, she is also barred from help, instruction, or consolation from her own mother, Till. That condition could only prevail in a slave society where the mistress can count on (and an author can believe the reader does not object to) the complicity of a mother in the seduction and rape of her own daughter. Because Till's loyalty to and responsibility for her mistress is so primary, it never occurs and need not occur to Sapphira that Till might be hurt or alarmed by the violence planned for her only child. That assumption is based on another—that slave women are not mothers; they are "natally dead," with no obligations to their offspring or their own parents.

This breach startles the contemporary reader and renders Till an unbelievable and unsympathetic character. It is a problem that Cather herself seems hard put to address. She both acknowledges and banishes this wholly unanalyzed mother-daughter relationship by inserting a furtive exchange between Till and Rachel in chapter 10:

> "...Till asked in a low, cautious murmur: 'You ain't heard nothin', Miss Rachel?'
>
> 'Not yet. When I do hear, I'll let you know. I saw her into good hands, Till. I don't doubt she's in Canada by this time, amongst English people.'
>
> 'Thank you, mam, Miss Rachel. I can't say no more. I don't want them niggers to see me cryin'. If she's up there with the English folks, she'll have some chance.' "[6]

The passage seems to come out of nowhere because there has been nothing in a hundred or so pages to prepare us for such maternal concern. "You ain't heard nothin'?" Till asks of Rachel. Just that—those four words—meaning: Is

---

[6]Willa Cather, *Sapphira and the Slave Girl* (New York: Alfred A. Knopf, 1940), p. 249.

Nancy all right? Did she arrive safely? Is she alive? Is anybody after her? All of these questions lie in the one she does manage to ask.

Surrounding this dialogue is the silence of four hundred years. It leaps out of the novel's void and out of the void of historical discourse on slave parent-child relationships and pain. The contemporary reader is relieved when Till finally finds the language and occasion to make this inquiry about the fate of her daughter. But nothing more is made of it. And the reader is asked to believe that the silence surrounding the inquiry as well as its delay are due to Till's greater concern about her status among dark-skinned "field" niggers. Clearly Cather was driven to create the exchange not to rehabilitate Till in our readerly eyes but because at some point the silence became an unbearable violence, even in a work full of violence and evasion. Consider the pressures exerted by the subject: the need to portray the faithful slave; the compelling attraction of exploring the possibilities of one woman's absolute power over the body of another woman; confrontation with an uncontested assumption of the sexual availability of black females; the need to make credible the bottomless devotion of the person on whom Sapphira is totally dependent. It is after all *hers*, this slave woman's body, in a way that her own invalid flesh is not. These fictional demands stretch to breaking all narrative coherence. It is no wonder that Nancy cannot think up her own escape and must be urged into taking the risk.

Nancy has to hide her interior life from hostile fellow slaves *and* her own mother. The absence of camaraderie between Nancy and the other slave women turns on the device of color fetish—the skin-color privilege that Nancy enjoys because she is lighter than the others and therefore enviable. The absence of mother love, always a troubling concern of Cather's, is connected to the assumption of a slave's natal isolation. These are bizarre and disturbing deformations of reality that normally lie mute in novels containing Africanist characters, but Cather does not repress them altogether. The character she creates is at once a fugitive within the household and a sign of the sterility of the fiction-making imagination when there is no available language to clarify or even name the source of unbelievability.

Interestingly, the other major cause of Nancy's constant state of flight is wholly credible: that she should be unarmed in the face of the nephew's sexual assault and that she alone is responsible for extracting herself from the crisis. We do not question her vulnerability. What becomes titillating in this wicked pursuit of innocence—what makes it something other than an American variant of *Clarissa*[7]—is the racial component. The nephew is not

---

[7]Novel by Samuel Richardson (1689–1761), among the first authors of the English novel; *Clarissa*, the tragic story of a seduced young woman, was published in seven volumes, in 1747–1748. [Ed. note.]

even required to court or flatter Nancy. After an unsuccessful reach for her from the branches of a cherry tree, he can, and plans to, simply arrive wherever she is sleeping. And since Sapphira has ordered her to sleep in the hall on a pallet, Nancy is forced to sneak away in the dark to quarters where she may be, but is not certain to be, safe. Other than Rachel, the pro-abolitionist, Nancy has access to no one to whom she can complain, explain, object, or from whom she can seek protection. We must accept her total lack of initiative, for there are no exits. She has no recourse—except in miserable looks that arouse Rachel's curiosity.

Nor is there any law, if the nephew succeeds in the rape, to entertain her complaint. If she becomes pregnant as a result of the violence, the issue is a boon to the economy of the estate, not an injury to it. There is no father or, in this case, "stepfather" to voice a protest on Nancy's behalf, since honor was the first thing stripped from the man. He is a "capon,"[8] we are told, given to Till so that she will have no more children and can give her full attention and energy to Mistress Sapphira.

Rendered voiceless, a cipher, a perfect victim, Nancy runs the risk of losing the reader's interest. In a curious way, Sapphira's plotting, like Cather's plot, is without reference to the characters and exists solely for the ego-gratification of the slave mistress. This becomes obvious when we consider what would have been the consequences of a successful rape. Given the novel's own terms, there can be no grounds for Sapphira's thinking that Nancy can be "ruined" in the conventional sense. There is no question of marriage to Martin, to Colbert, to anybody. Then, too, why would such an assault move her slave girl outside her husband's interest? The probability is that it would secure it. If Mr. Colbert is tempted by Nancy the chaste, is there anything in slavocracy to make him disdain Nancy the unchaste?

Such a breakdown in the logic and machinery of plot construction implies the powerful impact race has on narrative—and on narrative strategy. Nancy is not only the victim of Sapphira's evil, whimsical scheming. She becomes the unconsulted, appropriated ground of Cather's inquiry into what is of paramount importance to the author: the reckless, unabated power of a white woman gathering identity unto herself from the wholly available and serviceable lives of Africanist others. This seems to me to provide the coordinates of an immensely important moral debate.

This novel is not a story of a mean, vindictive mistress; it is the story of a desperate one. It concerns a troubled, disappointed woman confined to the prison of her defeated flesh, whose social pedestal rests on the sturdy spine of

---

[8] A capon is a castrated male chicken; the implication is that Till's husband has been similarly castrated. [Ed. note.]

racial degradation; whose privileged gender has nothing that elevates it except color, and whose moral posture collapses without a whimper before the greater necessity of self-esteem, even though the source of that esteem is a delusion. For Sapphira too is a fugitive in this novel, committed to escape: from the possibility of developing her own adult personality and her own sensibilities; from her femaleness; from motherhood; from the community of women; from her body.

She escapes the necessity of inhabiting her own body by dwelling on the young, healthy, and sexually appetizing Nancy. She has transferred its care into the hands of others. In this way she escapes her illness, decay, confinement, anonymity, and physical powerlessness. In other words, she has the leisure and the instruments to construct a self; but the self she constructs must be—is conceivable only as—white. The surrogate black bodies become her hands and feet, her fantasies of sexual ravish and intimacy with her husband, and, not inconsiderably, her sole source of love.

If the Africanist characters and their condition are removed from the text of *Sapphira and the Slave Girl* we will not have a Miss Havisham[9] immured or in flames. We have nothing: no process of deranged self-construction that can take for granted acquiescence in so awful an enterprise; no drama of limitless power. Sapphira can hide far more successfully than Nancy. She can, and does, remain outside the normal requirements of adult womanhood because of the infantilized Africanist population at her disposal.

The final fugitive in Cather's novel is the novel itself. The plot's own plotting to free the endangered slave girl (of no apparent interest, as we have seen, to the girl's mother or her slave associates) is designed for quite other purposes. It functions as a means for the author to meditate on the moral equivalence of free white women and enslaved black women. The fact that these equations are designed as mother-daughter pairings and relationships leads to the inescapable conclusion that Cather was dreaming and redreaming her problematic relationship with her own mother.

The imaginative strategy is a difficult one at best, an impossible one in the event—so impossible that Cather permits the novel to escape from the pages of fiction into nonfiction. For narrative credibility she substitutes her own determination to force the equation. It is an equation that must take place outside the narrative.

Sapphira and the Slave Girl turns at the end into a kind of memoir, the author's recollection of herself as a child witnessing the return, the reconciliation, and an imposed "all rightness" in untenable, outrageous circumstances.

---

[9] A central character, a spinster, in Charles Dickens's *Great Expectations*. [Ed.note.]

The silenced, acquiescent Africanist characters in the narrative are not less muzzled in the epilogue. The reunion—the drama of it, like its narrative function—is no more the slave characters' than their slave lives have been. The reunion is literally stage-managed for the author, now become a child. Till agrees to wait until little Willa is at the doorway before she permits herself the first sight she has had of her daughter in twenty-five years.

Only with Africanist characters is such a project thinkable: delayed gratification for the pleasure of a (white) child. When the embrace is over, Willa the white child accompanies the black mother and daughter into their narrative, listening to the dialogue but intervening in it at every turn. The shape and detail and substance of their lives are hers, not theirs. Just as Sapphira has employed these surrogate, serviceable black bodies for her own purposes of power without risk, so the author employs them in behalf of her own desire for a *safe* participation in loss, in love, in chaos, in justice.

But things go awry. As often happens, characters make claims, impose demands of imaginative accountability over and above the author's will to contain them. Just as Rachel's intervention foils Sapphira's plot, so Cather's urgent need to know and understand this Africanist mother and daughter requires her to give them center stage. The child Cather listens to Till's stories, and the slave, silenced in the narrative, has the final words of the epilogue.

Yet even, or especially, here where the novel ends Cather feels obliged to gesture compassionately toward slavery. Through Till's agency the elevating benevolence of the institution is invoked. Serviceable to the last, this Africanist presence is permitted speech only to reinforce the slaveholders' ideology, in spite of the fact that it subverts the entire premise of the novel. Till's voluntary genuflection is as ecstatic as it is suspicious.

In returning to her childhood, at the end of her writing career, Cather returns to a very personal, indeed private experience. In her last novel she works out and toward the meaning of female betrayal as it faces the void of racism. She may not have arrived safely, like Nancy, but to her credit she did undertake the dangerous journey.

[1993]

Zora Neale Hurston
[1901?–1960]

A multifaceted writer and intellectual, ZORA NEALE HURSTON published novels, an autobiography, and works on sociology and folklore. Though she was the most prolific female writer of the Harlem Renaissance, she fell out of the public eye during the fifties, supporting herself as a maid, and dying penniless and forgotten in 1960. She was buried in an unmarked grave.

Hurston's unique perspective on African-American life and culture derives in part from her upbringing in Eatonville, Florida, an all-black community. In this setting, free from the most immediate effects of white racism, she was able to develop a sense of herself and of black culture that later blossomed in her novel Their Eyes Were Watching God (1937), and also in her collections of African-American and Haitian folktales and legends, Mules and Men (1935) and Tell My Horse (1938). Unlike her Harlem Renaissance contemporary and sometime collaborator Langston Hughes, she was less concerned with the specific plight of African Americans, and more concerned with the nuances of human relationships, particularly those between men and women.

Hurston's mother was a schoolteacher, and she imbued her child with a sense of limitless potential. After her mother's early death, Hurston bounced between family members before setting out on her own. In 1918 Hurston entered Howard University in Washington, D.C., where she took literature classes in hopes of becoming a writer. Here she met Alain Locke, one of the earliest and most important writers of the Harlem Renaissance, who encouraged her to move to New York. After one of her stories was published in a New York literary journal, Hurston took his advice. In New York her vivacious personality and natural gifts as a storyteller quickly led her into the literary circles, and she soon landed a job as the secretary of prominent white novelist Fannie Hurst. At this time she also received a scholarship to study at Barnard College, where her contact with noted anthropologist Franz Boas kindled a lifelong passion to record the folkways of her native Florida and the Caribbean. She graduated from Barnard in 1928.

Hurston's first novel, Jonah's Gourd Vine, was published in 1934. A loose combination of the Southern folklore she had collected after graduation, and the history and experiences of her parents, the novel was featured as a Book-of-the-Month Club selection. This critical attention lead to the publication of Mules and Men, and to a Guggenheim fellowship for continued research into Southern folk culture. While conducting this research she completed Their Eyes Were Watching God (1937), her most acclaimed novel. In 1942 she published her autobiography, Dust Tracks on a Road, which was also a critical success. Members of the African-American community complained, however, that it failed to treat issues of racism and the suppression of blacks in America. Most notably, African-American writer Richard Wright excoriated her for neglecting to focus on racial politics. "The Gilded Six-Bits," first published in Story magazine in 1933, represents this inclination. Although the white world surrounding Eatonville is always understood as a presence, it has only a remote effect on this story of primarily intra-racial conflict.

Hurston's work is important because of the picture it presents of African-American folk culture, a culture full of humor, wry wit, wisdom, and humanity. Though her popularity declined during the last years of her life, partly due to her racial politics and partly due to an unsubstantiated charge of child molestation, Hurston inspires a generation of African-American woman writers such as Alice Walker. Her fiction and research display aspects of African-American and African diaspora culture to which white society has little access, but beyond this she demonstrates a sensitivity to the way human beings interact with one another that places her on a par with the best writers of her age.

—Lisa Perdigao, *Florida Institute of Technology*

The Gilded Six-Bits

ZORA NEALE HURSTON

IT WAS A NEGRO YARD around a Negro house in a Negro settlement that looked to the payroll of the G. and G. Fertilizer works for its support.

But there was something happy about the place. The front yard was parted in the middle by a sidewalk from gate to doorstep, a sidewalk edged on either side by quart bottles driven neck down into the ground on a slant. A mess of homey flowers planted without a plan but blooming cheerily from their helter-skelter places. The fence and house were whitewashed. The porch and steps scrubbed white.

The front door stood open to the sunshine so that the floor of the front room could finish drying after its weekly scouring. It was Saturday. Everything clean from the front gate to the privy house. Yard raked so that the strokes of the rake would make a pattern. Fresh newspaper cut in fancy edge on the kitchen shelves.

Missie May was bathing herself in the galvanized washtub[1] in the bedroom. Her dark-brown skin glistened under the soapsuds that skittered down from her washrag. Her stiff young breasts thrust forward aggressively, like broad-based cones with the tips lacquered in black.

She heard men's voices in the distance and glanced at the dollar clock on the dresser.

"Humph! Ah'm way behind time t'day! Joe gointer be heah 'fore Ah git mah clothes on if Ah don't make haste."

She grabbed the clean mealsack at hand and dried herself hurriedly and began to dress. But before she could tie her slippers, there came the ring of singing metal on wood. Nine times.

Missie May grinned with delight. She had not seen the big tall man come stealing in the gate and creep up the walk grinning happily at the joyful mischief he was about to commit. But she knew that it was her husband throwing

---

[1]Tub made from sheet tin that has been coated with rust-resistant zinc.

Reprinted from *The Complete Stories,* by permission of HarperCollins Publishers, Inc. Copyright © 1995 by Henry Louis Gates, Jr. and Sieglinde Lemke.

silver dollars in the door for her to pick up and pile beside her plate at dinner. It was this way every Saturday afternoon. The nine dollars hurled into the open door, he scurried to a hiding place behind the Cape jasmine bush and waited.

Missie May promptly appeared at the door in mock alarm.

"Who dat chunkin' money in mah do'way?" she demanded. No answer from the yard. She leaped off the porch and began to search the shrubbery. She peeped under the porch and hung over the gate to look up and down the road. While she did this, the man behind the jasmine darted to the chinaberry tree. She spied him and gave chase.

"Nobody ain't gointer be chunkin' money at me and Ah not do 'em nothin'," she shouted in mock anger. He ran around the house with Missie May at his heels. She overtook him at the kitchen door. He ran inside but could not close it after him before she crowded in and locked with him in a rough-and-tumble. For several minutes the two were a furious mass of male and female energy. Shouting, laughing, twisting, turning, tussling, tickling each other in the ribs; Missie May clutching onto Joe and Joe trying, but not too hard, to get away.

"Missie May, take yo' hand out mah pocket!" Joe shouted out between laughs.

"Ah ain't, Joe, not lessen you gwine gimme whateve' it is good you got in yo' pocket. Turn it go, Joe, do Ah'll tear yo' clothes."

"Go on tear 'em. You de one dat pushes de needles round heah. Move yo' hand, Missie May."

"Lemme git dat paper sak out yo' pocket. Ah bet it's candy kisses."

"Tain't. Move yo' hand. Woman ain't got no business in a man's clothes nohow. Go way."

Missie May gouged way down and gave an upward jerk and triumphed.

"Unhhunh! Ah got it! It 'tis so candy kisses. Ah knowed you had somethin' for me in yo' clothes. Now Ah got to see whut's in every pocket you got."

Joe smiled indulgently and let his wife go through all of his pockets and take out the things that he had hidden for her to find. She bore off the chewing gum, the cake of sweet soap, the pocket handkerchief as if she had wrested them from him, as if they had not been bought for the sake of this friendly battle.

"Whew! dat play-fight done got me all warmed up!" Joe exclaimed. "Got me some water in de kittle?"

"Yo' water is on de fire and yo' clean things is cross de bed. Hurry up and wash yo'self and git changed so we kin eat. Ah'm hongry." As Missie said this, she bore the steaming kettle into the bedroom.

"You ain't hongry, sugar," Joe contradicted her. "Youse jes' a little empty. Ah'm de one whut's hongry. Ah could eat up camp meetin', back off 'ssociation, and drink Jurdan[2] dry. Have it on de table when Ah git out de tub."

"Don't you mess wid mah business, man. You git in yo' clothes. Ah'm a real wife, not no dress and breath. Ah might not look lak one, but if you burn me, you won't git a thing but wife ashes."

Joe splashed in the bedroom and Missie May fanned around in the kitchen. A fresh red-and-white checked cloth on the table. Big pitcher of buttermilk beaded with pale drops of butter from the churn. Hot fried mullet,[3] crackling bread, ham hock atop a mound of string beans and new potatoes, and perched on the windowsill a pone of spicy potato pudding.

Very little talk during the meal but that little consisted of banter that pretended to deny affection but in reality flaunted it. Like when Missie May reached for a second helping of the tater pone. Joe snatched it out of her reach.

After Missie May had made two or three unsuccessful grabs at the pan, she begged, "Aw, Joe, gimme some mo' dat tater pone."

"Nope, sweetenin' is for us menfolks. Y'all pritty lil frail eels don't need nothin' lak dis. You too sweet already."

"Please, Joe."

"Naw, naw. Ah don't want you to git no sweeter than whut you is already. We goin' down de road a lil piece t'night so you go put on yo' Sunday-go-to-meetin' things."

Missie May looked at her husband to see if he was playing some prank. "Sho nuff, Joe?"

"Yeah. We goin' to de ice cream parlor."

"Where de ice cream parlor at, Joe?"

"A new man done come heah from Chicago and he done got a place and took and opened it up for a ice cream parlor, and bein' as it's real swell, Ah wants you to be one de first ladies to walk in dere and have some set down."

"Do Jesus, Ah ain't knowed nothin' bout it. Who de man done it?"

"Mister Otis D. Slemmons, of spots and places—Memphis, Chicago, Jacksonville, Philadelphia and so on."

"Dat heavyset man wid his mouth full of gold teeths?"

"Yeah. Where did you see 'im at?"

"Ah went down to de sto' tuh git a box of lye[4] and Ah seen 'im standin' on de corner talkin' to some of de mens, and Ah come on back and went to

---

[2]This allusion to the biblical river Jordan is consistent with Joe's playful religious theme.

[3]Bottom-dwelling freshwater fish.

[4]Soap made from caustic alkali ("lye").

scrubbin' de floor, and he passed and tipped his hat whilst Ah was scourin' de steps. Ah thought Ah never seen *him* befo'. "

Joe smiled pleasantly. "Yeah, he's up-to-date. He got de finest clothes Ah ever seen on a colored man's back."

"Aw, he don't look no better in his clothes than you do in yourn. He got a puzzlegut on 'im and be so chuckleheaded he got a pone behind his neck."[5]

Joe looked down at his own abdomen and said wistfully: "Wisht Ah had a build on me lak he got. He ain't puzzlegutted, honey. He jes' got a corperation.[6] Dat make 'm look lak a rich white man. All rich mens is got some belly on 'em."

"Ah seen de pitchers of Henry Ford and he's a spare-built man and Rockefeller look lak he ain't got but one gut. But Ford and Rockefeller[7] and dis Slemmons and all de rest kin be as many-gutted as dey please, Ah's satisfied wid you jes' lak you is baby. God took pattern after a pine tree and built you noble. Youse a pritty man, and if Ah knowed any way to make you mo' pritty still Ah'd take and do it."

Joe reached over gently and toyed with Missie May's ear. "You jes' say dat cause you love me, but Ah know Ah can't hold no light to Otis D. Slemmons. Ah ain't never been nowhere and Ah ain't got nothin' but you."

Missie May got on his lap and kissed him and he kissed back in kind. Then he went on. "All de womens is crazy 'bout 'im everywhere he go."

"How you know dat, Joe?"

"He tole us so hisself."

"Dat don't make it so. His mouf is cut crossways, ain't it? Well, he kin lie jes' lak anybody else."

"Good Lawd, Missie! You womens sho is hard to sense into things. He's got a five-dollar gold piece for a stickpin and he got a ten-dollar gold piece on his watch chain and his mouf is jes' crammed full of gold teeths. Sho wisht it wuz mine. And whut make it so cool, he got money 'cumulated. And womens give it all to 'im."

"Ah don't see whut de womens see on 'im. Ah wouldn't give 'im a wink if de sheriff wuz after 'im."

"Well, he tole us how de white womens in Chicago give 'im all dat gold money. So he don't 'low nobody to touch it at all. Not even put day finger on it. Dey told 'im not to. You kin make 'miration at it, but don't tetch it."

---

[5]The general impression offered here is that Slemmons is unattractively fat and stupid.

[6]Slang for physical build.

[7]Automobile manufacturer Henry Ford (1863–1947) and oil magnate John D. Rockefeller (1839–1937) were both wealthy American industrialists of the late nineteenth and early twentieth century.

"Whyn't he stay up dere where dey so crazy 'bout 'im?"

"Ah reckon dey done made 'im vast-rich and he wants to travel some. He says dey wouldn't leave 'im hit a lick of work. He got mo' lady people crazy 'bout him than he kin shake a stick at."

"Joe, Ah hates to see you so dumb. Dat stray nigger jes' tell y'all anything and y'all b'lieve it."

"Go 'head on now, honey, and put on yo' clothes. He talkin' 'bout his pritty womens—Ah want 'im to see *mine*."

Missie May went off to dress and Joe spent the time trying to make his stomach punch out like Slemmon's middle. He tried the rolling swagger of the stranger, but found that his tall bone-and-muscle stride fitted ill with it. He just had time to drop back into his seat before Missie May came in dressed to go.

On the way home that night Joe was exultant. "Didn't Ah say ole Otis was swell? Can't he talk Chicago talk? Wuzn't dat funny whut he said when great big fat ole Ida Armstrong come in? He asted me, 'Who is dat broad wid de forte shake?' Dat's a new word. Us always thought forty was a set of figgers but he showed us where it means a whole heap of things. Sometimes he don't say forty, he jes' say thirty-eight and two and dat mean de same thing. Know whut he told me when Ah wuz payin' for our ice cream? He say, Ah have to hand it to you, Joe. Dat wife of yours is jes' thirty-eight and two. Yessuh, she's forte!'[8] Ain't he killin'?"

"He'll do in case of a rush. But he sho is got uh heap uh gold on 'im. Dat's de first time Ah ever seed gold money. It lookted good on him sho nuff, but it'd look a whole heap better on you."

"Who, me? Missie May, youse crazy! Where would a po' man lak me git gold money from?"

Missie May was silent for a minute, then she said, "Us might find some goin' long de road some time. Us could."

"Who would be losin' gold money round heah? We ain't even seen none dese white folks wearin' no gold money on dey watch chain. You must be figgerin' Mister Packard or Mister Cadillac[9] goin' pass through heah."

"You don't know whut been lost 'round heah. Maybe somebody way back in memorial times lost they gold money and went on off and it ain't never been found. And then if we wuz to find it, you could wear some 'thout havin' no gang of womens lak dat Slemmons say he got."

---

[8]Italian for "strong," the word "forte" (pronounced "for-tay") can also mean loud (as in musical terminology) or can be used as a noun to mean "strength." Slemmons appears to be playing on the homonym "forty" to suggest forte as an adjective meaning "strong."

[9]Packard and Cadillac are expensive car makes.

Joe laughed and hugged her. "Don't be so wishful 'bout me. Ah'm satisfied de way Ah is. So long as Ah be yo' husband. Ah don't keer 'bout nothin' else. Ah'd ruther all de other womens in de world to be dead than for you to have de toothache. Less we go to bed and git our night rest."

It was Saturday night once more before Joe could parade his wife in Slemmons's ice cream parlor again. He worked the night shift and Saturday was his only night off. Every other evening around six o'clock he left home, and dying dawn saw him hustling home around the lake, where the challenging sun flung a flaming sword from east to west across the trembling water.

That was the best part of life—going home to Missie May. Their whitewashed house, the mock battle on Saturday, the dinner and ice cream parlor afterwards, church on Sunday nights when Missie outdressed any woman in town—all, everything, was right.

One night around eleven the acid ran out at the G. and G. The foreman knocked off the crew and let the steam die down. As Joe rounded the lake on his way home, a lean moon rode the lake in a silver boat. If anybody had asked Joe about the moon on the lake, he would have said he hadn't paid it any attention. But he saw it with his feelings. It made him yearn painfully for Missie. Creation obsessed him. He thought about children. They had been married more than a year now. They had money put away. They ought to be making little feet for shoes. A little boy child would be about right.

He saw a dim light in the bedroom and decided to come in through the kitchen door. He could wash the fertilizer dust off himself before presenting himself to Missie May. It would be nice for her not to know that he was there until he slipped into his place in bed and hugged her back. She always liked that.

He eased the kitchen door open slowly and silently, but when he went to set his dinner bucket on the table he bumped it into a pile of dishes, and something crashed to the floor. He heard his wife gasp in fright and hurried to reassure her.

"Iss me, honey. Don't git skeered."

There was a quick, large movement in the bedroom. A rustle, a thud, and a stealthy silence. The light went out.

What? Robbers? Murderers? Some varmint attacking his helpless wife, perhaps. He struck a match, threw himself on guard and stepped over the doorsill into the bedroom.

The great belt on the wheel of Time slipped and eternity stood still. By the match light he could see the man's legs fighting with his breeches in his frantic desire to get them on. He had both chance and time to kill the intruder in his helpless condition—half in and half out of his pants—but he was too weak to take action. The shapeless enemies of humanity that live in the hours of

Time had waylaid Joe. He was assaulted in his weakness. Like Samson awakening after his haircut.[10] So he just opened his mouth and laughed.

The match went out and he struck another and lit the lamp. A howling wind raced across his heart, but underneath its fury he heard his wife sobbing and Slemmons pleading for his life. Offering to buy it with all that he had. "Please, suh, don't kill me. Sixty-two dollars at de sto'. Gold money."

Joe just stood. Slemmons looked at the window, but it was screened. Joe stood out like a rough-backed mountain between him and the door. Barring him from escape, from sunrise, from life.

He considered a surprise attack upon the big clown that stood there laughing like a chessy cat. But before his fist could travel an inch, Joe's own rushed out to crush him like a battering ram. Then Joe stood over him.

"Git into yo' damn rags, Slemmons, and dat quick."

Slemmons scrambled to his feet and into his vest and coat. As he grabbed his hat, Joe's fury overrode his intentions and he grabbed at Slemmons with his left hand and struck at him with his right. The right landed. The left grazed the front of his vest. Slemmons was knocked a somersault into the kitchen and fled through the open door. Joe found himself alone with Missie May, with the golden watch charm clutched in his left fist. A short bit of broken chain dangled between his fingers.

Missie May was sobbing. Wails of weeping without words. Joe stood, and after a while he found out that he had something in his hand. And then he stood and felt without thinking and without seeing with his natural eyes. Missie May kept on crying and Joe kept on feeling so much, and not knowing what to do with all his feelings, he put Slemmons's watch charm in his pants pocket and took a good laugh and went to bed.

"Missie May, whut you cryin' for?"

"Cause Ah love you so hard and Ah know you don't love *me* no mo'. "

Joe sank his face into the pillow for a spell, then he said huskily, "You don't know de feelings of dat yet, Missie May."

"Oh Joe, honey, he said he wuz gointer give me dat gold money and he jes' kept on after me—"

Joe was very still and silent for a long time. Then he said, "Well, don't cry no mo', Missie May. Ah got yo' gold piece for you."

The hours went past on their rusty ankles. Joe still and quiet on one bed rail and Missie May wrung dry of sobs on the other. Finally the sun's tide crept upon the shore of night and drowned all its hours. Missie May with her face

---

[10]As described in the Book of Judges, the Biblical hero Samson was an Israelite hero whose superhuman strength was lost after his hair was cut by the Philistine seductress Delilah.

stiff and streaked towards the window saw the dawn come into her yard. It was day. Nothing more. Joe wouldn't be coming home as usual. No need to fling open the front door and sweep off the porch, making it nice for Joe. Never no more breakfast to cook; no more washing and starching of Joe's jumper-jackets and pants. No more nothing. So why get up?

With this strange man in her bed, she felt embarrassed to get up and dress. She decided to wait till he had dressed and gone. Then she would get up, dress quickly and be gone forever beyond reach of Joe's looks and laughs. But he never moved. Red light turned to yellow, then white.

From beyond the no-man's land between them came a voice. A strange voice that yesterday had been Joe's.

"Missie May, ain't you gonna fix me no breakfus'?"

She sprang out of bed. "Yeah, Joe. Ah didn't reckon you wuz hongry."

No need to die today. Joe needed her for a few more minutes anyhow.

Soon there was a roaring fire in the cookstove. Water bucket full and two chickens killed. Joe loved fried chicken and rice. She didn't deserve a thing and good Joe was letting her cook him some breakfast. She rushed hot biscuits to the table as Joe took his seat.

He ate with his eyes in his plate. No laughter, no banter.

"Missie May, you ain't eatin' yo' breakfus'. "

"Ah don't choose none, Ah thank yuh."

His coffee cup was empty. She sprang to refill it. When she turned from the stove and bent to set the cup beside Joe's plate, she saw the yellow coin on the table between them.

She slumped into her seat and wept into her arms.

Presently Joe said calmly, "Missie May, you cry too much. Don't look back lak Lot's wife and turn to salt."[11]

The sun, the hero of every day, the impersonal old man that beams as brightly on death as on birth, came up every morning and raced across the blue dome and dipped into the sea of fire every morning. Water ran downhill and birds nested.

Missie knew why she didn't leave Joe. She couldn't. She loved him too much, but she could not understand why Joe didn't leave her. He was polite, even kind at times, but aloof.

There were no more Saturday romps. No ringing silver dollars to stack beside her plate. No pockets to rifle. In fact, the yellow coin in his trousers was like a monster hiding in the cave of his pockets to destroy her.

---

[11]In the Biblical Book of Genesis, God spares Abraham's nephew Lot from the general destruction of Sodom and Gomorrah; Lot's wife turns into a pillar of salt, however, when she disobeys God's injunction against looking back at the doomed cities.

She often wondered if he still had it, but nothing could have induced her to ask nor yet to explore his pockets to see for herself. Its shadow was in the house whether or no.

One night Joe came home around midnight and complained of pains in the back. He asked Missie to rub him down with liniment. It had been three months since Missie had touched his body and it all seemed strange. But she rubbed him. Grateful for the chance. Before morning youth triumphed and Missie exulted. But the next day, as she joyfully made up their bed, beneath her pillow she found the piece of money with the bit of chain attached.

Alone to herself, she looked at the thing with loathing, but look she must. She took it into her hands with trembling and saw first thing that it was no gold piece. It was a gilded half dollar. Then she knew why Slemmons had forbidden anyone to touch his gold. He trusted village eyes at a distance not to recognize his stickpin as a gilded quarter, and his watch charm as a four-bit piece.

She was glad at first that Joe had left it there. Perhaps he was through with her punishment. They were man and wife again. Then another thought came clawing at her. He had come home to buy from her as if she were any woman in the longhouse. Fifty cents for her love. As if to say that he could pay as well as Slemmons. She slid the coin into his Sunday pants pocket and dressed herself and left his house.

Halfway between her house and the quarters she met her husband's mother, and after a short talk she turned and went back home. Never would she admit defeat to that woman who prayed for it nightly. If she had not the substance of marriage she had the outside show. Joe must leave *her*. She let him see she didn't want his old gold four-bits, too.

She saw no more of the coin for some time though she knew that Joe could not help finding it in his pocket. But his health kept poor, and he came home at least every ten days to be rubbed.

The sun swept around the horizon, trailing its robes of weeks and days. One morning as Joe came in from work, he found Missie May chopping wood. Without a word he took the ax and chopped a huge pile before he stopped.

"You ain't got no business choppin' wood, and you know it."

"How come? Ah been choppin' it for de last longest."

"Ah ain't blind. You makin' feet for shoes."

"Won't you be glad to have a lil baby chile, Joe?"

"You know dat 'thout astin' me."

"Iss gointer be a boy chile and de very spit of you."

"You reckon, Missie May?"

"Who else could it look lak?"

Joe said nothing, but he thrust his hand deep into his pocket and fingered something there.

It was almost six months later Missie May took to bed and Joe went and got his mother to come wait on the house.

Missie May was delivered of a fine boy. Her travail was over when Joe come in from work one morning. His mother and the old woman were drinking great bowls of coffee around the fire in the kitchen.

The minute Joe came into the room his mother called him aside.

"How did Missie May make out?" he asked quickly.

"Who, dat gal? She strong as a ox. She gointer have plenty mo'. We done fixed her wid de sugar and lard to sweeten her for de nex' one."

Joe stood silent awhile.

"You ain't ask 'bout de baby, Joe. You oughter be mighty proud cause he sho is de spittin' image[12] of yuh, son. Dat's yourn all right, if you never git another one, dat un is yourn. And you know Ah'm mighty proud too, son, cause Ah never thought well of you marryin' Missie May cause her ma used tuh fan her foot round right smart and Ah been mighty skeered dat Missie May wuz gointer git misput on her road."

Joe said nothing. He fooled around the house till late in the day, then, just before he went to work, he went and stood at the foot of the bed and asked his wife how she felt. He did this every day during the week.

On Saturday he went to Orlando to make his market. It had been a long time since he had done that.

Meat and lard, meal and flour, soap and starch. Cans of corn and tomatoes. All the staples. He fooled around town for a while and bought bananas and apples. Way after while he went around to the candy store.

"Hello, Joe," the clerk greeted him. "Ain't seen you in a long time."

"Nope, Ah ain't been heah. Been round in spots and places."

"Want some of them molasses kisses you always buy?"

"Yessuh." He threw the gilded half dollar on the counter. "Will dat spend?"

"What is it, Joe? Well, I'll be doggone! A gold-plated four-bit piece. Where'd you git it, Joe?"

"Offen a stray nigger dat come through Eatonville.[13] He had it on his watch chain for a charm—goin' round making out iss gold money. Ha ha! He had a quarter on his tiepin and it wuz all golded up too. Tryin' to fool people. Makin' out he so rich and everything. Ha! Ha! Tryin' to tole off folkses wives from home."

---

[12]The phrase means "exact likeness." One explanation is that "spit" is here a colloquial pronunciation of "spirit"; "spittin' image" therefore means "spirit and image."

[13]Hurston was raised in the small black community of Eatonville, near Orlando in central Florida.

"How did you git it, Joe? Did he fool you, too?"

"Who, me? Naw suh! He ain't fooled me none. Know whut Ah done? He come round me wid his smart talk. Ah hauled off and knocked 'im down and took his old four-bits away from 'im. Gointer buy my wife some good ole lasses kisses wid it. Gimme fifty cents worth of dem candy kisses."

"Fifty cents buys a mighty lot of candy kisses, Joe. Why don't you split it up and take some chocolate bars, too? They eat good, too."

"Yessuh, dey do, but Ah wants all dat in kisses. Ah got a lil boy chile home now. Tain't a week old yet, but he kin suck a sugar tit[14] and maybe eat one them kisses hisself."

Joe got his candy and left the store. The clerk turned to the next customer. "Wisht I could be like these darkies. Laughin' all the time. Nothin' worries 'em."

Back in Eatonville, Joe reached his own front door. There was the ring of singing metal on wood. Fifteen times. Missie May couldn't run to the door, but she crept there as quickly as she could.

"Joe Banks, Ah hear you chunkin' money in mah do'way. You wait till Ah got mah strength back and Ah'm gointer fix you for dat."

[1933]

---

[14]A "sugar tit" is a pacifier made by soaking a piece of cloth in sugar-water.

Gwendolyn Brooks
[1917–2000]

GWENDOLYN ELIZABETH BROOKS *was born and grew up in Topeka, Kansas, where her mother, Keziah Corine Wims Brooks, taught school and her father, David Anderson Brooks, provided her with a desk and allowed writing time early in her life. She published her first poem in a local newspaper,* Hyde Parker, *at age eleven and published poems again at age thirteen in* American Childhood. *At sixteen, she was publishing poems regularly in the* Chicago Defender. *At twenty-one she married Henry Lovington Blakeley II, with whom she had two children, Henry III and Nora. They moved to Chicago where she expanded her acquaintances and met famous writers of the Harlem Renaissance, including Langston Hughes who came to give a poetry reading in Chicago, and agreed to read her early poetry. Hughes later became a family friend as well as a mentor. By 1953, when she wrote an autobiographical novel,* Maud Martha, *she was a well-established poet. Her* A Street in Bronzeville *(1945) expressed the development of her powerful voice as she described the traumatized soldiers returning from World War II and the oppressed poor blacks who lived in rundown neighborhoods. In this collection she used the sonnet form to sing the woes of blacks in urban America during the thirties and forties. She described what she saw in Chicago and New York with a power that brought a wider community to feel and comprehend the plight of poor people.*

In The Bean Eaters *(1960) Brooks turned her attention to the civil rights movement, recounting the horrors of that time, for example, the murder of fourteen-year-old Emmet Till, in "A Bronzeville Mother Loiters in Mississippi. Meanwhile a Mississippi Mother Burns Bacon." She was accused by some as having become a political poet, but she wrote with a voice that was needed in the sixties. In* the Mecca *(1968) is a collection of her poems about false spirituality and deception, partially written about the time she worked for a spiritual leader who deceived his followers. During the first twenty-five years of her career, she also wrote many reviews for the* Chicago Daily News, *the* Sun Times, Black World, *the* New York Times, *and the* Tribune. *She taught poetry in colleges in Chicago (Columbia, Elmhurst, Northeastern Illinois) and at Wisconsin-Madison. In 1968, she became Poet Laureate of Illinois. In 1971, she wrote her first autobiography,* Report from Part One. *After this, she began to publish only with black presses and to write even more intensely about the lives of black people in the cities. Two volumes,* To Disembark *(1981) and* Children Coming Home *(1991), collect the poems that speak to black people about their lives. In 1996 she pro-*

duced a second autobiography, Report from Part Two, *which introduces and discusses some of her most well-known poems. Throughout the last years of her life, Brooks was generous with her time, traveling to give readings and to receive the scores of awards she received from admiring readers and listeners. Her work is loved and admired by both academics and non-academics, both in her adopted state and beyond.*

To the Diaspora[1]
You Did Not Know You Were Afrika

GWENDOLYN BROOKS

When you set out for Afrika
you did not know you were going.
Because
you did not know you were Afrika.
You did not know the Black continent   5
that had to be reached
was you.

I could not have told you then that some sun
would come,
somewhere over the road,   10
would come evoking the diamonds
of you, the Black continent—
somewhere over the road.
You would not have believed my mouth.

When I told you, meeting you somewhere close   15
to the heat and youth of the road,
liking my loyalty, liking belief,
you smiled and you thanked me but very little believed me.

Here is some sun. Some.
Now off into the places rough to reach.   20
Though dry, though drowsy, all unwillingly a-wobble,
into the dissonant and dangerous crescendo.
Your work, that was done, to be done to be done to be done.

[1981]

[1]Diaspora means the spreading of a people out from a central place to many other places.

Reprinted by permission from *Coming Home*. Copyright © 1981 by Gwendolyn Brooks.

A Street in Bronzeville: Southeast Corner

GWENDOLYN BROOKS

The School of Beauty's a tavern now.
The Madam is underground.
Out at Lincoln, among the graves
Her own is early found.
Where the thickest, tallest monument   5
Cuts grandly into the air
The Madam lies, contentedly.
Her fortune, too, lies there,
Converted into cool hard steel
And right red velvet lining;   10
While over her tan impassivity
Shot silk is shining.

[1945]

Reprinted by permission from *Blacks*. Copyright © 1945 by Gwendolyn Brooks.

The Bean Eaters

GWENDOLYN BROOKS

They eat beans mostly, this old yellow pair.
Dinner is a casual affair.
Plain chipware on a plain and creaking wood,
Tin flatware.

Two who are Mostly Good.   *5*
Two who have lived their day,

But keep on putting on their clothes
And putting things away.

And remembering . . .
Remembering, with twinklings and twinges,   *10*
As they lean over the beans in their rented back room that is
    full of beads and receipts and dolls and cloths, tobacco
    crumbs, vases and fringes.

[1960]

Reprinted by permission from *Blacks*. Copyright © 1960 by Gwendolyn Brooks.

Suzan-Lori Parks
[1964–   ]

In 2001, the American playwright **SUZAN-LORI PARKS** became the first black woman to win a Pulitzer Prize for Drama. She won the award for Topdog/Underdog (2001), a drama depicting the variable and troubled relationship between two brothers, Lincoln, the older "topdog," and Booth, the younger "underdog." This play was not, however, Parks's first foray into creative writing: She has been producing innovative work about race and history since taking a writing workshop at Mount Holyoke with the author James Baldwin, who first recommended she write plays.

In her work, Parks regularly appropriates familiar themes from American history and literature, and places them in harsh contemporary contexts. For instance, two of her plays offer heroines named Hester—women who suffer much like Hester Prynne, the heroine of Nathaniel Hawthorne's novel The Scarlet Letter. Her play In the Blood (1990) follows Hester, the homeless mother of five children, and Fucking A (2003), has for its protagonist an abortionist also named Hester. Likewise, a black Lincoln—suggestive of the sixteenth president of the United States, Abraham Lincoln—appears in The America Play (1994) and Topdog/Underdog. In the latter play, the character Lincoln performs nightly the assassination of President Lincoln at an amusement arcade, a job for which he wears whiteface and a top hat. Topdog/Underdog focuses simultaneously on the familial history of two African-American brother, Lincoln and Booth, and on the larger historical forces that shaped them. From their names, the destiny of Parks's characters Lincoln and Booth seems clear. In 1865, John Wilkes Booth assassinated President Lincoln at Ford's Theater, believing that Lincoln had betrayed the country by granting blacks not only freedom, but also citizenship and voting rights. Twelve days later, Booth was killed by federal troops. While popular history celebrates Lincoln for his endeavors on behalf of black Americans, recent historians reveal that in fact Lincoln was ambivalent about full racial equality and believed that whites would retain their status as "top dog" in American culture. The play addresses the ambiguities and power reversals that characterize not only the family, but also the nation.

Parks continues to be remarkably focused and prolific in a variety of genres. She produced the film Anemone Me (1990), and wrote the screenplay for the director Spike Lee's film Girl 6 (1996). She also adapted Zora Neale Hurston's Their Eyes Were Watching God and Toni Morrison's Paradise for film. Her novel, Getting Mother's Body (2003), was inspired in part by the work of William Faulkner, a Southern writer whose experimental work explores similar themes, including troubled race relations in America. Park is the recipient of a MacArthur Foundation "genius" grant, as well as of two Obie awards.

An Equation for Black People Onstage

SUZAN-LORI PARKS

Simply this:

The bulk of relationships Black people are engaged in onstage is the relationship between the Black and the White other. This is the stuff of high drama. I wonder if a drama involving Black people can exist without the presence of the White—no, not the *presence*—the presence is not the problem. As Toni Morrison writes in her essay "Black Matters," the presence of the White often signifies the presence of the Black. Within the subject is its other. So the mere *presence* of the other is not the problem. The interest in the other is. The use of the White in the dramatic equation is, I think, too often seen as the only way of exploring our Blackness; this equation reduces Blackness to merely a state of "non-Whiteness." Blackness in this equation is a people whose lives consist of a series of reactions and responses to the White ruling class. We have for so long been an "oppressed" people, but are Black people only blue? As African-Americans we have a history, a future and a daily reality in which a confrontation with a White ruling class is a central feature. This reality makes life difficult. This reality often traps us in a singular mode of expression. There are many ways of defining Blackness and there are many ways of presenting Blackness onstage. The Klan does not always have to be outside the door for Black people to have lives worthy of dramatic literature. Saying that "Whitey" has to be present in Black drama because Whitey is an inextricable aspect of Black reality is like saying that every play has to have a murder in it, is like saying that every drama involving Jews must reference Treblinka.[1] And what happens when we choose a concern other than the race problem to focus on? What kind of drama do we get? Let's look at the math:

BLACK PEOPLE + "WHITEY" =
        STANDARD DRAMATIC CONFLICT
        (STANDARD TERRITORY)

---

[1]Treblinka was a Nazi concentration camp located near Warsaw, Poland.

Copyright © 1995 by Suzan-Lori Parks. Used by permission of Theater Communications Group.

i.e.

"BLACK DRAMA" = the presentation of the Black as oppressed

so that

WHATEVER the dramatic dynamics, they are most often READ to EQUAL an explanation or relation of Black oppression. This is not only a false equation, this is bullshit.

so that

BLACK PEOPLE + x = NEW DRAMATIC CONFLICT (NEW TERRITORY)

where x is the realm of situations showing African-Americans in states other than the Oppressed by/Obsessed with "Whitey" state; where the White when present is not the oppressor, and where audiences are encouraged to see and understand and discuss these dramas in terms other than that same old shit.

An old acquaintance of mine, a somewhat revered theatre scholar, once suggested that a fabulous production of *The Importance of Being Earnest* would feature Black principals with Whites as the servants. This is NOT an interesting use of Black people. This is the thinnest sort of dramaturgy. Ideas like these—equations featuring this lack of complexity—are again and again held up to us as exemplar, as the ultimate possibilities for Black people onstage. Black presence on stage is more than a sign or messenger of some political point.

4 Questions

Can a White person be present onstage and not be an oppressor? Can a Black person be onstage and be other than oppressed? For the Black writer, are there Dramas other than race dramas? Does Black life consist of issues other than race issues?

And gee, there's another thing: There is no such thing as THE Black Experience; that is, there are many experiences of being Black which are included under the rubric. Just think of all the different kinds of African peoples.

A black man from Nigeria asked me once "What is this interest with water-melon you Black Americans have? I do not understand." His not understanding does not make him non-Black/White/an inauthentic Black man. His not understanding simply means that he grew up Black yes! but Black somewhere else.

I'm continually encouraging myself to explore The-Drama-of-the-Black-Person-as-an-Integral- Facet-of-the-Universe. This exploration takes me, in a very organic way, into new territory; because, in encouraging myself to listen to the stories beyond my default stories—because the story determines the shape of the play—the play assumes a new structure.

So. As a Black person writing for theatre, what is theatre good for? What can theatre do for us? We can "tell it like it is"; "tell it as it was"; "tell it as it could be." In my plays I do all 3; and the writing is rich because we are not an impoverished people, but a wealthy people fallen on hard times.

I write plays because I love Black people. As there is no single "Black Experience," there is no single "Black Aesthetic" and there is no one way to write or think or feel or dream or interpret or be interpreted. As African-Americans we should recognize this insidious essentialism for what it is: a fucked-up trap to reduce us to only one way of being. We should endeavor to show the world and ourselves our beautiful and powerfully infinite variety.

[1987]

Richard Wright
[1908–1960]

The grandson of former slaves, RICHARD WRIGHT *was born on Rucker's planta-
tion in rural Mississippi and grew up in Memphis, Tennessee and Jackson,
Mississippi. Wright suffered a tumultuous childhood. When he was six years old,
his father Nathaniel, a sharecropper, abandoned the family, forcing his mother
Ella into overwork and chronic illness. Richard and his brother Leon spent a brief
time in a Memphis orphanage. The family moved from Tennessee to Arkansas
where Richard grew close to his Uncle Silas; the relationship catastrophically
ended when Silas was murdered by whites in 1917. Ensuing poverty forced Wright
to leave school in order to find work; he was then sent to live with aunts and uncles
in Mississippi. Despite these trying circumstances, Wright resumed his formal education, graduating as the valedictorian from Smith Robertson Junior High School.
In a prophetic gesture, Wright refused to read the graduation address written for
him by the school principal and instead delivered his own speech.*

*Wright briefly returned to Memphis with his family before moving to Chicago
when he was nineteen. Unable to find work during the Great Depression he was
forced to go on relief. By 1938, however, he had published* Uncle Tom's Children,
*a collection of four long stories that won the Federal Writer's Project Story prize and
landed Wright a Guggenheim fellowship. During this time he also joined the
Communist Party and became an editor, in 1937, of the party newspaper the* Daily
Worker, *but left during the 1940s because of disagreements about how African-
American rights were neglected as part of the overall goal of communism. He would
register his dissatisfaction in the 1944 essay, "I Tried to Be a Communist."*

In 1940 Wright published Native Son, *the violent tale of Bigger Thomas, a
young African-American man from Chicago who accidentally kills a white woman.
This book sealed his reputation as an important naturalist author in the tradition
of Stephen Crane and Theodore Drieser. He later worked the novel into both a play
and a film, the latter (produced in 1950) starring Wright in the lead role. In 1947
Wright emigrated to Europe, dismayed by the racial prejudice that seemed endemic
to American society. Here he wrote and published* The Outsider *(1953), about a
black man's involvement with the Communist party. He wrote other novels, but
never achieved the power of his first books. Some critics argue that his separation
from the direct experience of race prejudice in the United States blunted the intensity of his work; but whatever the cause, his later works lack the ferocious intensity
that characterized his early writing. He died in France in 1960 of a heart attack.*

—David L.G. Arnold, *University of Wisconsin, Stevens Point*

"The Ethics of Living Jim Crow: An Autobiographical Sketch"

RICHARD WRIGHT

READING QUESTIONS: Describe the physical and psychological aspects of Jim Crow laws. Does Jim Crow rob African-Americans of their humanity? Constitutional rights? Explain.

1

My first lesson in how to live as a Negro came when I was quite small. We were living in Arkansas. Our house stood behind the railroad tracks. Its skimpy yard was paved with black cinders. Nothing green ever grew in that yard. The only touch of green we could see was far away, beyond the tracks, over where the white folks lived. But cinders were good enough for me, and I never missed the green growing things. And anyhow, cinders were fine weapons. You could always have a nice hot war with huge black cinders. All you had to do was crouch behind the brick pillars of a house with your hands full of gritty ammunition. And the first woolly black head you saw pop out from behind another row of pillars was your target. You tried your very best to knock it off. It was great fun.

I never fully realized the appalling disadvantages of a cinder environment till one day the gang to which I belonged found itself engaged in a war with the white boys who lived beyond the tracks. As usual we laid down our cinder barrage, thinking that this would wipe the white boys out. But they replied with a steady bombardment of broken bottles. We doubled our cinder barrage, but they hid behind trees, hedges, and the sloping embankments of their lawns. Having no such fortifications, we retreated to the brick pillars of our homes. During the retreat a broken milk bottle caught me behind the ear, opening a deep gash which bled profusely. The sight of blood pouring over my face completely demoralized our ranks. My fellow-combatants left me standing paralyzed in the center of the yard, and scurried for their homes. A kind neighbor saw me and rushed me to a doctor, who took three stitches in my neck.

Reprinted from *Uncle Tom's Children* (1940), by permission of HarperCollins Publishers, Inc., via Copyright Clearance Center. Copyright © 1993 by HarperCollins Publishers, Inc.

I sat brooding on my front steps, nursing my wound and waiting for my mother to come from work. I felt that a grave injustice had been done me. It was all right to throw cinders. The greatest harm a cinder could do was leave a bruise. But broken bottles were dangerous; they left you cut, bleeding, and helpless.

When night fell, my mother came from the white folks' kitchen. I raced down the street to meet her. I could just feel in my bones that she would understand. I knew she would tell me exactly what to do next time. I grabbed her hand and babbled out the whole story. She examined my wound, then slapped me.

"How come yuh didn't hide?" she asked me. "How come yuh awways fightin'?"

I was outraged, and bawled. Between sobs I told her that I didn't have any trees or hedges to hide behind. There wasn't a thing I could have used as a trench. And you couldn't throw very far when you were hiding behind the brick pillars of a house. She grabbed a barrel stave, dragged me home, stripped me naked, and beat me till I had a fever of one hundred and two. She would smack my rump with the stave, and, while the skin was still smarting, impart to me gems of Jim Crow wisdom. I was never to throw cinders any more. I was never to fight any more wars. I was never, never, under any conditions, to fight white folks again. And they were absolutely right in clouting me with the broken milk bottle. Didn't I know she was working hard every day in the hot kitchens of the white folks to make money to take care of me? When was I ever going to learn to be a good boy? She couldn't be bothered with my fights. She finished by telling me that I ought to be thankful to God as long as I lived that they didn't kill me.

All that night I was delirious and could not sleep. Each time I closed my eyes I saw monstrous white faces suspended from the ceiling, leering at me.

From that time on, the charm of my cinder yard was gone. The green trees, the trimmed hedges, the cropped lawns grew very meaningful, became a symbol. Even today when I think of white folks, the hard, sharp outlines of white houses surrounded by trees, lawns, and hedges are present somewhere in the background of my mind. Through the years they grew into an over-reaching symbol of fear.

It was a long time before I came in close contact with white folks again. We moved from Arkansas to Mississippi. Here we had the good fortune not to live behind the railroad tracks, or close to white neighborhoods. We lived in the very heart of the local Black Belt. There were black churches and black preachers; there were black schools and black teachers; black groceries and black clerks. In fact, everything was so solidly black that for a long time I did not even think of white folks, save in remote and vague terms. But this could not last forever. As one grows older one eats more. One's clothing costs more. When I finished grammar school I had to go to work. My mother could no longer feed and clothe me on her cooking job.

There is but one place where a black boy who knows no trade can get a job. And that's where the houses and faces are white, where the trees, lawns, and hedges are green. My first job was with an optical company in Jackson, Mississippi. The morning I applied I stood straight and neat before the boss, answering all his questions with sharp yessirs and nosirs. I was very careful to pronounce my sirs distinctly, in order that he might know that I was polite, that I knew where I was, and that I knew he was a white man. I wanted that job badly.

He looked me over as though he were examining a prize poodle. He questioned me closely about my schooling, being particularly insistent about how much mathematics I had had. He seemed very pleased when I told him I had had two years of algebra.

"Boy, how would you like to try to learn something around here?" he asked me.

"I'd like it fine, sir," I said, happy. I had visions of "working my way up." Even Negroes have those visions.

"All right," he said. "Come on."

I followed him to the small factory.

"Pease," he said to a white man of about thirty-five, "this is Richard. He's going to work for us."

Pease looked at me and nodded.

I was then taken to a white boy of about seventeen.

"Morrie, this is Richard, who's going to work for us."

"Whut yuh sayin' there, boy!" Morrie boomed at me.

"Fine!" I answered.

The boss instructed these two to help me, teach me, give me jobs to do, and let me learn what I could in my spare time.

My wages were five dollars a week.

I worked hard, trying to please. For the first month I got along O.K. Both Pease and Morrie seemed to like me. But one thing was missing. And I kept thinking about it. I was not learning anything, and nobody was volunteering to help me. Thinking they had forgotten that I was to learn something about the mechanics of grinding lenses, I asked Morrie one day to tell me about the work. He grew red.

"Whut yuh tryin' t' do, nigger, git smart?" he asked.

"Naw; I ain' tryin' t' git smart," I said.

"Well, don't, if yuh know whut's good for yuh!"

I was puzzled. Maybe he just doesn't want to help me, I thought. I went to Pease.

"Say, are you crazy, you black bastard?" Pease asked me, his gray eyes growing hard.

I spoke out, reminding him that the boss had said I was to be given a chance to learn something.

"Nigger, you think you're white, don't you?"

"Naw, sir!"

"Well, you're acting mighty like it!"

"But, Mr. Pease, the boss said . . ."

Pease shook his fist in my face.

"This is a white man's work around here, and you better watch yourself!"

From then on they changed toward me. They said good-morning no more. When I was just a bit slow in performing some duty, I was called a lazy black son-of-a-bitch.

Once I thought of reporting all this to the boss. But the mere idea of what would happen to me if Pease and Morrie should learn that I had "snitched" stopped me. And after all, the boss was a white man, too. What was the use?

The climax came at noon one summer day. Pease called me to his work-bench. To get to him I had to go between two narrow benches and stand with my back against a wall.

"Yes, sir," I said.

"Richard, I want to ask you something," Pease began pleasantly, not looking up from his work.

"Yes, sir," I said again.

Morrie came over, blocking the narrow passage between the benches. He folded his arms, staring at me solemnly.

I looked from one to the other, sensing that something was coming.

"Yes, sir," I said for the third time.

Pease looked up and spoke very slowly.

"Richard, Mr. Morrie here tells me you called me Pease."

I stiffened. A void seemed to open up in me. I knew this was the show-down.

He meant that I had failed to call him Mr. Pease. I looked at Morrie. He was gripping a steel bar in his hands. I opened my mouth to speak, to protest, to assure Pease that I had never called him simply Pease, and that I had never had any intentions of doing so, when Morrie grabbed me by the collar, ramming my head against the wall.

"Now, be careful, nigger!" snarled Morrie, baring his teeth. "I heard yuh call 'im Pease! 'N' if yuh say yuh didn't, yuh're callin' me a lie, see?" He waved the steel bar threateningly.

If I had said: No, sir, Mr. Pease, I never called you Pease, I would have been automatically calling Morrie a liar. And if I had said: Yes, sir, Mr. Pease, I called you Pease, I would have been pleading guilty to having uttered the worst insult that a Negro can utter to a southern white man. I stood hesitating, trying to frame a neutral reply.

"Richard, I asked you a question!" said Pease. Anger was creeping into his voice.

"I don't remember calling you Pease, Mr. Pease," I said cautiously. "And if I did, I sure didn't mean..."

"You black son-of-a-bitch! You called me Pease, then!" he spat, slapping me till I bent sideways over a bench. Morrie was on top of me, demanding:

"Didn't yuh call 'im Pease? If yuh say yuh didn't, I'll rip yo' gut string loose with this f—kin' bar, yuh black granny dodger! Yuh can't call a white man a lie 'n' git erway with it, you black son-of-a-bitch!"

I wilted. I begged them not to bother me. I knew what they wanted. They wanted me to leave.

"I'll leave," I promised. "I'll leave right now."

They gave me a minute to get out of the factory. I was warned not to show up again, or tell the boss.

I went.

When I told the folks at home what had happened, they called me a fool. They told me that I must never again attempt to exceed my boundaries. When you are working for white folks, they said, you got to "stay in your place" if you want to keep working.

2

My Jim Crow education continued on my next job, which was portering in a clothing store. One morning, while polishing brass out front, the boss and his twenty-year-old son got out of their car and half dragged and half kicked a Negro woman into the store. A policeman standing at the corner looked on, twirling his nightstick. I watched out of the corner of my eye, never slackening the strokes of my chamois upon the brass. After a few minutes, I heard shrill screams coming from the rear of the store. Later the woman stumbled out, bleeding, crying, and holding her stomach. When she reached the end of the block, the policeman grabbed her and accused her of being drunk. Silently I watched him throw her into a patrol wagon.

When I went to the rear of the store, the boss and his son were washing their hands at the sink. They were chuckling. The floor was bloody, and strewn with wisps of hair and clothing. No doubt I must have appeared pretty shocked, for the boss slapped me reassuringly on the back.

"Boy, that's what we do to niggers when they don't want to pay their bills," he said, laughing.

His son looked at me and grinned.

"Here, have cigarette," he said.

Not knowing what to do, I took it. He lit his and held the match for me. This was a gesture of kindness, indicating that even if they had beaten the poor old woman, they would not beat me if I knew enough to keep my mouth shut.

"Yes, sir," I said, and asked no questions.

After they had gone, I sat on the edge of a packing box and stared at the bloody floor till the cigarette went out.

That day at noon, while eating in a hamburger joint, I told my fellow Negro porters what had happened. No one seemed surprised. One fellow, after swallowing a huge bite, turned to me and asked:

"Huh. Is that all they did t' her?"

"Yeah. Wasn't that enough?" I asked.

"Shucks! Man, she's a lucky bitch!" he said, burying his lips deep into a juicy hamburger. "Hell, it's a wonder they didn't lay her when they got through."

3

I was learning fast, but not quite fast enough. One day, while I was delivering packages in the suburbs, my bicycle tire was punctured. I walked along the hot, dusty road, sweating and leading my bicycle by the handle-bars.

A car slowed at my side.

"What's the matter, boy?" a white man called.

I told him my bicycle was broken and I was walking back to town.

"That's too bad," he said. "Hop on the running board."

He stopped the car. I clutched hard at my bicycle with one hand and clung to the side of the car with the other.

"All set?"

"Yes, sir," I answered. The car started.

It was full of young white men. They were drinking. I watched the flask pass from mouth to mouth.

"Wanna drink, boy?" one asked.

I laughed, the wind whipping my face. Instinctively obeying the freshly planted precepts of my mother, I said:

"Oh, no!"

The words were hardly out of my mouth before I felt something hard and cold smash me between the eyes. It was an empty whisky bottle. I saw stars, and fell backwards from the speeding car into the dust of the road, my feet becoming entangled in the steel spokes of my bicycle. The white men piled out, and stood over me.

"Nigger, ain' yuh learned no better sense'n that yet?" asked the man who hit me. "ain' yuh learned t' say sir t' a white man yet?"

Dazed, I pulled to my feet. My elbows and legs were bleeding. Fists doubled, the white man advanced, kicking my bicycle out of the way.

"Aw, leave the bastard alone. He's got enough," said one.

They stood looking at me. I rubbed my shins, trying to stop the flow of blood. No doubt they felt a sort of contemptuous pity, for one asked:

"Yuh wanna ride t' town now, nigger? Yuh reckon yuh know enough t' ride now?"

"I wanna walk," I said, simply.

Maybe it sounded funny. They laughed.

"Well, walk, yuh black son-of-a-bitch!"

When they left they comforted me with:

"Nigger, yuh sho better be damn glad it wuz us yuh talked t' the' way. Yuh're a lucky bastard, 'cause if yuh'd said the' t' somebody else, yuh might've been a dead nigger now."

4

Negroes who have lived South know the dread of being caught alone upon the streets in white neighborhoods after the sun has set. In such a simple situation as this the plight of the Negro in America is graphically symbolized. While white strangers may be in these neighborhoods trying to get home, they can pass unmolested. But the color of a Negro's skin makes him easily recognizable, makes him suspect, converts him into a defenseless target.

Late one Saturday night I made some deliveries in a white neighborhood. I was pedaling my bicycle back to the store as fast as I could, when a police car, swerving toward me, jammed me into the curbing.

"Get down and put up your hands!" the policemen ordered.

I did. They climbed out of the car, guns drawn, faces set, and: advanced slowly.

"Keep still!" they ordered.

I reached my hands higher. They searched my pockets and packages. They seemed dissatisfied when they could find nothing incriminating. Finally, one of them said:

"Boy, tell your boss not to send you out in white neighborhoods this time of night."

As usual, I said:

"Yes, sir."

5

My next job was as hall-boy in a hotel. Here my Jim Crow education broadened and deepened. When the bell-boys were busy, I was often called to assist them. As many of the rooms in the hotel were occupied by prostitutes, I was constantly called to carry them liquor and cigarettes. These women were nude most of the time. They did not bother about clothing even for bell-boys. When you went into their rooms, you were supposed to take their nakedness for granted, as though it startled you no more than a blue vase or a red rug. Your presence awoke in them no sense of shame, for you were not regarded as human. If they were alone, you could steal sidelong glimpses at them. But if they were receiving men, not a flicker of your eyelids must show. I remember one incident vividly. A new woman, a huge, snowy-skinned blonde, took a room on my floor. I was sent to wait upon her. She was in bed with a thick-set man; both were nude and uncovered. She said she wanted some liquor, and slid out of bed and waddled across the floor to get her money from a dresser drawer. I watched her.

"Nigger, what in hell you looking at?" the white man asked me, raising himself upon his elbows.

"Nothing," I answered, looking miles deep into the blank wall of the room.

"Keep your eyes where they belong, if you want to be healthy!"

"Yes, sir," I said.

6

One of the bell-boys I knew in this hotel was keeping steady company with one of the Negro maids. Out of a clear sky the police descended upon his home and arrested him, accusing him of bastardy. The poor boy swore he had had no intimate relations with the girl. Nevertheless, they forced him to marry her. When the child arrived, it was found to be much lighter in complexion than either of the two supposedly legal parents. The white men around the hotel made a great joke of it. They spread the rumor that some white cow must have scared the poor girl while she was carrying the baby. If you were in their presence when this explanation was offered, you were supposed to laugh.

7

One of the bell-boys was caught in bed with a white prostitute. He was castrated, and run out of town. Immediately after this all the bell-boys and hall-boys were called together and warned. We were given to understand that the boy who had been castrated was a "mighty, mighty lucky bastard." We were impressed with the fact that next time the management of the hotel would not be responsible for the lives of "trouble-makin' niggers."

8

One night, just as I was about to go home, I met one of the Negro maids. She lived in my direction, and we fell in to walk part of the way home together. As we passed the white nightwatchman, he slapped the maid on her buttock. I turned around amazed. The watchman looked at me with a long, hard, fixed under stare. Suddenly he pulled his gun, and asked:

"Nigger, don't yuh like it?"

I hesitated.

"I asked yuh don't yuh like it?" he asked again, stepping forward.

"Yes, sir," I mumbled.

"Talk like it, them"

"Oh, yes, sir!" I said with as much heartiness as I could muster.

Outside, I walked ahead of the girl, ashamed to face her. She caught up with me and said:

"Don't be a fool; yuh couldn't help it!"

This watchman boasted of having killed two Negroes in self defense.

Yet, in spite of all this, the life of the hotel ran with an amazing smoothness. It would have been impossible for a stranger to detect anything. The maids, the hall-boys, and the bell-boys were all smiles. They had to be.

9

I had learned my Jim Crow lessons so thoroughly that I kept the hotel job till I left Jackson for Memphis. It so happened that while in Memphis I applied for a job at a branch of the optical company. I was hired. And for some reason, as long as I worked there, they never brought my past against me.

Here my Jim Crow education assumed quite a different form. It was no longer brutally cruel, but subtly cruel. Here I learned to lie, to steal, to dissemble. I learned to play that dual role which every Negro must play if he wants to eat and live.

For example, it was almost impossible to get a book to read. It was assumed that after a Negro had imbibed what scanty schooling the state furnished he had no further need for books. I was always borrowing books from men on the job. One day I mustered enough courage to ask one of the men to let me get books from the library in his name. Surprisingly, he consented. I cannot help but think that he consented because he was a Roman Catholic and felt a vague sympathy for Negroes, being himself an object of hatred.

Armed with a library card, I obtained books in the following manner: I would write a note to the librarian, saying: "Please let this nigger boy have the following books." I would then sign it with the white man's name.

When I went to the library, I would stand at the desk, hat in hand, looking as unbookish as possible. When I received the books desired I would take them home. If the books listed in the note happened to be out, I would sneak into the lobby and forge a new one. I never took any chances guessing with the white librarian about what the fictitious white man would want to read. No doubt if any of the white patrons had suspected that some of the volumes they enjoyed had been in the home of a Negro, they would not have tolerated it for an instant.

The factory force of the optical company in Memphis was much larger than that in Jackson, and more urbanized. At least they liked to talk, and would engage the Negro help in conversation whenever possible. By this means I found that many subjects were taboo from the white man's point of view. Among the topics they did not like to discuss with Negroes were the following: American white women; the Ku Klux Klan; France, and how Negro soldiers fared while there; French women; Jack Johnson; the entire northern part of the United States; the Civil War; Abraham Lincoln; U. S. Grant; General Sherman; Catholics; the Pope; Jews; the Republican Party; slavery; social equality; Communism; Socialism; the 13th and 14th Amendments to the Constitution; or any topic calling for positive knowledge or manly self-assertion on the part of the Negro. The most accepted topics were sex and religion.

There were many times when I had to exercise a great deal of ingenuity to keep out of trouble. It is a southern custom that all men must take off their hats when they enter an elevator. And especially did this apply to us blacks with rigid force. One day I stepped into an elevator with my arms full of packages. I was forced to ride with my hat on. Two white men stared at me coldly. Then one of them very kindly lifted my hat and placed it upon my armful of packages. Now the most accepted response for a Negro to make under such circumstances is to look at the white man out of the corner of his eye and grin. To have said: "Thank you!" would have made the white man think that you thought you were receiving from him a personal service. For such an act I have seen Negroes take a blow in the mouth. Finding the first alternative distasteful, and the second dangerous, I hit upon an acceptable course of action which fell safely between these two poles. I immediately—no sooner than my hat was lifted—pretended that my packages were about to spill, and appeared deeply distressed with keeping them in my arms. In this fashion I evaded having to acknowledge his service, and, in spite of adverse circumstances, salvaged a slender shred of personal pride.

How do Negroes feel about the way they have to live? How do they discuss it when alone among themselves? I think this question can be answered in a single sentence. A friend of mine who ran an elevator once told me:

"Lowd, man! Ef it wuzn't fer them polices 'n' them ol' lynch-mobs, there wouldn't be nothin' but uproar down here!"

Big Black Good Man

RICHARD WRIGHT

THROUGH THE OPEN WINDOW Olaf Jenson could smell the sea and hear the occasional foghorn of a freighter; outside, rain pelted down through an August night, drumming softly upon the pavements of Copenhagen, inducing drowsiness, bringing dreamy memory, relaxing the tired muscles of his work-wracked body. He sat slumped in a swivel chair with his legs outstretched and his feet propped atop an edge of his desk. An inch of white ash tipped the end of his brown cigar and now and then he inserted the end of the stogie into his mouth and drew gently upon it, letting wisps of blue smoke eddy from the corners of his wide, thin lips. The watery gray irises behind the thick lenses of his eyeglasses gave him a look of abstraction, of absent-mindedness, of an almost genial idiocy. He sighed, reached for his half-empty bottle of beer, and drained it into his glass and downed it with a long slow gulp, then licked his lips. Replacing the cigar, he slapped his right palm against his thigh and said half aloud:

"Well, I'll be sixty tomorrow. I'm not rich, but I'm not poor either . . . Really, I can't complain. Got good health. Traveled all over the world and had my share of the girls when I was young . . . And my Karen's a good wife. I own my home. Got no debts. And I love digging in my garden in the spring . . . Grew the biggest carrots of anybody last year. Ain't saved much money, but what the hell . . . Money ain't everything. Got a good job. Night portering ain't too bad." He shook his head and yawned. "Karen and I could of had some children, though. Would of been good company . . . 'Specially for Karen. And I could of taught 'em languages . . . English, French, German, Danish, Dutch, Swedish, Norwegian, and Spanish . . ." He took the cigar out of his mouth and eyed the white ash critically. "Hell of a lot of good language learning did me . . . Never got anything out of it. But those ten years in New York were fun . . . Maybe I could of got rich if I'd stayed in America . . . Maybe. But I'm satisfied. You can't have everything."

Behind him the office door opened and a young man, a medical student occupying room number nine, entered.

Reprinted from *Eight Men,* by permission of HarperCollins Publishers, Inc. Copyright © 1957 by Esquire, Inc.

"Good evening," the student said.

"Good evening," Olaf said, turning.

The student went to the keyboard and took hold of the round, brown knob that anchored his key.

"Rain, rain, rain," the student said.

"That's Denmark for you," Olaf smiled at him.

"This dampness keeps me clogged up like a drainpipe," the student complained.

"That's Denmark for you," Olaf repeated with a smile.

"Good night," the student said.

"Good night, son," Olaf sighed, watching the door close.

Well, my tenants are my children, Olaf told himself. Almost all of his children were in their rooms now . . . Only seventy-two and forty-four were missing . . . Seventy-two might've gone to Sweden . . . And forty-four was maybe staying at his girl's place tonight, like he sometimes did . . . He studied the pear-shaped blobs of hard rubber, reddish brown like ripe fruit, that hung from the keyboard, then glanced at his watch. Only room thirty, eighty-one, and one hundred and one were empty . . . And it was almost midnight. In a few moments he could take a nap. Nobody hardly ever came looking for accommodations after midnight, unless a stray freighter came in, bringing thirsty, women-hungry sailors. Olaf chuckled softly. Why in hell was I ever a sailor? The whole time I was at sea I was thinking and dreaming about women. Then why didn't I stay on land where women could be had? Hunh? Sailors are crazy . . .

But he liked sailors. They reminded him of his youth, and there was something so direct, simple, and childlike about them. They always said straight out what they wanted, and what they wanted was almost always women and whisky . . . "Well, there's no harm in that . . . Nothing could be more natural," Olaf sighed, looking thirstily at his empty beer bottle. No; he'd not drink any more tonight; he'd had enough; he'd go to sleep . . .

He was bending forward and loosening his shoelaces when he heard the office door crack open. He lifted his eyes, then sucked in his breath. He did not straighten; he just stared up and around at the huge black thing that filled the doorway. His reflexes refused to function; it was not fear; it was just simple astonishment. He was staring at the biggest, strangest, and blackest man he'd ever seen in all his life.

"Good evening," the black giant said in a voice that filled the small office. "Say, you got a room?"

Olaf sat up slowly, not to answer but to look at this brooding black vision; it towered darkly some six and a half feet into the air, almost touching the ceiling; and its skin was so black that it had a bluish tint. And the sheer bulk of the man!... His chest bulged like a barrel; his rocklike and humped shoulders hinted of mountain ridges; the stomach ballooned like a threatening stone; and the legs were like telephone poles... The big black cloud of a man now lumbered into the office, bending to get its buffalolike head under the door frame, then advanced slowly upon Olaf, like a stormy sky descending.

"You got a room?" the big black man asked again in a resounding voice.

Olaf now noticed that the ebony giant was well dressed, carried a wonderful new suitcase, and wore black shoes that gleamed despite the raindrops that peppered their toes.

"You're American?" Olaf asked him.

"Yeah, man; sure," the black giant answered.

"Sailor?"

"Yeah. American Continental Lines."

Olaf had not answered the black man's question. It was not that the hotel did not admit men of color; Olaf took in all comers—blacks, yellows, whites, and browns... To Olaf, men were men, and, in his day, he'd worked and eaten and slept and fought with all kinds of men. But this particular black man... Well, he didn't seem human. Too big, too black, too loud, too direct, and probably too violent to boot... Olaf's five feet seven inches scarcely reached the black giant's shoulder and his frail body weighed less, perhaps, than one of the man's gigantic legs... There was something about the man's intense blackness and ungamely bigness that frightened and insulted Olaf; he felt as though this man had come here expressly to remind him how puny, how tiny, and how weak and how white he was. Olaf knew, while registering his reactions, that he was being irrational and foolish; yet, for the first time in his life, he was emotionally determined to refuse a man a room solely on the basis of the man's size and color... Olaf's lips parted as he groped for the right words in which to couch his refusal, but the black giant bent forward and boomed:

"I asked you if you got a room. I got to put up somewhere tonight, man."

"Yes, we got a room," Olaf murmured.

And at once he was ashamed and confused. Sheer fear had made him yield. And he seethed against himself for his involuntary weakness. Well, he'd look over his book and pretend that he'd made a mistake; he'd tell this hunk of blackness that there was really no free room in the hotel, and that he was so sorry... Then, just as he took out the hotel register to make believe that he was poring over it, a thick roll of American bank notes, crisp and green, was thrust under his nose.

"Keep this for me, will you?" the black giant commanded. "'Cause I'm gonna get drunk tonight and I don't wanna lose it."

Olaf stared at the roll; it was huge, in denominations of fifties and hundreds. Olaf's eyes widened.

"How much is there?" he asked.

"Two thousand six hundred," the giant said. "Just put it into an envelope and write 'Jim' on it and lock it in your safe, hunh?"

The black mass of man had spoken in a manner that indicated that it was taking it for granted that Olaf would obey. Olaf was licked. Resentment clogged the pores of his wrinkled white skin. His hands trembled as he picked up the money. No; he couldn't refuse this man . . . The impulse to deny him was strong, but each time he was about to act upon it something thwarted him, made him shy off. He clutched about desperately for an idea. Oh, yes, he could say that if he planned to stay for only one night, then he could not have the room, for it was against the policy of the hotel to rent rooms for only one night . . .

"How long are you staying? Just tonight?" Olaf asked.

"Naw. I'll be here for five or six days, I reckon," the giant answered offhandedly.

"You take room number thirty," Olaf heard himself saying. "It's forty kronor a day."

"That's all right with me," the giant said.

With slow, stiff movements, Olaf put the money in the safe and then turned and stared helplessly up into the living, breathing blackness looming above him. Suddenly he became conscious of the outstretched palm of the black giant; he was silently demanding the key to the room. His eyes downcast, Olaf surrendered the key, marveling at the black man's tremendous hands . . . He could kill me with one blow, Olaf told himself in fear.

Feeling himself beaten, Olaf reached for the suitcase, but the black hand of the giant whisked it out of his grasp.

"That's too heavy for you, big boy; I'll take it," the giant said.

Olaf let him. He thinks I'm nothing . . . He led the way down the corridor, sensing the giant's lumbering presence behind him. Olaf opened the door of number thirty and stood politely to one side, allowing the black giant to enter. At once the room seemed like a doll's house, so dwarfed and filled and tiny it was with a great living blackness . . . Flinging his suitcase upon a chair, the giant turned. The two men looked directly at each other now. Olaf saw that the giant's eyes were tiny and red, buried, it seemed, in muscle and fat. Black cheeks spread, flat and broad, topping the wide and flaring nostrils. The mouth was the biggest that Olaf had ever seen on a human face; the lips were thick, pursed, parted, showing snow-white teeth. The black neck was like a bull's . . . The giant advanced upon Olaf and stood over him.

"I want a bottle of whisky and a woman," he said. "Can you fix me up?"

"Yes," Olaf whispered, wild with anger and insult.

But what was he angry about? He'd had requests like this every night from all sorts of men and he was used to fulfilling them; he was a night porter in a cheap, water-front Copenhagen hotel that catered to sailors and students. Yes, men needed women, but this man, Olaf felt, ought to have a special sort of woman. He felt a deep and strange reluctance to phone any of the women whom he habitually sent to men. Yet he had promised. Could he lie and say that none was available? No. That sounded too fishy. The black giant sat upon the bed, staring straight before him. Olaf moved about quickly, pulling down the window shades, taking the pink coverlet off the bed, nudging the giant with his elbow to make him move as he did so ... That's the way to treat 'im ... Show 'im I ain't scared of 'im ... But he was still seeking for an excuse to refuse. And he could think of nothing. He felt hypnotized, mentally immobilized. He stood hesitantly at the door.

"You send the whisky and the woman quick, pal?" the black giant asked, rousing himself from a brooding stare.

"Yes," Olaf grunted, shutting the door.

Goddamn, Olaf sighed. He sat in his office at his desk before the phone. Why did *he* have to come here? ... I'm not prejudiced ... No, not at all ... But ... He couldn't think any more. God oughtn't make men as big and black as that ... But what the hell was he worrying about? He'd sent women of all races to men of all colors ... So why not a woman to the black giant? Oh, only if the man were small, brown, and intelligent-looking ... Olaf felt trapped.

With a reflex movement of his hand, he picked up the phone and dialed Lena. She was big and strong and always cut him in for fifteen per cent instead of the usual ten per cent. Lena had four small children to feed and clothe. Lena was willing; she was, she said, coming over right now. She didn't give a good goddamn about how big and black the man was ...

"Why you ask me that?" Lena wanted to know over the phone. "You never asked that before ..."

"But this one is *big*," Olaf found himself saying.

"He's just a man," Lena told him, her voice singing stridently, laughingly over the wire. "You just leave that to me. You don't have to do anything. *I'll* handle 'im."

Lena had a key to the hotel door downstairs, but tonight Olaf stayed awake. He wanted to see her. Why? He didn't know. He stretched out on the sofa in his office, but sleep was far from him. When Lena arrived, he told her again how big and black the man was.

"You told me that over the phone," Lena reminded him.

Olaf said nothing. Lena flounced off on her errand of mercy. Olaf shut the office door, then opened it and left it ajar. But why? He didn't know. He lay upon the sofa and stared at the ceiling. He glanced at his watch; it was almost two o'clock . . . She's staying in there a long time . . . Ah, God, but he could do with a drink . . . Why was he so damned worked up and nervous about a nigger and a white whore? . . . He'd never been so upset in all his life. Before he knew it, he had drifted off to sleep. Then he heard the office door swinging creakingly open on its rusty hinges. Lena stood in it, grim and businesslike, her face scrubbed free of powder and rouge. Olaf scrambled to his feet, adjusting his eyeglasses, blinking.

"How was it?" he asked her in a confidential whisper.

Lena's eyes blazed.

"What the hell's that to you?" she snapped. "There's your cut," she said, flinging him his money, tossing it upon the covers of the sofa. "You're sure nosy tonight. You wanna take over my work?"

Olaf's pasty cheeks burned red.

"You go to hell," he said, slamming the door.

"I'll meet you there!" Lena's shouting voice reached him dimly.

He was being a fool; there was no doubt about it. But, try as he might, he could not shake off a primitive hate for that black mountain of energy, of muscle, of bone; he envied the easy manner in which it moved with such a creeping and powerful motion; he winced at the booming and commanding voice that came to him when the tiny little eyes were not even looking at him; he shivered at the sight of those vast and clawlike hands that seemed always to hint of death . . .

Olaf kept his counsel. He never spoke to Karen about the sordid doings at the hotel. Such things were not for women like Karen. He knew instinctively that Karen would have been amazed had he told her that he was worried sick about a nigger and a blonde whore . . . No; he couldn't talk to anybody about it, not even the hard-bitten old bitch who owned the hotel. She was concerned only about money; she didn't give a damn about how big and black a client was as long as he paid his room rent.

Next evening, when Olaf arrived for duty, there was no sight or sound of the black giant. A little later after one o'clock in the morning he appeared, left his key, and went out wordlessly. A few moments past two the giant returned, took his key from the board, and paused.

"I want that Lena again tonight. And another bottle of whisky," he said boomingly.

"I'll call her and see if she's in," Olaf said.

"Do that," the black giant said and was gone.

He thinks he's God, Olaf fumed. He picked up the phone and ordered Lena and a bottle of whisky, and there was a taste of ashes in his mouth. On the third night came the same request: Lena and whisky. When the black giant appeared on the fifth night, Olaf was about to make a sarcastic remark to the effect that maybe he ought to marry Lena, but he checked it in time . . . After all, he could kill me with one hand, he told himself.

Olaf was nervous and angry with himself for being nervous. Other black sailors came and asked for girls and Olaf sent them, but with none of the fear and loathing that he sent Lena and a bottle of whisky to the giant . . . All right, the black giant's stay was almost up. He'd said that he was staying for five or six nights; tomorrow night was the sixth night and that ought to be the end of this nameless terror.

On the sixth night Olaf sat in his swivel chair with his bottle of beer and waited, his teeth on edge, his fingers drumming the desk. But what the hell am I fretting for? . . . The hell with 'im . . . Olaf sat and dozed. Occasionally he'd awaken and listen to the foghorns of freighters sounding as ships came and went in the misty Copenhagen harbor. He was half asleep when he felt a rough hand on his shoulder. He blinked his eyes open. The giant, black and vast and powerful, all but blotted out his vision.

"What I owe you, man?" the giant demanded. "And I want my money."

"Sure," Olaf said, relieved, but filled as always with fear of this living wall of black flesh.

With fumbling hands, he made out the bill and received payment, then gave the giant his roll of money, laying it on the desk so as not to let his hands touch the flesh of the black mountain. Well, his ordeal was over. It was past two o'clock in the morning. Olaf even managed a wry smile and muttered a guttural "Thanks" for the generous tip that the giant tossed him.

Then a strange tension entered the office. The office door was shut and Olaf was alone with the black mass of power, yearning for it to leave. But the black mass of power stood still, immobile, looking down at Olaf. And Olaf could not, for the life of him, guess at what was transpiring in that mysterious black mind. The two of them simply stared at each other for a full two minutes, the giant's tiny little beady eyes blinking slowly as they seemed to measure and search Olaf's face. Olaf's vision dimmed for a second as terror seized him and he could feel a flush of heat overspread his body. Then Olaf sucked in his breath as the devil of blackness commanded:

"Stand up!"

Olaf was paralyzed. Sweat broke on his face. His worst premonitions about this black beast were coming true. This evil blackness was about to attack him, maybe kill him . . . Slowly Olaf shook his head, his terror permitting him to breathe:

"What're you talking about?"

"Stand up, I say!" the black giant bellowed.

As though hypnotized, Olaf tried to rise: then he felt the black paw of the beast helping him roughly to his feet.

They stood an inch apart. Olaf's pasty-white features were lifted to the giant's swollen black face. The ebony ensemble of eyes and nose and mouth and cheeks looked down at Olaf, silently; then, with a slow and deliberate movement of his gorillalike arms, he lifted his mammoth hands to Olaf's throat. Olaf had long known and felt that this dreadful moment was coming; he felt trapped in a nightmare. He could not move. He wanted to scream, but could find no words. His lips refused to open; his tongue felt icy and inert. Then he knew that his end had come when the giant's black fingers slowly, softly encircled his throat while a horrible grin of delight broke out on the sooty face . . . Olaf lost control of the reflexes of his body and he felt a hot stickiness flooding his underwear . . . He stared without breathing, gazing into the grinning blackness of the face that was bent over him, feeling the black fingers caressing his throat and waiting to feel the sharp, stinging ache and pain of the bones in his neck being snapped, crushed . . . He knew all along that I hated 'im . . . Yes, and now he's going to kill me for it, Olaf told himself with despair.

The black fingers still circled Olaf's neck, not closing, but gently massaging it, as it were, moving to and fro, while the obscene face grinned into his. Olaf could feel the giant's warm breath blowing on his eyelashes and he felt like a chicken about to have its neck wrung and its body tossed to flip and flap dyingly in the dust of the barnyard . . . Then suddenly the black giant withdrew his fingers from Olaf's neck and stepped back a pace, still grinning. Olaf sighed, trembling, his body seeming to shrink; he waited. Shame sheeted him for the hot wetness that was in his trousers. Oh, God, he's teasing me . . . He's showing me how easily he can kill me . . . He swallowed, waiting, his eyes stones of gray.

The giant's barrel-like chest gave forth a low, rumbling chuckle of delight.

"You laugh?" Olaf asked whimperingly.

"Sure I laugh," the giant shouted.

"Please don't hurt me," Olaf managed to say.

"I wouldn't hurt you, boy," the giant said in a tone of mockery. "So long."

And he was gone. Olaf fell limply into the swivel chair and fought off losing consciousness. Then he wept. He was showing me how easily he could kill me . . . He made me shake with terror and then laughed and left . . . Slowly, Olaf recovered, stood, then gave vent to a string of curses:

"Goddamn 'im! My gun's right there in the desk drawer; I should of shot 'im. Jesus, I hope the ship he's on sinks . . . I hope he drowns and the sharks eat 'im . . ."

Later, he thought of going to the police, but sheer shame kept him back; and, anyway, the giant was probably on board his ship by now. And he had to get home and clean himself. Oh, Lord, what could he tell Karen? Yes, he would say that his stomach had been upset . . . He'd change clothes and return to work. He phoned the hotel owner that he was ill and wanted an hour off; the old bitch said that she was coming right over and that poor Olaf could have the evening off.

Olaf went home and lied to Karen. Then he lay awake the rest of the night dreaming of revenge. He saw that freighter on which the giant was sailing; he saw it springing a dangerous leak and saw a torrent of sea water flooding, gushing into all the compartments of the ship until it found the bunk in which the black giant slept. Ah, yes, the foamy, surging waters would surprise that sleeping black bastard of a giant and he would drown, gasping and choking like a trapped rat, his tiny eyes bulging until they glittered red, the bitter water of the sea pounding his lungs until they ached and finally burst . . . The ship would sink slowly to the bottom of the cold, black, silent depths of the sea and a shark, a *white* one, would glide aimlessly about the shut portholes until it found an open one and it would slither inside and nose about until it found that swollen, rotting, stinking carcass of the black beast and it would then begin to nibble at the decomposing mass of tarlike flesh, eating the bones clean . . . Olaf always pictured the giant's bones as being jet black and shining.

Once or twice, during these fantasies of cannibalistic revenge, Olaf felt a little guilty about all the many innocent people, women and children, all white and blonde, who would have to go down into watery graves in order that that white shark could devour the evil giant's black flesh . . . But, despite feelings of remorse, the fantasy lived persistently on, and when Olaf found himself alone, it would crowd and cloud his mind to the exclusion of all else, affording him the only revenge he knew. To make me suffer just for the pleasure of it, he fumed. Just to show me how strong he was . . . Olaf learned how to hate, and got pleasure out of it.

Summer fled on wings of rain. Autumn flooded Denmark with color. Winter made rain and snow fall on Copenhagen. Finally spring came, bringing violets and roses. Olaf kept to his job. For many months he feared the return of the black giant. But when a year had passed and the giant had not put in an appearance, Olaf allowed his revenge fantasy to peter out, indulging in it only when recalling the shame that the black monster had made him feel.

Then one rainy August night, a year later, Olaf sat drowsing at his desk, his bottle of beer before him, tilting back in his swivel chair, his feet resting atop a corner of his desk, his mind mulling over the more pleasant aspects of his life. The office door cracked open. Olaf glanced boredly up and around. His heart jumped and skipped a beat. The black nightmare of terror and shame that he had hoped that he had lost forever was again upon him . . . Resplendently dressed, suitcase in hand, the black looming mountain filled the doorway. Olaf's thin lips parted and a silent moan, half a curse, escaped them.

"Hy," the black giant boomed from the doorway.

Olaf could not reply. But a sudden resolve swept him: this time he would even the score. If this black beast came within so much as three feet of him, he would snatch his gun out of the drawer and shoot him dead, so help him God . . .

"No rooms tonight," Olaf heard himself announcing in a determined voice.

The black giant grinned; it was the same infernal grimace of delight and triumph that he had had when his damnable black fingers had been around his throat . . .

"Don't want no room tonight," the giant announced.

"Then what are you doing here?" Olaf asked in a loud but tremulous voice.

The giant swept toward Olaf and stood over him; and Olaf could not move, despite his oath to kill him . . .

"What do you want then?" Olaf demanded once more, ashamed that he could not lift his voice above a whisper.

The giant still grinned, then tossed what seemed the same suitcase upon Olaf's sofa and bent over it; he zippered it open with a sweep of his clawlike hand and rummaged in it, drawing forth a flat, gleaming white object done up in glowing cellophane. Olaf watched with lowered lids, wondering what trick was now being played on him. Then, before he could defend himself, the giant had whirled and again long, black, snakelike fingers were encircling Olaf's throat . . . Olaf stiffened, his right hand clawing blindly for the drawer where the gun was kept. But the giant was quick.

"Wait," he bellowed, pushing Olaf back from the desk.

The giant turned quickly to the sofa and, still holding his fingers in a wide circle that seemed a noose for Olaf's neck, he inserted the rounded fingers into the top of the flat, gleaming object. Olaf had the drawer open and his sweaty fingers were now touching his gun, but something made him freeze. The flat, gleaming object was a shirt and the black giant's circled fingers were fitting themselves into its neck . . .

"A perfect fit!" the giant shouted.

Olaf stared, trying to understand. His fingers loosened about the gun. A mixture of a laugh and a curse struggled in him. He watched the giant plunge his hands into the suitcase and pull out other flat, gleaming shirts.

"One, two, three, four, five, six," the black giant intoned, his voice crisp and businesslike. "Six nylon shirts. And they're all yours. One shirt for each time Lena came . . . See, Daddy-O?"

The black, cupped hands, filled with billowing nylon whiteness, were extended under Olaf's nose. Olaf eased his damp fingers from his gun and pushed the drawer closed, staring at the shirts and then at the black giant's grinning face.

"Don't you like 'em?" the giant asked.

Olaf began to laugh hysterically, then suddenly he was crying, his eyes so flooded with tears that the pile of dazzling nylon looked like snow in the dead of winter. Was this true? Could he believe it? Maybe this too was a trick? But, no. There were six shirts, all nylon, and the black giant had had Lena six nights.

"What's the matter with you, Daddy-O?" the giant asked. "You blowing your top? Laughing and crying . . ."

Olaf swallowed, dabbed his withered fists at his dimmed eyes; then he realized that he had his glasses on. He took them off and dried his eyes and sat up. He sighed, the tension and shame and fear and haunting dread of his fantasy went from him, and he leaned limply back in his chair . . .

"Try one on," the giant ordered.

Olaf fumbled with the buttons of his shirt, let down his suspenders, and pulled the shirt off. He donned a gleaming nylon one and the giant began buttoning it for him.

"Perfect, Daddy-O," the giant said.

His spectacled face framed in sparkling nylon, Olaf sat with trembling lips. So he'd not been trying to kill me after all.

"You want Lena, don't you?" he asked the giant in a soft whisper. "But I don't know where she is. She never came back here after you left—"

"I know where Lena is," the giant told him. "We been writing to each other. I'm going to her house. And, Daddy-O, I'm late." The giant zippered the suitcase shut and stood a moment gazing down at Olaf, his tiny little red eyes blinking slowly. Then Olaf realized that there was a compassion in that stare that he had never seen before.

"And I thought you wanted to kill me," Olaf told him. "I was scared of you . . ."

"Me? Kill you?" the giant blinked. "When?"

"That night when you put your fingers about my throat—"

"What?" the giant asked, then roared with laughter. "Daddy-O, you're a funny little man. I wouldn't hurt you. I like you. You a *good* man. You helped me."

Olaf smiled, clutching the pile of nylon shirts in his arms.

"You're a good man too," Olaf murmured. Then loudly: "You're a big black good man."

"Daddy-O, you're crazy," the giant said.

He swept his suitcase from the sofa, spun on his heel, and was at the door in one stride.

"Thanks!" Olaf cried after him.

The black giant paused, turned his vast black head, and flashed a grin.

"Daddy-O, drop dead," he said and was gone.

[1958]

Maxine Hong Kingston
[1940–   ]

The daughter of Chinese immigrant parents, MAXINE HONG KINGSTON *was born in Stockton, California and grew up in various Chinese-American communities throughout central California. She received a bachelor of arts from the University of California at Berkeley in 1962 and a teacher's certificate in 1965, and subsequently taught high school in California and Hawai'i. In 1977 she became a member of the faculty of the University of Hawai'i, and in 1990 joined the faculty at the University of California at Berkeley, where she teaches creative writing.*

Kingston was teaching school in Hawai'i when she wrote The Woman Warrior: Memoirs of a Girlhood Among Ghosts, *published in 1976. This pastiche of myth and legend, family history and imagination, demonstrates Kingston's ambivalence toward her Chinese heritage, but also her acknowledgment of its richness. As a young girl growing up in California, she was confronted by the sometimes incomprehensible traditions her family adhered to and struggled to reconcile these with a mainstream culture that regarded them as foreign. In her attempts to navigate between the sexism of her native culture and the racism of mainstream American society she finds power in her own voice as a storyteller.* The Woman Warrior *earned Kingston a National Book Critics Circle Award for nonfiction and was named one of the top ten nonfiction works of the decade by* Time *magazine. Kingston followed* The Woman Warrior *with the limited edition of* Hawai'i One Summer *in 1978. Her next major work was* China Men, *published in 1980. In this novel, as in* The Woman Warrior, *Kingston fuses history and legend to describe the experiences of young male Chinese immigrants to the United States, as well as the cultural confusion faced by their children. Though raising the same questions of culture and heritage as* Woman Warrior, China Men *also explores the social and cultural constructions of masculinity and the challenges men face as they confront alien and alienating cultures.* China Men *was followed in 1989 by* Tripmaster Monkey, *which was awarded the John Dos Passos Prize for Literature in 1998. Kingston's other distinctions include the title of "Living Treasure of Hawai'i" (1980) and the award of a National Humanities Medal by President Bill Clinton, in 1997.*

The selection reprinted here, "No Name Woman," is drawn from The Woman Warrior *and deals with a young Chinese-American girl's discovery that her aunt, whom she never knew existed, had dishonored her family in China by becoming pregnant out of wedlock. The narrator's response to her aunt's "un-naming," to the functional erasure of her identity, foregrounds the sometimes brutal traditions of her ancestors, particularly with regard to the treatment of women.*

—David L. G. Arnold, *University of Wisconsin, Stevens Point*

No Name Woman

MAXINE HONG KINGSTON

"YOU MUST NOT TELL anyone," my mother said, "what I am about to tell you. In China your father had a sister who killed herself. She jumped into the family well. We say that your father has all brothers because it is as if she had never been born.

"In 1924 just a few days after our village celebrated seventeen hurry-up weddings—to make sure that every young man who went 'out on the road' would responsibly come home—your father and his brothers and your grandfather and his brothers and your aunt's new husband sailed for America, the Gold Mountain. It was your grandfather's last trip. Those lucky enough to get contracts waved good-bye from the decks. They fed and guarded the stowaways and helped them off in Cuba, New York, Bali, Hawaii. 'We'll meet in California next year,' they said. All of them sent money home.

"I remember looking at your aunt one day when she and I were dressing; I had not noticed before that she had such a protruding melon of a stomach. But I did not think, 'She's pregnant,' until she began to look like other pregnant women, her shirt pulling and the white tops of her black pants showing. She could not have been pregnant, you see, because her husband had been gone for years. No one said anything. We did not discuss it. In early summer she was ready to have the child, long after the time when it could have been possible.

"The village had also been counting. On the night the baby was to be born the villagers raided our house. Some were crying. Like a great saw, teeth strung with lights, files of people walked zigzag across our land, tearing the rice. Their lanterns doubled in the disturbed black water, which drained away through the broken bunds.[1] As the villagers closed in, we could see that some of them, probably men and women we knew well, wore white masks. The people with long hair hung it over their faces. Women with short hair made it stand up on end. Some had tied white bands around their foreheads, arms, and legs.

---

[1]Bunds are a damn-like embankment used to control the flow of water.

Reprinted from *The Woman Warrior,* by permission of Alfred A. Knopf, a division of Random House, Inc. Copyright © 1975, 1976 by Maxine Hong Kingston.

"At first they threw mud and rocks at the house. Then they threw eggs and began slaughtering our stock. We could hear the animals scream their deaths—the roosters, the pigs, a last great roar from the ox. Familiar wild heads flared in our night windows; the villagers encircled us. Some of the faces stopped to peer at us, their eyes rushing like searchlights. The hands flattened against the panes, framed heads, and left red prints.

"The villagers broke in the front and the back doors at the same time, even though we had not locked the doors against them. Their knives dripped with the blood of our animals. They smeared blood on the doors and walls. One woman swung a chicken, whose throat she had slit, splattering blood in red arcs about her. We stood together in the middle of our house, in the family hall with the pictures and tables of the ancestors around us, and looked straight ahead.

"At that time the house had only two wings. When the men came back, we would build two more to enclose our courtyard and a third one to begin a second courtyard. The villagers rushed through both wings, even your grandparents' rooms, to find your aunt's, which was also mine until the men returned. From this room a new wing for one of the younger families would grow. They ripped up her clothes and shoes and broke her combs, grinding them underfoot. They tore her work from the loom. They scattered the cooking fire and rolled the new weaving in it. We could hear them in the kitchen breaking our bowls and banging the pots. They overturned the great waist-high earthenware jugs; duck eggs, pickled fruits, vegetables burst out and mixed in acrid torrents. The old woman from the next field swept a broom through the air and loosed the spirits-of-the-broom over our heads. 'Pig.' 'Ghost.' 'Pig,' they sobbed and scolded while they ruined our house.

"When they left, they took sugar and oranges to bless themselves. They cut pieces from the dead animals. Some of them took bowls that were not broken and clothes that were not torn. Afterward we swept up the rice and sewed it back up into sacks. But the smells from the spilled preserves lasted. Your aunt gave birth in the pigsty that night. The next morning when I went for the water, I found her and the baby plugging up the family well.

"Don't let your father know that I told you. He denies her. Now that you have started to menstruate, what happened to her could happen to you. Don't humiliate us. You wouldn't like to be forgotten as if you had never been born. The villagers are watchful."

Whenever she had to warn us about life, my mother told stories that ran like this one, a story to grow up on. She tested our strength to establish realities. Those in the emigrant generations who could not reassert brute survival died young and far from home. Those of us in the first American generations have had to figure out how the invisible world the emigrants built around our childhoods fit in solid America.

The emigrants confused the gods by diverting their curses, misleading them with crooked streets and false names. They must try to confuse their off-spring as well, who, I suppose, threaten them in similar ways—always trying to get things straight, always trying to name the unspeakable. The Chinese I know hide their names; sojourners take new names when their lives change and guard their real names with silence.

Chinese-Americans, when you try to understand what things in you are Chinese, how do you separate what is peculiar to childhood, to poverty, insanities, one family, your mother who marked your growing with stories, from what is Chinese? What is Chinese tradition and what is the movies?

If I want to learn what clothes my aunt wore, whether flashy or ordinary, I would have to begin, "Remember Father's drowned-in-the-well sister?" I cannot ask that. My mother has told me once and for all the useful parts. She will add nothing unless powered by Necessity, a riverbank that guides her life. She plants vegetable gardens rather than lawns; she carries the odd-shaped tomatoes home from the fields and eats food left for the gods.

Whenever we did frivolous things, we used up energy; we flew high kites. We children came up off the ground over the melting cones our parents brought home from work and the American movie on New Year's Day—*Oh, You Beautiful Doll* with Betty Grable one year, and *She Wore a Yellow Ribbon* with John Wayne another year.[2] After the one carnival ride each, we paid in guilt; our tired father counted his change on the dark walk home.

Adultery is extravagance. Could people who hatch their own chicks and eat the embryos and the heads for delicacies and boil the feet in vinegar for party food, leaving only the gravel, eating even the gizzard lining—could such people engender a prodigal aunt? To be a woman, to have a daughter in starvation time was a waste enough. My aunt could not have been the lone romantic who gave up everything for sex. Women in the old China did not choose. Some man had commanded her to lie with him and be his secret evil. I wonder whether he masked himself when he joined the raid on her family.

Perhaps she encountered him in the fields or on the mountain where the daughters-in-law collected fuel. Or perhaps he first noticed her in the market-place. He was not a stranger because the village housed no strangers. She had to have dealings with him other than sex. Perhaps he worked an adjoining field, or he sold her the cloth for the dress she sewed and wore. His demand must have surprised, then terrified her. She obeyed him; she always did as she was told.

---

[2]Both of the films mentioned here were released in 1949. *Oh You Beautiful Doll,* directed by John M. Stahl, stars June Haver (Betty Grable starred in the 1949 comedy-western *The Beautiful Blonde from Bashful Bend,* directed by Preston Sturges). John Wayne plays Capt. Brittles in John Ford's *She Wore a Yellow Ribbon.*

When the family found a young man in the next village to be her husband, she stood tractably beside the best rooster, his proxy, and promised before they met that she would be his forever. She was lucky that he was her age and she would be the first wife, an advantage secure now. The night she first saw him, he had sex with her. Then he left for America. She had almost forgotten what he looked like. When she tried to envision him, she only saw the black and white face in the group photograph the men had had taken before leaving.

The other man was not, after all, much different from her husband. They both gave orders: she followed. "If you tell your family, I'll beat you. I'll kill you. Be here again next week." No one talked sex, ever. And she might have separated the rapes from the rest of living if only she did not have to buy her oil from him or gather wood in the same forest. I want her fear to have lasted just as long as rape lasted so that the fear could have been contained. No drawn-out fear. But women at sex hazarded birth and hence lifetimes. The fear did not stop but permeated everywhere. She told the man, "I think I'm pregnant." He organized the raid against her.

On nights when my mother and father talked about their life back home, sometimes they mentioned an "outcast table" whose business they still seemed to be settling, their voices tight. In a commensal tradition, where food is precious, the powerful older people made wrongdoers eat alone. Instead of letting them start separate new lives like the Japanese, who could become samurais and geishas, the Chinese family, faces averted but eyes glowering sideways, hung on to the offenders and fed them leftovers. My aunt must have lived in the same house as my parents and eaten at an outcast table. My mother spoke about the raid as if she had seen it, when she and my aunt, a daughter-in-law to a different household, should not have been living together at all. Daughters-in-law lived with their husbands' parents, not their own; a synonym for marriage in Chinese is "taking a daughter-in-law." Her husband's parents could have sold her, mortgaged her, stoned her. But they had sent her back to her own mother and father, a mysterious act hinting at disgraces not told me. Perhaps they had thrown her out to deflect the avengers.

She was the only daughter; her four brothers went with her father, husband, and uncles "out on the road" and for some years became western men. When the goods were divided among the family, three of the brothers took land, and the youngest, my father, chose an education. After my grandparents gave their daughter away to her husband's family, they had dispensed all the adventure and all the property. They expected her alone to keep the traditional ways, which her brothers, now among the barbarians, could fumble without detection. The heavy, deep-rooted women were to maintain the past against the flood, safe for returning. But the rare urge west had fixed upon our family, and so my aunt crossed boundaries not delineated in space.

The work of preservation demands that the feelings playing about in one's guts not be turned into action. Just watch their passing like cherry blossoms. But perhaps my aunt, my forerunner, caught in a slow life, let dreams grow and fade and after some months or years went toward what persisted. Fear at the enormities of the forbidden kept her desires delicate, wire and bone. She looked at a man because she liked the way the hair was tucked behind his ears, or she liked the question-mark line of a long torso curving at the shoulder and straight at the hip. For warm eyes or a soft voice or a slow walk—that's all—a few hairs, a line, a brightness, a sound, a pace, she gave up family. She offered us up for a charm that vanished with tiredness, a pigtail that didn't toss when the wind died. Why, the wrong lighting could erase the dearest thing about him.

It could very well have been, however, that my aunt did not take subtle enjoyment of her friend, but, a wild woman, kept rollicking company. Imagining her free with sex doesn't fit, though. I don't know any women like that, or men either. Unless I see her life branching into mine, she gives me no ancestral help.

To sustain her being in love, she often worked at herself in the mirror, guessing at the colors and shapes that would interest him, changing them frequently in order to hit on the right combination. She wanted him to look back.

On a farm near the sea, a woman who tended her appearance reaped a reputation for eccentricity. All the married women blunt-cut their hair in flaps about their ears or pulled it back in tight buns. No nonsense. Neither style blew easily into heart-catching tangles. And at their weddings they displayed themselves in their long hair for the last time. "It brushed the backs of my knees," my mother tells me. "It was braided, and even so, it brushed the backs of my knees."

At the mirror my aunt combed individuality into her bob. A bun could have been contrived to escape into black streamers blowing in the wind or in quiet wisps about her face, but only the older women in our picture album wear buns. She brushed her hair back from her forehead, tucking the flaps behind her ears. She looped a piece of thread, knotted into a circle between her index fingers and thumbs, and ran the double strand across her forehead. When she closed her fingers as if she were making a pair of shadow geese bite, the string twisted together catching the little hairs. Then she pulled the thread away from her skin, ripping the hairs out neatly, her eyes watering from the needles of pain. Opening her fingers, she cleaned the thread, then rolled it along her hairline and the tops of her eyebrows. My mother did the same to me and my sisters and herself. I used to believe that the expression "caught by the short hairs" meant a captive held with a depilatory string. It especially hurt at the temples, but my mother said we were lucky we didn't have to have our feet bound when we were seven. Sisters used to sit on their beds and cry together, she said, as their mothers or their slave removed the bandages for a few minutes each night and let the blood gush back into their veins. I hope that the man my aunt loved appreciated a smooth brow, that he wasn't just a tits-and-ass man.

Once my aunt found a freckle on her chin, at a spot that the almanac said predestined her for unhappiness. She dug it out with a hot needle and washed the wound with peroxide.

More attention to her looks than these pullings of hairs and pickings at spots would have caused gossip among the villagers. They owned work clothes and good clothes, and they wore good clothes for feasting the new seasons. But since a woman combing her hair hexes beginnings, my aunt rarely found an occasion to look her best. Women looked like great sea snails—the corded wood, babies, and laundry they carried were the whorls on their backs. The Chinese did not admire a bent back; goddesses and warriors stood straight. Still there must have been a marvelous freeing of beauty when a worker laid down her burden and stretched and arched.

Such commonplace loveliness, however, was not enough for my aunt. She dreamed of a lover for the fifteen days of New Year's, the time for families to exchange visits, money, and food. She plied her secret comb. And sure enough she cursed the year, the family, the village, and herself.

Even as her hair lured her imminent lover, many other men looked at her. Uncles, cousins, nephews, brothers would have looked, too, had they been home between journeys. Perhaps they had already been restraining their curiosity, and they left, fearful that their glances, like a field of nesting birds, might be startled and caught. Poverty hurt, and that was their first reason for leaving. But another, final reason for leaving the crowded house was the never-said.

She may have been unusually beloved, the precious only daughter, spoiled and mirror gazing because of the affection the family lavished on her. When her husband left, they welcomed the chance to take her back from the in-laws; she could live like the little daughter for just a while longer. There are stories that my grandfather was different from other people, "crazy ever since the little Jap bayoneted him in the head." He used to put his naked penis on the dinner table, laughing. And one day he brought home a baby girl, wrapped up inside his brown western-style greatcoat. He had traded one of his sons, probably my father, the youngest, for her. My grandmother made him trade back. When he finally got a daughter of his own, he doted on her. They must have all loved her, except perhaps my father, the only brother who never went back to China, having once been traded for a girl.

Brothers and sisters, newly men and women, had to efface their sexual color and present plain miens. Disturbing hair and eyes, a smile like no other, threatened the ideal of five generations living under one roof. To focus blurs, people shouted face to face and yelled from room to room. The immigrants I know have loud voices, unmodulated to American tones even after years away from the village where they called their friendships out across the fields. I have not been able to stop my mother's screams in public libraries or over telephones. Walking erect (knees straight, toes pointed forward, not pigeon-toed, which is Chinese-feminine) and speaking in an inaudible voice, I have tried to turn myself American-feminine. Chinese communication was loud, public. Only sick people had to whisper. But at the dinner table, where the family members came nearest one another, no one could talk, not the outcasts nor any eaters. Every word that falls from the mouth is a coin lost. Silently they gave and accepted food with both hands. A preoccupied child who took his bowl with one hand got a sideways glare. A complete moment of total attention is due everyone alike. Children and lovers have no singularity here, but my aunt used a secret voice, a separate attentiveness.

She kept the man's name to herself throughout her labor and dying; she did not accuse him that he be punished with her. To save her inseminator's name she gave silent birth.

He may have been somebody in her own household, but intercourse with a man outside the family would have been no less abhorrent. All the village were kinsmen, and the titles shouted in loud country voices never let kinship be forgotten. Any man within visiting distance would have been neutralized as a lover—"brother," "younger brother," "older brother"—one hundred and fifteen relationship titles. Parents researched birth charts probably not so much to assure good fortune as to circumvent incest in a population that has but one hundred surnames. Everybody has eight million relatives. How useless then sexual mannerisms, how dangerous.

As if it came from an atavism deeper than fear, I used to add "brother" silently to boys' names. It hexed the boys, who would or would not ask me to dance, and made them less scary and as familiar and deserving of benevolence as girls.

But, of course, I hexed myself also—no dates. I should have stood up, both arms waving, and shouted out across libraries, "Hey, you! Love me back." I had no idea, though, how to make attraction selective, how to control its direction and magnitude. If I made myself American-pretty so that the five or six Chinese boys in the class fell in love with me, everyone else—the Caucasian, Negro, and Japanese boys—would too. Sisterliness, dignified and honorable, made much more sense.

Attraction eludes control so stubbornly that whole societies designed to organize relationships among people cannot keep order, not even when they bind people to one another from childhood and raise them together. Among the very poor and the wealthy, brothers married their adopted sisters, like doves. Our family allowed some romance, paying adult brides' prices and providing dowries so that their sons and daughters could marry strangers. Marriage promises to turn strangers into friendly relatives—a nation of siblings.

In the village structure, spirits shimmered among the live creatures, balanced and held in equilibrium by time and land. But one human being flaring up into violence could open up a black hole, a maelstrom that pulled in the sky. The frightened villagers, who depended on one another to maintain the real, went to my aunt to show her a personal, physical representation of the break she had made in the "roundness." Misallying couples snapped off the future, which was to be embodied in true offspring. The villagers punished her for acting as if she could have a private life, secret and apart from them.

If my aunt had betrayed the family at a time of large grain yields and peace, when many boys were born, and wings were being built on many houses, perhaps she might have escaped such severe punishment. But the men—hungry, greedy, tired of planting in dry soil, cuckolded—had had to leave the village in order to send food-money home. There were ghost plagues, bandit plagues, wars with the Japanese, floods. My Chinese brother and sister had died of an unknown sickness. Adultery, perhaps only a mistake during good times, became a crime when the village needed food.

The round moon cakes and round doorways, the round tables of graduated size that fit one roundness inside another, round windows and rice bowls—these talismans had lost their power to warn this family of the law: a family must be whole, faithfully keeping the descent line by having sons to feed the old and the dead, who in turn look after the family. The villagers came to show my aunt and her lover-in-hiding a broken house. The villagers were speeding up the circling of events because she was too shortsighted to see that her infidelity had already harmed the village, that waves of consequences would return unpredictably, sometimes in disguise, as now, to hurt her. This roundness had to be made coin-sized so that she would see its circumference: punish her at the birth of her baby. Awaken her to the inexorable. People who refused fatalism because they could invent small resources insisted on culpability. Deny accidents and wrest fault from the stars.

After the villagers left, their lanterns now scattering in various directions toward home, the family broke their silence and cursed her. "Aiaa, we're going to die. Death is coming. Death is coming. Look what you've done. You've killed us. Ghost! Dead ghost! Ghost! You've never been born." She ran out into the fields, far enough from the house so that she could no longer hear their voices, and pressed herself against the earth, her own land no more. When she felt the birth coming, she thought that she had been hurt. Her body seized together. "They've hurt me too much," she thought. "This is gall, and it will kill me." With forehead and knees against the earth, her body convulsed and then relaxed. She turned on her back, lay on the ground. The black well of sky and stars went out and out and out forever; her body and her complexity seemed to disappear, without home, without a companion, in eternal cold and silence. An agoraphobia rose in her, speeding higher and higher, bigger and bigger; she would not be able to contain it; there would be no end to fear.

Flayed, unprotected against space, she felt pain return, focusing her body. This pain chilled her—a cold, steady kind of surface pain. Inside, spasmodically, the other pain, the pain of the child, heated her. For hours she lay on the ground, alternately body and space. Sometimes a vision of normal comfort obliterated reality: she saw the family in the evening gambling at the dinner table, the young people massaging their elders' backs. She saw them congratulating one another, high joy on the mornings the rice shoots came up. When these pictures burst, the stars drew yet further apart. Black space opened.

She got to her feet to fight better and remembered that old-fashioned women gave birth in their pigsties to fool the jealous, pain-dealing gods, who do not snatch piglets. Before the next spasms could stop her, she ran to the pigsty, each step a rushing out into emptiness. She climbed over the fence and knelt in the dirt. It was good to have a fence enclosing her, a tribal person alone.

Laboring, this woman who had carried her child as a foreign growth that sickened her every day, expelled it at last. She reached down to touch the hot, wet, moving mass, surely smaller than anything human, and could feel that it was human after all—fingers, toes, nails, nose. She pulled it up on to her belly, and it lay curled there, butt in the air, feet precisely tucked one under the other. She opened her loose shirt and buttoned the child inside. After resting, it squirmed and thrashed and she pushed it up to her breast. It turned its head this way and that until it found her nipple. There, it made little snuffling noises. She clenched her teeth at its preciousness, lovely as a young calf, a piglet, a little dog.

She may have gone to the pigsty as a last act of responsibility: she would protect this child as she had protected its father. It would look after her soul, leaving supplies on her grave. But how would this tiny child without family find her grave when there would be no marker for her anywhere, neither in the earth nor the family hall? No one would give her a family hall name. She had taken the child with her into the wastes. At its birth the two of them had felt the same raw pain of separation, a wound that only the family pressing tight could close. A child with no descent line would not soften her life but only trail after her, ghost-like, begging her to give it purpose. At dawn the villagers on their way to the fields would stand around the fence and look.

Full of milk, the little ghost slept. When it awoke, she hardened her breasts against the milk that crying loosens. Toward morning she picked up the baby and walked to the well.

Carrying the baby to the well shows loving. Otherwise abandon it. Turn its face into the mud. Mothers who love their children take them along. It was probably a girl; there is some hope of forgiveness for boys.

"Don't tell anyone you had an aunt. Your father does not want to hear her name. She has never been born." I have believed that sex was unspeakable and words so strong and fathers so frail that "aunt" would do my father mysterious harm. I have thought that my family, having settled among immigrants who had also been their neighbors in the ancestral land, needed to clean their name, and a wrong word would incite the kinspeople even here. But there is more to this silence: they want me to participate in her punishment. And I have.

In the twenty years since I heard this story I have not asked for details nor said my aunt's name; I do not know it. People who can comfort the dead can also chase after them to hurt them further—a reverse ancestor worship. The real punishment was not the raid swiftly inflicted by the villagers, but the family's deliberately forgetting her. Her betrayal so maddened them, they saw to it that she would suffer forever, even after death. Always hungry, always needing, she would have to beg food from other ghosts, snatch and steal it from those whose living descendants give them gifts. She would have to fight the ghosts massed at crossroads for the buns a few thoughtful citizens leave to decoy her away from village and home so that the ancestral spirits could feast unharassed. At peace, they could act like gods, not ghosts, their descent lines providing them with paper suits and dresses, spirit money, paper houses, paper automobiles, chicken, meat, and rice into eternity—essences delivered up in smoke and flames, steam and incense rising from each rice bowl. In an attempt to make the Chinese care for people outside the family, Chairman Mao[3] encourages us now to give our paper replicas to the spirits of outstanding soldiers and workers, no matter whose ancestors they may be. My aunt remains forever hungry. Goods are not distributed evenly among the dead.

My aunt haunts me—her ghost drawn to me because now, after fifty years of neglect, I alone devote pages of paper to her, though not origamied[4] into

---

[3]Mao Zedong (1893–1976) was chairman of the Communist Party of China from 1935 until his death.

[4]Origami is the Japanese art of paper folding.

houses and clothes. I do not think she always means me well. I am telling on her, and she was a spite suicide, drowning herself in the drinking water. The Chinese are always very frightened of the drowned one, whose weeping ghost, wet hair hanging and skin bloated, waits silently by the water to pull down a substitute.

[1975]

Nancy Chodorow
[1944–   ]

Sociologist and psychologist **NANCY CHODOROW** *is a pioneer in the field of the psychology of gender; her first book,* The Reproduction of Mothering: Psychoanalysis and the Sociology of Gender *(1978), numbers among the most influential texts of late twentieth century feminist theory. In* The Reproduction of Mothering, *Chodorow argues against the biological determinism so often ascribed to gender formations, and particularly against the notion that women are biologically predisposed toward nurturing; she instead points out the ways that gender identity is shaped within social institutions and relationships such as the family. Chodorow likewise contests traditional Freudian understandings of femininity, arguing that psychoanalysis has treated identity formation as an ahistorical process, failing to consider the cultural and social conditions within which identities are formed. She extends that critique of Freudianism into her subsequent book,* Feminities, Masculinities, Sexualities: Freud and Beyond *(1994), in which she explores traditional psychoanalytic theories of sexuality, paying particular attention to the ways such theories attempt to universalize masculinity and heterosexuality as the "normal" from which all others deviate. Chodorow, by contrast, treats heterosexuality and homosexuality as equally in need of analysis; these revisions of contemporary understandings of both gender and sexuality have made her a leading thinker in the field of feminist psychology.*

Heterosexuality As a Compromise Formation

NANCY CHODOROW

THE PRECEDING CHAPTER CONTRASTS the wide variety of Freudian accounts of women (and men) with the account of normal femininity (and masculinity) that we often take to be—and that Freud also takes to be—*the* Freudian theory. This theory of "normal femininity," an account of the normative desiderata of female development, fits itself best into an account of women in heterosexual relationship to men. Along with a complementary account of male development and character, and with Freud's various accounts of perversion and typical masculine object choices, we find in these writings the origins of a psychoanalytic theory of sexuality. Sexuality has always been central to psychoanalysis, and accordingly, there has continued to be since Freud much psychoanalytic attention to sexuality. Yet as we read this literature, we must be struck that it has not much advanced our understanding of heterosexuality.

This chapter unpacks what seem to be psychoanalytic assumptions that take as given a psychosexuality of normal heterosexual development in which deviation from this norm needs explanation but norm-following does not. By "normal" or "ordinary" heterosexuality, I have in mind socially and culturally taken-for-granted assumptions that seem to encompass notions both of the normative and of the statistically prevalent or typical. Within psychoanalysis, normal heterosexuality is represented in Freud's descriptions of the path to normal femininity in girls and the positive oedipal resolution in boys. We can also define normal heterosexuality negatively, as that which psychoanalysts have tended to see as *not* requiring special notice, in contrast to homosexuality and the perversions. (To say "normal" does not imply that there is no variety within heterosexuality or that such sexuality might not be intensely meaningful to participants.)

I make two intertwined arguments. First, because heterosexuality has been assumed, its origins and vicissitudes have not been described: psychoanalysis does not have a developmental account of "normal" heterosexuality (which is, of course, a wide variety of heterosexualities) that compares in richness and specificity to accounts we have of the development of the various homosexualities and what are called perversions. Psychoanalytic writers have not paid the kind of attention to heterosexuality that they have to these other

Reprinted by permission from *Feminities, Masculinities, Sexualities.* Copyright © 1994 by University Press of Kentucky.

identities and practices; after Freud, most of what one can tease out about the psychoanalytic theory of "normal" heterosexuality comes by reading between the lines in writings on perversions and homosexuality.[1]

Second, insofar as we do have a developmental or clinical account of heterosexuality, it seems either to be relatively empty and general or to imply that heterosexuality is not different in kind from homosexuality, perversion, or *any* sexual outcome or practice. Depending upon which theory is relied on, it is a symptom, a defensive complex, a neurosis, a disorder, a meshing of self-development, narcissistic restitutions, object relations, unconscious fantasy, and drive derivatives. Within the theory, therefore, it is difficult to find persuasive grounds for distinguishing heterosexuality from homosexuality according to criteria of "health," "maturity," "neurosis," "symptom," or any other evaluative terms, or in terms that contrast "normal" and "abnormal" in other than the statistical or normative sense. Both are similarly constructed and experienced compromise formations; at most, we may be able according to these terms to distinguish perverse from nonperverse within both categories. Since the onus seems to be on homosexuality to prove its nonsymptomatic character, we need to add, moreover, that the almost definitional encoding in heterosexuality of intrapsychic and interpersonal male dominance contributes to its defensive, symptomatic, or restitutive character.

My discussion, of necessity, skirts a problem of connotation in the literature. When this literature refers to homosexuality, homosexuals, homosexual object choice, or a variety of perversions, it seems (apparently reflecting everyday culture) to be referring specifically to sexuality, sexual object choice, fantasy, erotization, or desire—and, in the case of both male homosexuals and lesbians, to someone with a conscious sexual identity.[2] By contrast, accounts

---

[1]This chapter is not a review of the literature but, as a quick check on these impressions about psychoanalytic attention to sexuality, Karin Martin surveyed eight major psychoanalytic journals for the past ten years, finding only a couple of articles on love, and a few that address heterosexuality tangentially. (David W. Hershey, "On a Type of Heterosexuality, and the Fluidity of Object Relations," *Journal of the American Psychoanalytic Association* 37 (1989): 147–71, stands out as one article that takes heterosexuality as problematic.) Martin's conclusion (personal communication): "It struck me that it is not just normal heterosexuality that is neglected by psycho-analysis but more specifically normal male heterosexuality. Female sexuality, heterosexual or not, has been continuously understood as problematic if not deviant by psychoanalysis, and there are accounts of how and why it is so problematic."

[2]A large contemporary historical and theoretical literature documents persuasively the relatively recent construction of such notions of sexual identity or of sexuality. Formerly, Western culture conceptualized sexuality in terms of individual prescribed and proscribed acts, and the terms and conceptions of "homosexual" and "heterosexual" as unitary stances, kinds of persons, or object choices were unknown. See Michel Foucault, *The History of Sexuality*, vol. 1, *An Introduction* (New York: Pantheon, 1978); Jonathan N. Katz, *The Gay/Lesbian Almanac* (New York: Harper and Row, 1983); Katz, "The Invention of Heterosexuality," *Socialist Review* 20 (1990): 7–34; Arlene Stein, "Three Models of Sexuality: Drives, Identities and Practices," *Sociological Theory* 7 (1989): 1–13; and Jeffrey Weeks, *Sexuality* (London: Tavistock, 1986).

of the development or experience of normal heterosexuality seem to mean something more than or "larger than" sex: we are in the realm of "falling in love," "mature love," "romantic passion," "true object love," or "genital love." This love may *include* sexual pleasures and meanings, but it goes beyond them. It is as though heterosexuality is more than a matter of erotic or orgasmic satisfaction, whereas other sexualities are not.[3]

My discussion too addresses only inconsistently the relations between sexuality and gender difference. Given what we know about men and women, their sexuality and its development, there is some question whether we can or should talk generically of either homosexuality or heterosexuality. Nonpsychoanalytic writings on sexuality, as well as contemporary sexual politics, tangle with questions concerning whether "queerness" or gender most defines sexuality, and most psychoanalytic writing tends to differentiate male homosexual from lesbian, focusing on one or the other.[4] Similar considerations would also seem to apply in the heterosexual case. A woman's choice of a male sexual object or lover is typically so different—developmentally, experientially, dynamically, and in its meaning for her womanliness or femininity—from a man's choice of a female sexual object or lover that it is not at all clear whether we should identify these by the same term. We can do so behaviorally and definitionally—a hetero-object is other than or different from the self, whereas a homo-object is like the self—and there is certainly a culturally

---

[3]See, e.g., Ethel S. Person, *Dreams of Love and Fateful Encounters: The Power of Romantic Passion* (New York: Norton, 1988); Otto Kernberg, "Barriers to Falling and Remaining in Love," in *Object Relations Theory and Clinical Psycho-Analysis* (New York: Aronson, 1976), 185–213; Kernberg, "Mature Love: Prerequisites and Characteristics," in *Object Relations Theory*, 215–39; and Kernberg, "Boundaries and Structures in Love Relations," in *Internal World and External Reality* (New York: Aronson, 1980), 277–305. For an earlier period, see Michael Balint, "Eros and Aphrodite," 59–73, "On Genital Love," 109–20, and "Perversions and Genitality," 136–47, all in his *Primary Love and Psycho-Analytic Technique* (New York: Liveright, 1965). Balint and Kernberg address sexuality and, in Kernberg's case, aggression, specifically. See Balint, "Eros and Aphrodite" and "Perversions and Genitality"; Kernberg, "Between Conventionality and Aggression: the Boundaries of Passion," in Willard Gaylin and Ethel Person, eds., *Passionate Attachments: Thinking about Love* (New York: Free Press, 1988), 63–83; Kernberg, "Aggression and Love in the Relationship of the Couple," *Journal of the American Psychoanalytic Association* 39 (1991): 45–70; and Kernberg, "Sadomasochism, Sexual Excitement, and Perversion," *Journal of the American Psychoanalytic Association* 39 (1991): 333–62,

[4]Katz, in "Invention of Heterosexuality," 10, 14, provides useful historical insight into this problem, pointing out that the first medical writer to use the term "homosexual" referred exclusively to gender conceptions ("persons whose 'general mental state is that of the opposite sex' "). He also suggests that the turn-of-the-century term "invert" allows gender-crossing—deviation from True Womanhood and True Manhood—to stand for homoerotic desire. Karin Martin, in "Gender and Sexuality: Medical Opinion on Homosexuality, 1900–1950," *Gender and Society* 7 (1993): 246–60, reviews the medical and psychiatric literature and finds that gender behavior, physiology, and sexual orientation are intertwined in discussions of homosexuals of both sexes. Theoretically, as I noted in the preceding chapter, Freud construed gender identity and personality almost exclusively as issues of sexuality.

normative distinction that conflates heterosexuals of both genders, but we may thereby confuse our psychological understanding.[5]

In what follows, I focus on specific theorists, but I also consider what I regard as widespread unelaborated, paradigmatic accounts and assumptions found in clinical reports, case discussions, theoretical and clinical discussions of men or women, and even in articles that do not particularly focus on sexuality or gender. My point is not to condemn or to universalize about psychoanalytic writings but to indicate trends in psychoanalytic thinking that I think warrant reflection. I suggest a need for more explicit attention to the development of heterosexuality in both men and women (and imply a need for more explicit attention to the development of love and passion in homosexuals).

Certain biological assumptions or understandings, I believe, underlie the striking lack of interest in detailed investigation of the developmental genesis of heterosexuality. The simplest of these—what many psychoanalysts probably think—is that heterosexuality is innate or natural; it is how humans "naturally" develop as we follow our evolutionary heritage and that of other animal species, especially our primate ancestors. Such a position is regarded as obvious and not in need of defense or argument.[6]

There are a number of problems with this kind of psychoanalytic account. To begin on the level of logical consistency, it implies that we need an explanation for the development of homosexuality or perversion in the individual but that heterosexuality doesn't need explaining. As psychoanalyst Robert Stoller, discussing problems with the assumption of a biologically "natural" heterosexuality, puts it: "Are there really psychoanalysts who believe that human psychic development proceeds 'naturally' with preprogrammed facility?"[7]

A more complex empirical problem with the claim or assumption that people are biologically programmed to be heterosexual is that normal heterosexuality, like all sexual desire, is specified in its object. If it were not, *any* man would suit a heterosexual woman's sexual or relational object need, and vice versa, whereas in fact there is great cultural and individual psychological

---

[5]Kenneth Lewes, in *Psychoanalytic Theory of Male Homosexuality* [New York: Simon & Schuster, 1988] 232, suggests that modern psychoanalysis, uncharacteristically, does just this, defining homosexuality in terms of its behavior rather than its dynamics or phenomenology.

[6]E.g., noted psychoanalytic feminist Juliet Mitchell, in "Eternal Divide," [London] *Times Higher Education Supplement*, Nov. 17, 1989, 20, takes me to task for claiming that the "distinction between the sexes . . . is neither necessary nor universal," and she goes on to assert: "The problem of the social and psychological reproduction of heterosexuality for the propagation of the species comes after that. . . . for reasons of heterosexuality, all societies have made some, however different, distinction between the sexes which has, so far, been universal and necessary."

[7]Stoller, *Observing the Erotic Imagination* (New Haven: Yale Univ. Press, 1985), 101.

specificity to sexual object choice, erotic attraction, and fantasy. Any *particular* heterosexual man or woman chooses *particular* objects of desire (or types of objects), and in each case we probably need a cultural and individual developmental story to account for these choices.

By cultural story, I mean the fairytales, myths, tales of love and loss and betrayal, movies, and books that members of a culture grow up with and thus share with others. Since even unconscious fantasy must be constituted at least partially through language, we are not surprised to find that sexual fantasy has partial resonance with these stories, which are individually appropriated in what Ernst Kris has called a "personal myth."[8] As we would expect from this cultural component, notions of sexual attraction and attractiveness vary historically and cross-culturally. In the West, cultural fantasies are almost exclusively heterosexual (Greek myths and tales of male friendship are a notable exception, and of course homosexual love was sanctioned in classic Greek culture, while it has been largely proscribed in ours). In a sense, it is easier to construct heterosexual fantasies because the ingredients are nearer to hand.

Heterosexual fantasy and desire also have an individual component, a private heterosexual erotism that contrasts with or specifies further the cultural norm. To take an everyday example that we all immediately recognize, different ethnicities are likely to have different norms of attractiveness. For both cultural and oedipal reasons (and I do not wish to minimize the influence of hegemonic cultural concepts of attractiveness on these), people who grow up in these ethnicities are likely to build such norms (directly or indirectly, positively or negatively) into their sexual orientation and object choice.[9] Those who are called or who consider themselves heterosexual are, in all likelihood, tall-blond-Wasposexual, short-curly-haired zaftig-Jewishosexual, African-American-with-a-southern-accentosexual, erotically excited only by members of their own ethnic group or only by those outside that group. Some women find themselves repeatedly attracted to men who turn out to be depressed, others to men who are aggressive or violent, still others to narcissists. Some men are attracted to women who are chattery and flirtatious, others to those who are quiet and distant. Some choose lovers or spouses who are like a parent (and it can be either parent for either gender or a mixture of the two); others choose lovers or spouses as much unlike their parents as possible (often to find these mates recapitulating parental characteristics after all, or to find

---

[8]Ernst Kris, "The Personal Myth," *Journal of the American Psychoanalytic Association* 4 (1956): 653–81.

[9]On the effects of culturally hegemonic beauty concepts, see Robin Lakoff and Raquel Scherr, "Beauty and Ethnicity," in their *Face Value* (Boston: Routledge, 1984), 245–76.

themselves discontented when they don't). These choices have both cultural and individual psychological resonance.

My point is that biology cannot explain the content of either cultural fantasy or private erotism. We need a psychodynamic story to account for the development of any particular person's particular heterosexuality, such that it is difficult to claim that we can draw the line between what needs accounting for and what does not in anyone's sexual development or object choice. Any clinician knows this, but clinicians have tended for pretheoretical reasons to assume that such variety is less important than the overarching division of sexual orientation that our culture has made primary since the nineteenth century.

[1994]

"The Rape of Mr. Smith"

Reading Questions: What are the main points of this article? How accurate is this article in depicting rape cases? If you were on a jury, would you consider the evidence presented in the article? Why or why not?

"Mr. Smith, you were held up at gunpoint on the corner of 16th and Locust?"

"Yes."

"Did you struggle with the robber?"

"No."

"Why not?"

"He was armed."

"Then you made a conscious decision to comply with his demands rather than to resist?"

"Yes."

"Did you scream? Cry out?"

"No. I was afraid."

"I see. Have you ever been held up before?"

"No."

"Have you ever given money away?"

"Yes, of course —"

"And did you do so willingly?"

"What are you getting at?"

"Well, let's put it like this, Mr. Smith. You've given away money in the past — in fact, you have quite a reputation for philanthropy. How can we be sure that you weren't contriving to have your money taken from you by force?"

"Listen, if I wanted —"

"Never mind. What time did this holdup take place, Mr. Smith?"

"About 11 p.m."

"You were out on the streets at 11 p.m.? Doing what?"

"Just walking."

"Just walking? You know it's dangerous being out on the street that late at night. Weren't you aware that you could have been held up?"

"I hadn't thought about it."

"What were you wearing at the time, Mr. Smith?"

"Let's see. A suit. Yes, a suit."

"An expensive suit?"

"Well — yes."

"In other words, Mr. Smith, you were walking around the streets late at night in a suit that practically advertised the fact that you might be a good target for some easy money, isn't that so? I mean, if we didn't know better, Mr. Smith, we might even think you were asking for this to happen, mightn't we?"

"Look, can't we talk about the past history of the guy who did this to me?"

"I'm afraid not, Mr. Smith. I don't think you would want to violate his rights, now, would you?"

The law discriminates against rape victims in a manner which would not be tolerated by victims of any other crime. In the following example, a holdup victim is asked questions similar in form to those usually asked a victim of rape.

The Constitution of the United States: A Brief Transcription

Reading Questions: What rights does the Constitution guarantee? Does racial profiling violate your Constitutional rights? What about Amendment IV or V? Why or why not?

We the People of the United States, in Order to form a more perfect Union, establish Justice, insure domestic Tranquility, provide for the common defense, promote the general Welfare, and secure the Blessings of Liberty to ourselves and our Posterity, do ordain and establish this Constitution for the United States of America.

The Bill of Rights

Amendment I
Congress shall make no law respecting an establishment of religion, or prohibiting the free exercise thereof; or abridging the freedom of speech, or of the press; or the right of the people peaceably to assemble, and to petition the Government for a redress of grievances.

Amendment II
A well regulated Militia, being necessary to the security of a free State, the right of the people to keep and bear Arms, shall not be infringed.

Amendment III
No Soldier shall, in time of peace be quartered in any house, without the consent of the Owner, nor in time of war, but in a manner to be prescribed by law.

Amendment IV
The right of the people to be secure in their persons, houses, papers, and effects, against unreasonable searches and seizures, shall not be violated, and no Warrants shall issue, but upon probable cause, supported by Oath or affirmation, and particularly describing the place to be searched, and the persons or things to be seized.

Amendment V
No person shall be held to answer for a capital, or otherwise infamous crime, unless on a presentment or indictment of a Grand Jury, except in cases arising in the land or naval forces, or in the Militia, when in actual service in time of War or public danger; nor shall any person be subject for the same offence to be twice put in jeopardy of life or limb; nor shall be compelled in any criminal case to be a witness against himself, nor be deprived of life, liberty, or property, without due process of law; nor shall private property be taken for public use, without just compensation.

Amendment VI

In all criminal prosecutions, the accused shall enjoy the right to a speedy and public trial, by an impartial jury of the State and district wherein the crime shall have been committed, which district shall have been previously ascertained by law, and to be informed of the nature and cause of the accusation; to be confronted with the witnesses against him; to have compulsory process for obtaining witnesses in his favor, and to have the Assistance of Counsel for his defence.

Amendment VII
In Suits at common law, where the value in controversy shall exceed twenty dollars, the right of trial by jury shall be preserved, and no fact tried by a jury, shall be otherwise re-examined in any Court of the United States, than according to the rules of the common law.

Amendment VIII
Excessive bail shall not be required, nor excessive fines imposed, nor cruel and unusual punishments inflicted.

Amendment IX
The enumeration in the Constitution, of certain rights, shall not be construed to deny or disparage others retained by the people.

Amendment X
The powers not delegated to the United States by the Constitution, nor prohibited by it to the States, are reserved to the States respectively, or to the people.

AMENDMENT XI
Passed by Congress March 4, 1794. Ratified February 7, 1795.
Note: Article III, section 2, of the Constitution was modified by amendment 11.
The Judicial power of the United States shall not be construed to extend to any suit in law or equity, commenced or prosecuted against one of the United States by Citizens of another State, or by Citizens or Subjects of any Foreign State.

AMENDMENT XII
Passed by Congress December 9, 1803. Ratified June 15, 1804.
Note: A portion of Article II, section 1 of the Constitution was superseded by the 12th amendment.
The Electors shall meet in their respective states and vote by ballot for President and Vice-President, one of whom, at least, shall not be an inhabitant of the same state with themselves; they shall name in their ballots the person voted for as President, and in distinct ballots the person voted for as Vice-President, and they shall make distinct lists of all persons voted for as President, and of all persons voted for as Vice-President, and of the number of votes for each, which lists they shall sign and certify, and transmit sealed to the seat of the government of the United States, directed to the President of the Senate; -- the President of the Senate shall, in the presence of the Senate and House of Representatives, open all the certificates and the votes shall then be counted; -- The person having the greatest number of votes for President, shall be the President,

if such number be a majority of the whole number of Electors appointed; and if no person have such majority, then from the persons having the highest numbers not exceeding three on the list of those voted for as President, the House of Representatives shall choose immediately, by ballot, the President. But in choosing the President, the votes shall be taken by states, the representation from each state having one vote; a quorum for this purpose shall consist of a member or members from two-thirds of the states, and a majority of all the states shall be necessary to a choice. [And if the House of Representatives shall not choose a President whenever the right of choice shall devolve upon them, before the fourth day of March next following, then the Vice-President shall act as President, as in case of the death or other constitutional disability of the President. --]* The person having the greatest number of votes as Vice-President, shall be the Vice-President, if such number be a majority of the whole number of Electors appointed, and if no person have a majority, then from the two highest numbers on the list, the Senate shall choose the Vice-President; a quorum for the purpose shall consist of two-thirds of the whole number of Senators, and a majority of the whole number shall be necessary to a choice. But no person constitutionally ineligible to the office of President shall be eligible to that of Vice-President of the United States.

*Superseded by section 3 of the 20th amendment.

AMENDMENT XIII
Passed by Congress January 31, 1865. Ratified December 6, 1865.
Note: A portion of Article IV, section 2, of the Constitution was superseded by the 13th amendment.
Section 1.
Neither slavery nor involuntary servitude, except as a punishment for crime whereof the party shall have been duly convicted, shall exist within the United States, or any place subject to their jurisdiction.
Section 2.
Congress shall have power to enforce this article by appropriate legislation.

AMENDMENT XIV
Passed by Congress June 13, 1866. Ratified July 9, 1868.
Note: Article I, section 2, of the Constitution was modified by section 2 of the 14th amendment.
Section 1.
All persons born or naturalized in the United States, and subject to the jurisdiction thereof, are citizens of the United States and of the State wherein they reside. No State shall make or enforce any law which shall abridge the privileges or immunities of citizens of the United States; nor shall any State deprive any person of life, liberty, or property, without due process of law; nor deny to any person within its jurisdiction the equal protection of the laws.
Section 2.
Representatives shall be apportioned among the several States according to their

respective numbers, counting the whole number of persons in each State, excluding Indians not taxed. But when the right to vote at any election for the choice of electors for President and Vice-President of the United States, Representatives in Congress, the Executive and Judicial officers of a State, or the members of the Legislature thereof, is denied to any of the male inhabitants of such State, being twenty-one years of age,* and citizens of the United States, or in any way abridged, except for participation in rebellion, or other crime, the basis of representation therein shall be reduced in the proportion which the number of such male citizens shall bear to the whole number of male citizens twenty-one years of age in such State.

Section 3.
No person shall be a Senator or Representative in Congress, or elector of President and Vice-President, or hold any office, civil or military, under the United States, or under any State, who, having previously taken an oath, as a member of Congress, or as an officer of the United States, or as a member of any State legislature, or as an executive or judicial officer of any State, to support the Constitution of the United States, shall have engaged in insurrection or rebellion against the same, or given aid or comfort to the enemies thereof. But Congress may by a vote of two-thirds of each House, remove such disability.

Section 4.
The validity of the public debt of the United States, authorized by law, including debts incurred for payment of pensions and bounties for services in suppressing insurrection or rebellion, shall not be questioned. But neither the United States nor any State shall assume or pay any debt or obligation incurred in aid of insurrection or rebellion against the United States, or any claim for the loss or emancipation of any slave; but all such debts, obligations and claims shall be held illegal and void.

Section 5.
The Congress shall have the power to enforce, by appropriate legislation, the provisions of this article.

Changed by section 1 of the 26th amendment.

AMENDMENT XV
Passed by Congress February 26, 1869. Ratified February 3, 1870.
Section 1.
The right of citizens of the United States to vote shall not be denied or abridged by the United States or by any State on account of race, color, or previous condition of servitude--

Section 2.
The Congress shall have the power to enforce this article by appropriate legislation.

AMENDMENT XVI
Passed by Congress July 2, 1909. Ratified February 3, 1913.
Note: Article I, section 9, of the Constitution was modified by amendment 16.

The Congress shall have power to lay and collect taxes on incomes, from whatever source derived, without apportionment among the several States, and without regard to any census or enumeration.

AMENDMENT XVII
Passed by Congress May 13, 1912. Ratified April 8, 1913.
Note: Article I, section 3, of the Constitution was modified by the 17th amendment.
The Senate of the United States shall be composed of two Senators from each State, elected by the people thereof, for six years; and each Senator shall have one vote. The electors in each State shall have the qualifications requisite for electors of the most numerous branch of the State legislatures.
When vacancies happen in the representation of any State in the Senate, the executive authority of such State shall issue writs of election to fill such vacancies: *Provided*, That the legislature of any State may empower the executive thereof to make temporary appointments until the people fill the vacancies by election as the legislature may direct. This amendment shall not be so construed as to affect the election or term of any Senator chosen before it becomes valid as part of the Constitution.

AMENDMENT XVIII
Passed by Congress December 18, 1917. Ratified January 16, 1919. Repealed by amendment 21.
Section 1.
After one year from the ratification of this article the manufacture, sale, or transportation of intoxicating liquors within, the importation thereof into, or the exportation thereof from the United States and all territory subject to the jurisdiction thereof for beverage purposes is hereby prohibited.
Section 2.
The Congress and the several States shall have concurrent power to enforce this article by appropriate legislation.
Section 3.
This article shall be inoperative unless it shall have been ratified as an amendment to the Constitution by the legislatures of the several States, as provided in the Constitution, within seven years from the date of the submission hereof to the States by the Congress.

AMENDMENT XIX
Passed by Congress June 4, 1919. Ratified August 18, 1920.
The right of citizens of the United States to vote shall not be denied or abridged by the United States or by any State on account of sex.
Congress shall have power to enforce this article by appropriate legislation.

AMENDMENT XX

Passed by Congress March 2, 1932. Ratified January 23, 1933.
Note: Article I, section 4, of the Constitution was modified by section 2 of this amendment. In addition, a portion of the 12th amendment was superseded by section 3.

Section 1.
The terms of the President and the Vice President shall end at noon on the 20th day of January, and the terms of Senators and Representatives at noon on the 3d day of January, of the years in which such terms would have ended if this article had not been ratified; and the terms of their successors shall then begin.

Section 2.
The Congress shall assemble at least once in every year, and such meeting shall begin at noon on the 3d day of January, unless they shall by law appoint a different day.

Section 3.
If, at the time fixed for the beginning of the term of the President, the President elect shall have died, the Vice President elect shall become President. If a President shall not have been chosen before the time fixed for the beginning of his term, or if the President elect shall have failed to qualify, then the Vice President elect shall act as President until a President shall have qualified; and the Congress may by law provide for the case wherein neither a President elect nor a Vice President shall have qualified, declaring who shall then act as President, or the manner in which one who is to act shall be selected, and such person shall act accordingly until a President or Vice President shall have qualified.

Section 4.
The Congress may by law provide for the case of the death of any of the persons from whom the House of Representatives may choose a President whenever the right of choice shall have devolved upon them, and for the case of the death of any of the persons from whom the Senate may choose a Vice President whenever the right of choice shall have devolved upon them.

Section 5.
Sections 1 and 2 shall take effect on the 15th day of October following the ratification of this article.

Section 6.
This article shall be inoperative unless it shall have been ratified as an amendment to the Constitution by the legislatures of three-fourths of the several States within seven years from the date of its submission.

AMENDMENT XXI
Passed by Congress February 20, 1933. Ratified December 5, 1933.

Section 1.
The eighteenth article of amendment to the Constitution of the United States is hereby repealed.

Section 2.
The transportation or importation into any State, Territory, or Possession of the United States for delivery or use therein of intoxicating liquors, in violation of the laws thereof, is hereby prohibited.

Section 3.

This article shall be inoperative unless it shall have been ratified as an amendment to the Constitution by conventions in the several States, as provided in the Constitution, within seven years from the date of the submission hereof to the States by the Congress.

AMENDMENT XXII

Passed by Congress March 21, 1947. Ratified February 27, 1951.

Section 1.

No person shall be elected to the office of the President more than twice, and no person who has held the office of President, or acted as President, for more than two years of a term to which some other person was elected President shall be elected to the office of President more than once. But this Article shall not apply to any person holding the office of President when this Article was proposed by Congress, and shall not prevent any person who may be holding the office of President, or acting as President, during the term within which this Article becomes operative from holding the office of President or acting as President during the remainder of such term.

Section 2.

This article shall be inoperative unless it shall have been ratified as an amendment to the Constitution by the legislatures of three-fourths of the several States within seven years from the date of its submission to the States by the Congress.

AMENDMENT XXIII

Passed by Congress June 16, 1960. Ratified March 29, 1961.

Section 1.

The District constituting the seat of Government of the United States shall appoint in such manner as Congress may direct:

A number of electors of President and Vice President equal to the whole number of Senators and Representatives in Congress to which the District would be entitled if it were a State, but in no event more than the least populous State; they shall be in addition to those appointed by the States, but they shall be considered, for the purposes of the election of President and Vice President, to be electors appointed by a State; and they shall meet in the District and perform such duties as provided by the twelfth article of amendment.

Section 2.

The Congress shall have power to enforce this article by appropriate legislation.

AMENDMENT XXIV

Passed by Congress August 27, 1962. Ratified January 23, 1964.

Section 1.

The right of citizens of the United States to vote in any primary or other election for President or Vice President, for electors for President or Vice President, or for Senator or Representative in Congress, shall not be denied or abridged by the United States or any State by reason of failure to pay poll tax or other tax.

Section 2.
The Congress shall have power to enforce this article by appropriate legislation.

AMENDMENT XXV
Passed by Congress July 6, 1965. Ratified February 10, 1967.
Note: Article II, section 1, of the Constitution was affected by the 25th amendment.
Section 1.
In case of the removal of the President from office or of his death or resignation, the Vice President shall become President.
Section 2.
Whenever there is a vacancy in the office of the Vice President, the President shall nominate a Vice President who shall take office upon confirmation by a majority vote of both Houses of Congress.
Section 3.
Whenever the President transmits to the President pro tempore of the Senate and the Speaker of the House of Representatives his written declaration that he is unable to discharge the powers and duties of his office, and until he transmits to them a written declaration to the contrary, such powers and duties shall be discharged by the Vice President as Acting President.
Section 4.
Whenever the Vice President and a majority of either the principal officers of the executive departments or of such other body as Congress may by law provide, transmit to the President pro tempore of the Senate and the Speaker of the House of Representatives their written declaration that the President is unable to discharge the powers and duties of his office, the Vice President shall immediately assume the powers and duties of the office as Acting President.
Thereafter, when the President transmits to the President pro tempore of the Senate and the Speaker of the House of Representatives his written declaration that no inability exists, he shall resume the powers and duties of his office unless the Vice President and a majority of either the principal officers of the executive department or of such other body as Congress may by law provide, transmit within four days to the President pro tempore of the Senate and the Speaker of the House of Representatives their written declaration that the President is unable to discharge the powers and duties of his office. Thereupon Congress shall decide the issue, assembling within forty-eight hours for that purpose if not in session. If the Congress, within twenty-one days after receipt of the latter written declaration, or, if Congress is not in session, within twenty-one days after Congress is required to assemble, determines by two-thirds vote of both Houses that the President is unable to discharge the powers and duties of his office, the Vice President shall continue to discharge the same as Acting President; otherwise, the President shall resume the powers and duties of his office.

AMENDMENT XXVI

Passed by Congress March 23, 1971. Ratified July 1, 1971.
Note: Amendment 14, section 2, of the Constitution was modified by section 1 of the 26th amendment.
Section 1.
The right of citizens of the United States, who are eighteen years of age or older, to vote shall not be denied or abridged by the United States or by any State on account of age.
Section 2.
The Congress shall have power to enforce this article by appropriate legislation.

AMENDMENT XXVII
Originally proposed Sept. 25, 1789. Ratified May 7, 1992.
No law, varying the compensation for the services of the Senators and Representatives, shall take effect, until an election of representatives shall have intervened.